The Family in History

*the text of this book is printed
on 100% recycled paper*

Editorial Note   All of the essays in this book originally appeared in the *Journal of Interdisciplinary History*, edited by Robert I. Rotberg and Theodore K. Rabb and published by the Massachusetts Institute of Technology Press.

The article by Pierre Goubert appeared in the very first number of the *Journal* (Autumn 1970). The Bibliographic Note by C. John Somerville appeared in volume III (Autumn 1972). All of the other contributions originally constituted a special number of the *Journal* (II, 2) on "The Family in History," which was published in Autumn 1971.

The article by Peter Laslett on "Menarche" has been extensively revised and supplemented for this book. Alterations have also been made in the articles by Edward Shorter and Emily Coleman. All of the others appear here without major changes since their original publication.

The
Family in History
Interdisciplinary Essays

Edited by

Theodore K. Rabb and Robert I. Rotberg

HARPER TORCHBOOKS
Harper & Row, Publishers
New York, Hagerstown, San Francisco, London

First HARPER TORCHBOOK edition published 1973

LIBRARY OF CONGRESS CATALOG CARD NUMBER: 73-12978

ISBN: 0-06-131757-8

78 79 80   12 11 10 9 8 7 6 5

Contents

Editorial Note   ii

Preface   vii

Medieval Marriage Characteristics:
A Neglected Factor in the History
of Medieval Serfdom   Emily R. Coleman   1

Historical Demography and the Reinterpretation
of Early Modern French History:
A Research Review   Pierre Goubert   16

Age at Menarche in Europe since the
Eighteenth Century   Peter Laslett   28

Illegitimacy, Sexual Revolution, and
Social Change in Modern Europe   Edward Shorter   48

Demographic Change and the Life Cycle
of American Families   Robert V. Wells   85

Adolescence and Youth
in Nineteenth-Century America   Joseph F. Kett   95

Patterns of Work and Family Organization:
Buffalo's Italians   Virginia Yans McLaughlin   111

Developmental Perspectives
on the History of Childhood   John Demos   127

Psychological Development and
Historical Change   Kenneth Keniston   141

On Writing Women's History   Lois W. Banner   159

Recent Approaches to Past Childhoods   Etienne van de Walle   171

Documents in Search of a Historian:
Toward a History of Children and
Youth in America   David J. Rothman   179

The Morphology of New England Society
in the Colonial Period   James A. Henretta   191

The History of the Family as an
Interdisciplinary Field   Tamara K. Hareven   211

Bibliographic Note:
Toward a History of Childhood
and Youth   C. John Sommerville   227

Preface
to the
Torchbook Edition

In recent years a variety of subjects largely ignored by earlier generations has captured the attention of historians. One of the most fruitful has been the life of ordinary men and women, whose habits and beliefs were virtually unknown until, during the last two decades, scholars brought to light information about social groups who previously had been considered too obscure (or unimportant) to merit exploration. Topics as diverse as popular culture, fertility, and disease have attracted notice and have stimulated the development of such pioneering research techniques as historical demography.

By their nature investigations of "grass roots" history focus on all levels of society, breaking from the traditional concentration on elites and the upper classes. For that very reason, however, they require different kinds of evidence and different ways of handling sources. Fortunately, both inspiration and guidance in solving these problems has been available from other disciplines, especially psychology, sociology, demography, anthropology, the creative arts, genetics, and medicine, whose contributions have given the new studies an interdisciplinary character that sets them apart from most historical research.

The history of the family, a relative newcomer even to so young a body of literature, epitomizes the particular qualities of these seemingly mundane subjects. Nowhere can one perceive more clearly that as our knowledge of prosaic, everyday activities increases, we gain a far richer and more thorough understanding of human behavior in bygone ages. An interest that has long been the preserve of genealogists has thus been transformed, in a few short years, into one of the most lively and influential areas in the study of history. Perhaps the happiest result of the rise of this new genre has been its illumination of the single most neglected historical subject—women. In the family their importance cannot be ignored, and this book shows them taking decisive roles in places as distinct as ninth-century France and twentieth-century Buffalo.

Despite their occasionally tentative conclusions, therefore, the essays which follow, drawn from the *Journal of Interdisciplinary History*, indicate both the range and the novelty of this field of inquiry, whose impact on the methods and goals of historical scholarship is already strikingly apparent.

The Editors

The Family in History

A major stimulus to the historian's adoption of techniques from other disciplines has been his interest in subjects largely ignored by earlier generations. One of the most fruitful of these unexplored territories has been the life of ordinary men and women, and during the last two decades scholars have brought to light considerable information about the habits and beliefs of social groups who previously had been considered too obscure (or unimportant) to bear investigation. Topics as diverse as popular culture, fertility, and disease have attracted attention, inspiring borrowings from psychology, sociology, demography, anthropology, the creative arts, genetics, and medicine. The teachings of the first four of these disciplines will be particularly evident in the pages that follow, and they indicate the extent to which "grass roots" history is dependent upon interdisciplinary methods.

That studies of the family should set the theme of this issue is noteworthy, first, because they focus on *all* levels of society. Minimal attention is paid to elites or upper classes. Equally significant, though, is the number of people pursuing this type of research. Not only are the approaches novel (in an area long the preserve of genealogists), but they are clearly winning a wide following. And it is implicit in current work that as we learn more about this most fundamental of social organizations we will be able to gain a deeper understanding of human behavior in past eras.

Perhaps the happiest result of the rise of this new genre is its illumination of the single most neglected subject in history—women. In the family their importance cannot be ignored, and the articles and reviews in this issue show them taking decisive roles in places as different as ninth-century France and twentieth-century Buffalo. It is worth observing that this changing emphasis has a parallel in the prominent contribution made by women historians to this issue, and indeed to our last two issues—yet another scholarly interaction that is more than welcome.

The Family in History

Emily R. Coleman

Medieval Marriage Characteristics: A Neglected Factor in the History of Medieval Serfdom

Only recently have historians come to appreciate the role which demographic factors have played in the social history of the Middle Ages. In the traditional view, medieval society remained rigidly stratified and static; change, when it came, was attributable largely to external factors playing upon the medieval world—the opening of frontiers, the expansion of trade, and the growth of towns. All of this is true, but it does not represent a complete picture of the forces working to transform medieval society. This paper examines another factor, hitherto neglected by scholars, which apparently played a major role in the social history of the Middle Ages, and, particularly, in the history of medieval serfdom: the marriage patterns characteristic of the servile population.

I have utilized one of the magnificent documents of medieval social history—the Polyptych of the Abbot Irminon, redacted probably between c. 801 and c. 820. It describes the lands and the some 2,000 families belonging to the monastry of Saint Germain-des-Prés near Paris. This polyptych of Saint Germain-des-Prés is an extraordinary example of the medieval *censier* or manorial extent of the estates and benefices which comprised and/or were dependent upon an abbey or church. There is a *breve*, or chapter, describing each part of the seigneury, relating in some detail the type and size of the elements of the demesne, the amount of arable tenanted land, the number of people on the land, the dues they owed, and information on mills and churches.

The polyptych has been the worthy object of intense and careful study for over a century. The manuscript, which is preserved in the Bibliothèque Nationale (*Fonds latin*, manuscript no. 12832), has been edited twice. The first edition (1844) was by Guérard, whose detailed introduction has become a starting point for all studies of the document.[1] Fifty years later Longnon revised some of Guérard's paleographic interpretations and reduced the introduction to more manageable

Emily R. Coleman is Assistant Professor of History, University of Pittsburgh.

The author wishes to express her gratitude to David Herlihy of the University of Wisconsin for his guidance and encouragement. She also wishes to thank Maureen F. Mazzaoui of Indiana University.

1 Benjamin Guérard, *Polyptyque de l'Abbé Irminon ... avec des Prolégomènes* (Paris, 1844), 2v.

proportions.[2] Since then, the document has revealed and confirmed numerous findings for its patient researchers.[3] It is interesting to note, however, that these diligent scholars have concentrated almost wholly upon the tenurial aspect of the document.[4] The material that it contains on early ninth-century demography has not been systematically analyzed.[5]

The document is unusually rich in demographic information. It is not a total census for the Île-de-France, but it is far more than a tenurial document (in the sense of being concerned more with property than with people). The redactors were closely interested in the people who lived on the monastery's land and/or who owed personal dues to Saint Germain-des-Prés.[6] Even a cursory glance at some of the *brevia* reveals the strict attention given in the census to the dependents on those ecclesiastical lands. Each fisc (villa) is broken down by manse (the dependent family farm), and those on the manse are denoted individually, by status and by name—including, in most cases, the children.[7] Moreover, the census listed those peasants who lived on these

2 Auguste Longnon, *Polyptyque de l'abbaye de Saint Germain-des-Prés rédigé au temps de l'abbé Irminon* (Paris, 1886–1895), 2v.
3 The best bibliography for the monastery is still L. H. Cottineau, *Répertoire topo-bibliographique des abbayes et prieures* (Macon, 1939–40), 2v. The most recent general works of which I am aware are *Mémorial du XIVe Centenaire de l'Abbaye de Saint Germain-des-Prés* (Paris, 1959); L.-R. Ménager, "Considérations sociologiques sur la démo-graphique des grands domaines ecclésiastiques carolingiens," in *Etudes d'histoire du droit canonique dédiées à Gabriel Le Bras* (Sirey, 1965), II. Unfortunately, these sources do not contain a bibliography of recently published works. For additional bibliography, see the *Cambridge Economic History* (Cambridge, 1966), I, or the concluding bibliography in Georges Duby, *Rural Economy and Country Life in the Medieval West* (Columbia, S.C., 1968). For sources on the use of land measures such as *aripenna* (arpents) and *bunuaria*, see Guérard, *Polyptyque*; P. Guilhiermoz, "De l'équivalence des anciennes mesures à propos d'une publication récente," *Bibliothèque de l'Ecole des Chartes* (Paris, 1913), LXXIV, 267–328; Lucien Musset, "Observations historiques sur une mesure agraire: le bonnier," *Mélanges d'histoire du Moyen Age dédiés à Louis Halphen* (Paris, 1951), 535–541.
4 For an exceedingly fine example of the type of work that has been done, as well as an additional bibliographical source, see Charles-Edmund Perrin, "Observations sur le manse dans la région parisienne au début de IXe siècle," *Annales d'Histoire Sociale*, VII (1945), 39–52.
5 The most ambitious attempt at a demographic analysis was by Ferdinand Lot, "Conjectures démographique sur la France au IXe siècle," *Le Moyen Age*, XXXII (1921), 1–27, 107–137. This study has been acutely and variously criticized by Henri Sée, "Peut-on évaluer la population de l'ancienne France," *Revue d'Économie Politique*, XXXVIII (1924), 647–655; Charles-Edmund Perrin, "Note sur la population de Villeneuve-Saint-Georges au IXe siècle," *Le Moyen Age*, LXIX (1963), 75–86; Ménager, "Considerations sociologiques," 1316–1335.
6 For example, see Perrin, "Note sur la population," 80–81.
7 Longnon, *Polyptyque*, Brevia I, II, III, IV, *passim*.

lands, even if they belonged personally to other seigneuries.[8] The monastery's interest in more than just a head count is also made clear by the attention paid to familial relationships, noting even when children had a mother different from the woman with whom they were living.[9] If we utilize the available data, we find a wealth of information dealing with sex ratios, family size, and, especially, medieval marriage characteristics.

The working and personal relationships associated with the seigneurial regime of Saint Germain-des-Prés display a hierarchical society with subtle, but important, distinctions in rank. These range from the descendants of simple slaves to the descendants of purely free men, and cover most of the ground in between. In an entirely predictable manner, the 9,219 peasants composed four main categories: *liberi* (making up a diminutive 1.30 per cent of the total census), *coloni* (82.74 per cent), *lidi* (3.17 per cent), and *servi* (comprising a surprisingly small 5.02 per cent), with 7.77 per cent of the population of undeterminable status.[10] Although these groups were in theory supposed to have their own rather distinct set of responsibilities and taxes due to their various positions in the social and economic hierarchy, a close examination of the polyptych reveals that the different types of tenures basically determined the redevances (dues) that their inhabitants, of whatever status or varieties of status, had to pay.

By the ninth century, the manse was no longer the area delegated to one family. There was no determinable relationship between the size of the plots and the services due from the peasants, and still less relationship between the size and the number of villein households that they supported.[11] In Abbot Irminon's polyptych, the number of manses supporting more than one family ranged from about 8 per cent to about 67 per cent; 701 out of 1,726 manses had multiple households

8 For instance, *Polyptyque*, IX: 145, 157, 289, 290; XXI: 1, 3, 81, 82, 86; XXII: 53, 72, 84; and other examples might easily be found.

9 For example, *ibid.*, XXI: 25, 27, 33; XXIV: 25.

10 The *liberi*, technically, were legally free individuals. The *coloni* were, for the most part, the descendants of Roman peasants who were tied to the land they worked by the late imperial legislation of Constantine and Diocletian. The *lides* are believed to have originally been *laeti*—the barbarians introduced into Gaul as auxiliaries during Diocletian's reign. They came as both farmers and soldiers, but, during the decline of the Roman world by the barbarian invasions, they became servile laborers. The *servi* were simply the descendants of slaves. For more on these groups and the redevances owed by them, see Guérard, *Polyptyque . . . Prolégomènes*; Longnon, *Polyptyque,* Introduction; Henri Sée, *Les classes rurales et le régime domanial en France au Moyen Age* (Paris, 1901).

11 Duby, *Rural Economy*, 51; Perrin, "Observations sur le manse," 47.

—equaling 40.61 per cent of the total population.[12] The fact that over 40 per cent of the manses were supporting at least twice the number of people than was originally intended would be explained, at least in part, by a growth in population which exceeded the ability of the seigneury to clear new lands and create new manses quickly enough.[13] This picture of a dense population and vigorous expansion is substantiated and reinforced by what seems to have been a definite upward demographic trend during the Carolingian period.[14]

Yet, while there was an increase in population, the manors belonging to Saint Germain-des-Prés did not show a trend toward large families. The average number of children ranged from slightly more than one child per couple to slightly over three children per couple.[15] Rarely did the households include other than those in the immediate family.[16]

However, although familial characteristics were surprisingly modern, Saint Germain's seigneuries showed a startlingly high sex ratio, quite unlike that which one would ordinarily expect. The sex ratio is generally defined as:

> the number of men to each 100 women in a population. The normal [modern] ratio at birth is about 105. However, this declines with the greater mortality of males until most [modern] populations show an equal number of men and women in the total.[17]

12　See Appendix I for a more visual demonstration of the following statistics: Breve I had 12.20 per cent of its manses supporting multiple households. Breve II: 44.34 per cent; III: 34.29 per cent; IV: 19.35 per cent; V: 58.88 per cent; VI: 25.00 per cent; VII: 29.87 per cent; VIII: 8.34 per cent; IX: 63.74 per cent; X: no demographic information; XI: 66.67 per cent; XII: no demographic information; XIII: 67.61 per cent; XIV: 56.66 per cent; XV: 53.36 per cent; XVI: 27.27 per cent; XVII: 11.11 per cent; XVIII: 66.67 per cent; XIX: 67.39 per cent; XX: 30.95 per cent; XXI: 14.12 per cent; XXII: 19.23 per cent; XXIII: 8.34 per cent; XXIV: 30.17 per cent; XXV: 30.95 per cent; *Fragmento Duo*: 33.34 per cent.

13　This demographic evidence is also supported by the prevalence of demi-manses. See, for example, Perrin, "Observations sur le manse."

14　This phenomenon has been noted by B. H. Slicher van Bath, *The Agrarian History of Western Europe, A.D. 500–1850* (London, 1966), 77ff, esp. fig. 9; Perrin, "Observations sur le manse"; David Herlihy, "The Agrarian Revolution in Southern France and Italy, 801–1150," *Speculum*, XXXIII (1958), 23–41, for southern Europe.

15　*Polyptyque*, I: 2.53 children per couple; II: 2.32; III: 2.82; IV: 1.92; V: 2.73; VI: 2.30; VII: 2.81; VIII: 2.04; IX: 2.60; XI: 2.60; XIII: 2.59; XIV: 2.41; XV: 2.20; XVI: 2.18; XVII: 1.12; XVIII: 1.08; XIX: 2.54; XX: 2.40; XXI: 2.72; XXII: 3.03; XXIII: 2.13; XXIV: 1.70; XXV: undeterminable; *Fragmento Duo*: 2.78.

16　Duby, *Rural Economy*, 53. *Polyptyque*, VIII, I, XVIII, XI, IV, *passim*.

17　J. C. Russell, *Late Ancient and Medieval Population* (Philadelphia, 1958), XLVIII, Pt. 3, 13–14.

The polyptych shows different characteristics. The ratios among the adult populations on the manors of Saint Germain-des-Prés ran from 110.3 to 252.9 men for each 100 women; if the entire population (where determinable) is taken into account, the ratio still ranged from 115.7 to 156.2—both of which may be seen in Table 1 below.[18]

The causes for such a marked predominance of men, especially in certain areas, are difficult to determine; we must assume that more factors are involved than a communal genetic freak. It is probably safe to discount the under-reporting of women, however. Polyptychs were relatively sophisticated and carefully constructed tax rolls. They gave information relevant to manorial income with a uniformity that would suggest methodical planning. It is unlikely that a monastic management possessing the ability to conceive and execute a project on so large a scale, and employing what appears to have been a definite basic formula of inquisition, would have simply neglected real taxable units in the form of some women. The redactors took care to mention those women who did not belong to Saint Germain-des-Prés when they were married to the monastery's peasants; and women not tied to any particular manse were mentioned regularly among those who paid the head tax at the end of the *brevia*.[19] The importance of women in a peasant society was undeniable; they made up an important labor source, aside from their more obvious role in childbearing. Moreover, women were of especial importance in Saint Germain-des-Prés because it was they who passed on the status valuation to their children.[20]

There are several plausible reasons for the unbalanced sex ratio. Certainly, one must not ignore the possibility of female infanticide. That, and the death of many women during parturition, would account for a certain disequilibrium in the sex ratio. Undoubtedly, ninth-century midwives and medical practices produced many widowers. This might also account for the marked inequality we find generally, or for the inequality apparent in children's sex ratios. It is possible,

---

18 This male preponderance, as anomalous to modern times as it is, was not peculiar to the estates of Saint Germain-des-Prés. The Salic Law, both in its first redaction under Clovis and in the more extensive version under Charlemagne, stipulates a *wergeld* three times higher for a woman of childbearing age than for an adult male—which suggests a scarcity of women. See Andrée Lehmann, *Le rôle de la femme dans l'histoire de France au moyen âge* (Paris, 1952), 42.

19 See above, note 9; Perrin, "Note sur la population," 80–81; *Polyptyque*, III: 61; V: 94–116; VII: 81; IX: 30; *passim*.

20 See below, 214.

however, that the estates which showed a definite preponderance of men as opposed to women may have been in the process of clearing the forest for cultivatable fields. In those areas, women would have been of less use. They would have followed the men and boys to the untamed regions slowly, as conditions of life gradually softened and their skills and abilities could be more profitably utilized. In other words, the sex ratio might be an indication of an internal frontier clearance in the Île-de-France that provided more fields and food to supply the rising population of the ninth century.[21] Yet, it is also possible that the numerical masculine superiority was the result of an immigration of men who had hoped to find work and protection on these monastic lands.[22] Taken together, infanticide, maternal mortality, frontier clearance, and masculine mobility suggest a possible complex of factors explaining the high sex ratios displayed by the polyptych.

What is important is the indisputable fact of the high sex ratio, for whatever reason. The important point to note about this preponderance of men is that, as a result, the marriage market should have been auspicious for women. Since the number of men to each woman was so high and the economic advantages of a wife in a peasant society were so obvious, one would have expected the women to make excellent marriages in terms of both economics and status. Yet these two assumptions seem to be erroneous.

Many of the scholars who have studied the polyptych have noted, in passing, the odd marriage characteristics of the inhabitants.[23] There was, in addition, an unusually high proportion of socially unequal marriages—among the different peasant statuses—for which no apparent reason has hitherto been suggested. In 251 out of a total of 1,827 marriages, or 13.74 per cent, in which the statuses of both spouses were determinable, that of the man and woman were different. On the individual estates, the percentages ran from 1.28 per cent to 80 per cent, as seen in Table 1.

In 61 out of 251 cases, the man married beneath himself. In 190 cases or 75.69 per cent of the unequal matches, it was the woman, who may be assumed to have been in an ideal position, who married below her status. And it is interesting to note that in these cases, the average

---

21 This is a highly theoretical suggestion. The subject of sex ratios deserves more detailed treatment.
22 Ménager, "Considerations sociologiques," 1334–1335, and n. 66.
23 Among them, Longnon, Polyptyque, Introduction; Duby, Rural Economy; Guérard, Polyptyque . . . Prolégomènes.

Table 1 Sex Ratios and Marriages

Breve	TOTAL SEX RATIO	ADULT SEX RATIO	ADULT *Coloni* SEX RATIO	UNEQUAL MARRIAGES			
1.	177.1	252.9	207.6	21.40% or	3	out of	14
2.	133.3	136.6	129.6	10.17%	12		118
3.	148.6	150.0	152.19	18.87%	10		53
4.	153.1	126.6	106.66	10.70%	3		28
5.[a]	146.9?	146.9	135.5	1.28%	1		78
6.[a]	115.8?	115.8	101.81	6.38%	3		47
7.[a]	149.24?	149.24	124.07	15.00%	9		60
8.	130.6	140.0	119.23	25.93%	7		27
9.	128.0	125.38	112.14	8.94%	32		358
11.[b]	143.3	112.5	no male coloni	80.00%	12		15
13.[b]	141.6	119.8	91.86	37.19%	61		164
14.	124.3	125.8	115.12	3.64%	4		110
15.	131.6	114.6	106.48	9.18%	9		98
16.	125.3	125.84	116.25	8.86%	7		79
17.	134.3	125.0	127.77	5.41%	2		37
18.	118.1	142.8	257.14	38.48%	5		13
19.[a]	110.3?	110.3	110.99	4.31%	4		93
20.	144.0	123.3	119.23	20.69%	6		29
21.	128.8	121.5	104.76	24.00%	18		75
22.	128.6	112.1	107.06	18.63%	19		102
23.	122.7	118.1	141.17	15.00%	3		20
24.	115.7	120.2	122.92	12.65%	22		174
25.[a]	145.6?	145.6	123.07	11.92%	5		42
Fragmento Duo	156.2	133.3	123.07	9.09%	1		11

a The sex ratio among children is undeterminable.
b Brevia 10 and 12 contain no demographic materials.

number of children per couple ran to 2.04 as opposed to 1.76 where the man was the socially superior partner.

Why would so many of the available women—almost one sixth of the married population—marry men socially inferior? It could not have been due merely to a lack of eligible men of the same status. As was noted, the vast majority of people on the seigneuries were *coloni*, and it was the *colonae* who took the major role in this social transformation when the sex ratio averaged 117.06 among adults.[24] Even so, there was no dearth of marriageable *servi*. For example, in the Breve

24 See Table 1.

de Gaugiaco, there were four unmarried *servi* and only one unmarried *ancilla* (female *servus*). In the Breve de Nuviliaco, there were two to one. In fact, the overall sex ratio among *servi* adults was an incredible 297.56. Furthermore, it is unlikely that the unattached men of the corresponding status would be in the wrong age group. This was the least important of qualifications in an age untouched by concepts of "romantic love." Also, in some cases, the sex ratio was even more favorable among the children—which would indicate a rough similarity of age—than among adults.

We can rule out, too, any connection between personal and tenurial status as a factor in marriage. Unequal marriages appeared on free manses[25] and servile manses.[26] The extent of the holding made no difference, either. They occurred on manses whose territory ranged from twenty-eight *bunuaria* of arable land and four arpents of vineyards to eight *bunuaria* of arable land, one and one-half arpents of vineyards, and one and one-half arpents of meadow to two *bunuaria* of arable alone, with gradations in between, above, and below.[27]

It has been suggested, by Bloch among others, that by the time when the polyptych was redacted, social stratifications had become devoid of practical significance.[28] He suggested that the classes found within the manorial surveys were administrative anachronisms. In the day-to-day life of the individual they were meaningless, and were kept alive only by the fact that scribes and other servants of administration usually utilized terminology and categories of social analysis that were at least a generation behind the times. To an extent, this was certainly true. The dues relevant to personal service had generally fallen into disuse. Yet this unfortunately does not explain the marital mismatching that occurred on the manors of Saint Germain-des-Prés. If the solution were simply that no one really took the status hierarchy seriously, there would inevitably have been a statistically parallel number of cases of men making misalliances; and the average number of children in both groups would have been more evenly balanced. Yet this was not so—over three-fourths of these mixed marriages show that the women married below their status. Thus, while the social hierarchy had less and less meaning in economic life, it apparently retained some importance within a hierarchically-conscious society; every group had

25 For example, *Polyptyque*, VII: 7, 14, 15, 42; I: 6; XVIII: 6, 7, 8; *passim*.
26 See, for instance, *ibid.*, I: 13, 14; IV: 28; *passim*.
27 See, for example, *ibid.*, XI: 4; VII: 14; XVIII: 6; I: 13; etc.
28 Marc Bloch, *French Rural History* (Berkeley, 1966), 70.

its own "pecking order"—in fact, this was of particular psychological importance when the distinctions came to mean very little in practical life.

It is nevertheless possible to suggest a hypothesis as to the cause of the peculiar situation. On the manors of Saint Germain, the status of the mother decided the condition of the children, as prescribed in the laws of the Emperors Gratian, Valentinian II, and Theodoric.[29] Now this may not have always held true, but it apparently was a general rule, enhanced by the occasional exception. If the difference in status between husband and wife were very large, the position of the children sometimes became a compromise; this unusual situation was specifically mentioned by the redactors of the document. In the rules of inheriting status, however, Longnon agrees with Guérard that the condition of the mother seems to have been the determining factor. Their interpretation, as one would expect, is verified by an examination of the polyptych itself, in such passages as: "Frotcarius, Frudoldus, Frotbertus. These three are *lidi* because they were born of a *lida* mother; Martinus, a *servus*, and his wife, an *ancilla*, named Frotlindis, are people of Saint Germain. These are their children: Raganbolda, their daughter, is an *ancilla*, Faregaus, Widericus, and Winevoldus are *lidi* because their mother was a *colona*" (an example of the occasional compromise); or "These are the children of Dudoinus by another woman, and they are *servi*: Berhaus, Aclevertus, Dodo, Faregaus, Acleverga, Audina," or "Witbolda, an *ancilla*, and her sons, who are *servi*. . . ."[30]

There are many more examples.[31] In the Breve de Murcincto, on the eighth manse, the redactors took unusual care in recording the status of the children: "Alveus, a *colonus*, and his wife, a *colona*, named Ermoildis, are people of Saint Germain; they have four children— *also coloni*. . . ."[32] The reason would seem to be that the scribe had

---

29 P. Krueger (ed.), *Corpus Juris Civilis* (Berlin, 1959); *Codex Justinianus*, XI, 68, 4. "Ex ingenuo et colonis ancillisque nostris natasve origini, ex qua matres eorum sunt, facies deputari."

30 "Frotcarius, Frudoldus, Frotbertus. Isti tres sunt lidi, quoniam de lida matre sunt nati, Martinus servus et uxor ejus ancilla, nomine Frotlindis homines sancti Germani. Isti sunt eorum infantes: Raganbolda, filia eorum, est ancilla; Faregaus, Widericus, Winevoldus sunt lidi, quoniam de colona sunt nati. Isti sunt filii Dudoini de alia femina, et sunt servi: Berhaus, Aclevertus, Dodo, Faregaus, Acleverga, Audina. Witbolda ancilla et filii ejus servi. . . ."

31 *Polyptyque*, IX: 25; XIII: 65, 67, 68; also see, e.g., XIX: 18; XVII: 45; XXIV: 3, 169; XXV: 42.

32 "Alveus colonus et uxor ejus colona, nomine Ermoildis, homines sancti Germani, havent secum infantes IIII, *similiter coloni* . . ." *Polyptyque*, XVII: 8. Italics mine.

initially mistaken the status of Ermoildis; originally he had recorded her as an *ancilla*, caught the error, and corrected it by replacing that word with "*colona*." [33] As always, the names of the children followed their parents' names and statuses. But here the uncommon step was taken of adding "*similiter coloni*" so that there would be no error in calculating the children's status by misreading Ermoildis as an *ancilla*—because her condition devolved on her children. And, in other instances as mentioned above, the redactors carefully noted when children had mothers other than the women with whom they were living.[34]

Although social hierarchy made no effective difference in the life style of a couple, and mixed marriages were apparently not frowned upon, a consciousness of status did exist, and the woman herself passed on this status. This being so, one might suggest that the marriage characteristics exhibited by the polyptych represented a conscious pattern, if not a policy, on the part of at least some of the peasants. Is it not possible that men knowingly looked for a woman of higher social position for the psychological pride and prestige of an advantageous match and/or in order to improve the condition of his progeny? Certainly, the latter possibility was a result, whatever the original reason. This thesis can be graphically shown by both Appendix II and Table 2, where status comparisons for the children as opposed to adults show a trend toward higher status in the younger generation. Of the 8,377 people whose status is determinable, 87.81 per cent of the adults were *coloni* and 7.56 per cent were *servi*. In the next generation, however, their children were 90.34 per cent *coloni* and only 4.31 per cent *servi*.

This conclusion may be shown from another angle as well. The original status that a manse received corresponded to that of its original tenant and remained the same in perpetuity. It is extremely difficult to be definite because of the large number of manses of unspecified status and the possibility that old *hospicia*, or cottars' holdings, may have been absorbed into the seigneury as free manses. Yet, it would seem fair to posit that the entire population of the manors of Saint Germain-des-Prés at the time of the polyptych's redaction contained a larger proportion of *coloni* as compared to *servi* than at the time of the land's original division into free and servile manses.

In the overall picture of these medieval marriage characteristics,

33 See Longnon, *Polyptyque*, 250, n. 2.
34 See above, 209, and note 9.

Table 2 Status Change Comparison[a]

Breve	TOTAL ADULTS	TOTAL CHILDREN	ADULT Coloni	Coloni CHILDREN	ADULT Servi	Servi CHILDREN
1.	53	34	40 or 75.47%	29 or 90.63%	6 or 11.32%	0 or 0.00%
2.	304	330	287 94.41%	320 96.97%	14 4.61%	5 1.52%
3.	130	134	116 89.23%	123 91.79%	8 6.15%	3 2.24%
4.	67	54	62 92.54%	54 100.00%	5 7.46%	0 0.00%
5.	221	226	219 99.09%	226 100.00%	2 0.09%	0 0.00%
6.	117	117	111 94.87%	114 97.44%	3 2.56%	0 0.00%
7.	138	147	121 87.68%	117 79.59%	17 12.32%	30 20.41%
8.	64	68	57 89.06%	58 85.29%	3 4.69%	4 5.88%
9.	816	812	734 89.95%	755 92.98%	35 4.29%	23 2.83%
11.	34	36	6 17.65%	5 13.89%	15 44.12%	9 25.00%
13.	353	415	237 67.14%	302 72.77%	51 14.45%	45 10.81%
14.	271	189	256 94.46%	183 97.34%	13 4.80%	1 0.53%
15.	256	196	223 87.11%	186 94.88%	29 11.33%	8 4.08%
16.	192	91	173 90.10%	79 86.81%	18 6.77%	8 8.79%
17.	88	51	82 93.18%	44 86.27%	4 4.55%	0 0.00%
18.	31	9	25 80.65%	6 66.67%	2 6.45%	2 22.20%
19.	198	237	192 96.97%	229 96.62%	0 0.00%	0 0.00%
20.	78	64	57 73.08%	55 85.94%	19 24.36%	6 9.38%
21.	157	195	129 82.17%	169 86.67%	17 10.83%	8 4.10%
22.	207	259	176 85.02%	250 95.53%	24 11.59%	0 0.00%
23.	46	46	41 89.13%	37 80.43%	3 6.52%	5 10.87%
24.	360	307	321 89.17%	285 92.83%	35 9.72%	18 5.86%
25.	101	undeterminable	96 95.05%	undeterminable	3 2.97%	undeterminable
Frag. Duo	34	43	29 85.29%	41 95.35%	5 14.71%	2 4.65%
OVERALL	4,316	4,060	3,789 87.81%	3,667 90.34%	326 7.56%	175 4.31%

a Breve XI shows a loss in both *coloni* and *servi*; on this fisc the loss was absorbed by the more fluid intermediate group of *lidi*. Conceivably the trend could continue in the next generation or the *lidi* could buy their emancipation. Brevia VII, VIII, XVIII, and XXIII do not show the characteristic we have been tracing in the two to three generations which characterize the polyptych. There is no need to assume that the upward demographic spiral would have taken place consistently and at the same rate in all places. Again the trend could conceivably continue in the next generation. The overall characteristics for the polyptych are visually demonstrated in Appendix II.

women would not necessarily have resented or objected to marrying beneath themselves because, in essence, it made no effective change to their lives, nor would their children lose caste. But there could be a more positive reason. One can assume, with the sex ratio being as generally high as it was, that in many cases a woman would have had a fair number of brothers. While the number of children in a family averaged between two and three, there would obviously be cases of five, six, seven, even eight or more children in a ménage.[35] At the same time, on the lands belonging to Saint Germain-des-Prés, women could work and control their manses themselves if there were no men in the households; for the most part, we see this in the case of widows.[36] Therefore, it would appear reasonable to suggest that where a woman had a large number of brothers, the possibility of her attaining control of the family plot was slim. As a consequence, she would offer little economic incentive toward marriage to a man of her own status.[37] Yet, at the same time, her very status—without the economic inducement of land—would offer positive motivation to a man in a lower social position. In other words, a man would marry up for psychological reasons or with the conscious intention of improving the status of his progeny; a woman would marry down due to the force of economic circumstance. The result was the transformation of the class structure. One confirmation of this interpretation is the larger number of children in these families, by contrast with those in which the male was of a higher status. The hypothesis is reinforced, too, by the fact that— aside from discernible widows—the unmarried women of these fiscs were quite often, though not always, from a low social situation.

This explanation also helps to account for the fact noted above— the larger proportion of *coloni* as opposed to *lidi* and *servi*. *Lidi* could have bought themselves into a higher situation[38] and thereby reduced their numbers. But *servi* had no way of improving their positions in their lifetimes unless they successfully ran away and became *hôtes* on some other seigneury, as many of them undoubtedly did. Many more, however, must have found it difficult to leave; and is it not possible to suggest that while they could not ameliorate their own

35 *Polyptyque*, II: 30, 36; III: 12, 13; V: 15, 47, 62; VII: 16, 8, 40, 58; IX: 92, 119; XI: 3, 8; XIII: 5, 67, 81; XIV: 9, 11, 30; these are just isolated examples of which many more could easily be found.
36 See, for example, *ibid.*, XV: 66; XVI: 86, 41; XX: 38–41; *passim.*
37 This point was suggested by William Courtenay.
38 Longnon, *Polyptyque*, Introduction, 41.

plight economically, they might do so psychologically or even aid their children's condition by a judiciously chosen marriage.[39] The lords would not object, for they lost virtually nothing in personal dues (what they lost in *manoperae* [*corvées*], they made up in *censive*), and the dues of the tenure remained the same.

While it is impossible to argue back from a ninth-century document to a fourth-century situation, one may wonder if the thesis of virtual slave nonreproduction and mass manumission[40] is as satisfactory an answer to the problem of the decline of slavery as has been supposed. If one ventures to wander into the dubious world of pure hypothesis, the polyptych of Saint Germain-des-Prés might conceivably represent an indication—a link in a chain—of a gradual but persistent improvement in status through calculated marriage arrangements, by selection on a basis of heritable status. It is a thesis that certainly suggests another basis for future investigation into the fact that slaves declined in percentage and absolute numerical importance throughout most of the Middle Ages. There are obviously other problems which the polyptych suggests for investigation, but they are too diverse and detailed to be discussed here. One thing, at least, is clear: within Saint Germain-des-Prés, by slow degrees, a statistically interesting proportion of the peasantry moved up a rung of the status ladder.

---

39 This pattern of unequal marriages was not a situation unique to the ninth century or Saint Germain-des-Prés. Cinzio Violante, in his *La Società Milanese Nell'età Precomunale* (Bari, 1953), noted that clerics would marry free women so that their children would inherit the mother's free status and the father's ecclesiastical benefices. These clerics were *coloni* (159), and, c. 1000, Otto III questioned this abuse in a diploma to the Vercelli church: "Statuimus quoqui, ut omnes filii vel filie colonorum ex familia sancti Eusebii in servitute ecclesie maneant neque libertas matris, se colone servo adhesit, hiis qui nati fuerint, prosit volumus." Sickel [ed.], (*Monumenta Germaniae Historica, Diplomata regum et imperatorum Germaniae* [Hanover, 1888], II, pt. 2, 811–812, no. 383.)

40 Marc Bloch, "Le servage dans la société européenne," *Mélanges historiques* (Paris, 1963), I, 259–528.

Appendix I

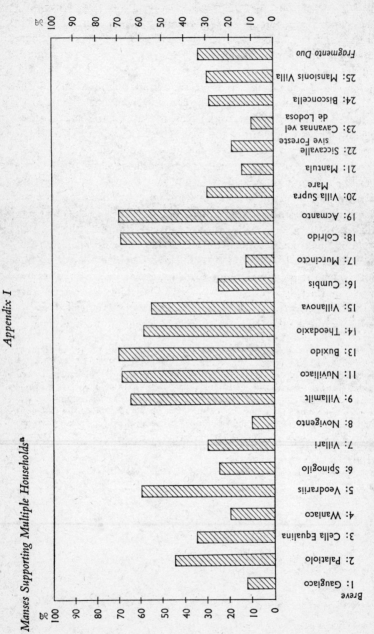

Manses Supporting Multiple Households[a]

a I intend to discuss the varying degrees of population pressure against the land at a later date.

Appendix II

Improvement in Status over the course of two to three Generations[a]

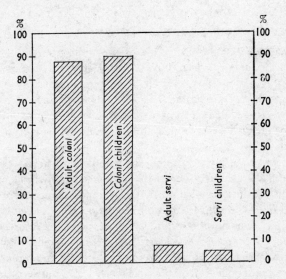

a This chart represents the characteristics exhibited by 8,377 people whose status can be determined. Over the course of two to three generations, as determinable in the polyptych of Saint Germain-des-Prés, there has been a small but definite and significant improvement in the status of the monastery's peasants.

Pierre Goubert

Historical Demography and the Reinterpretation of Early Modern French History:

A Research Review   One of the most fruitful of the historical techniques developed since World War II has been in the field of historical demography. Although demographic history had been practiced before 1945, a dramatically different approach appeared in the post-war period. The French have been among the leaders of this new branch of the discipline, and it is to their contribution that this article will be devoted.

The origins of this new approach are difficult to trace. Traditional historians had ceased to dominate the field after 1929, when a group of non-traditional historians led by Marc Bloch and Lucien Febvre formed the small Ecole des Annales. But the innovators paid little attention to demography. One historian who was quite close to the Annales group, Henri Sée, even wrote an article asserting the impossibility of discovering the size of the French population in the seventeenth century.[1]

The demographic revolution in French history proved to be the child of two distinct groups—a few historians who became interested in demography in 1944,[2] and a number of statisticians and demographers who became interested in history two or three years later.[3] The two groups eventually merged, and now the Société de Démographie Historique has more than two hundred members. If we examine the concerns of the two original groups, we can see how they transformed

Pierre Goubert is Professor at the Sorbonne and the Ecole Pratique des Hautes Etudes, Paris. He is the author of *Beauvais et le Beauvaisis de 1600 à 1730* (Paris, 1960), *Louis XIV et Vingt Millions de Français* (Paris, 1966; New York, 1970), and *L'Ancien Régime* (Paris, 1969).

1   Henri Sée, "Peut-on évaluer la population de l'ancienne France?" *Revue d'Economie Politique*, XXXVIII (1924), 647ff.
2   Jean Meuvret, "Les mouvements des prix de 1661 à 1715 et leurs répercussions," *Journal de la société de statistique de Paris*, LXXV (1944), 109–119; Claude Ernest Labrousse, *La crise de l'économie française à la fin de l'Ancien Régime et au début de la Révolution* (Paris, 1944), 183ff.
3   The first issue of *Population* appeared in January 1946; the names Alfred Sauvy, Jean Bourgeois, Jean Daric, Alain Girard, Jean Stoetzel, Jean Sutter, and Paul Vincent, all statisticians, were among the first to appear in the journal.

our knowledge of early modern French history, and how the more recent generation (which will be discussed below) has built on their work.

The first group consisted of a handful of historians who specialized in economic and social history. The three principal figures, Ernest Labrousse, Jean Meuvret, and Marcel Reinhard, all began to publish at the same time. Today these three men are all approximately seventy years old. Their primary and almost identical purposes can be summarized as follows:

1. By linking economic problems with demographic problems, they hoped to explain economic growth (in the eighteenth century) or economic stagnation (in the seventeenth) by reference to demographic circumstances. This topic has now become a sort of "Tarte à la Crême."[4] The difficulty with such an approach is that frequently we do not know the exact percentages of economic growth and population growth.

2. Their second purpose was to point out the many differences between seventeenth- and eighteenth-century French demography. As they have shown, national population growth during the seventeenth century was halted by frequent demographic crises—notably in 1630, 1650, 1662, and 1710. During the eighteenth century, the crises became less and less frequent, and less and less severe—as a result, the population began to grow: from about 20 to 26 million in the course of the century.[5]

3. One member of the group, Jean Meuvret, sought to reveal the nature of a demographic crisis during the Ancien Régime.[6] It was a real crisis—very short in time (one or two years), but very powerful in effect: the number of deaths multiplying by two, three, four, or more times; the number of marriages reduced to very few; the number of births divided by two, three, or four; and an increase of beggars and

4 It has occupied primarily English-speaking historians. In France two works have served as the point of departure: François Simiand, *Le salaire, l'évolution sociale et la monnaie* (Paris, 1932); and Claude Ernest Labrousse, *Esquisse du mouvement des prix et des revenus en France au XVIIIᵉ siècle* (Paris, 1933). The current state of the question is presented by Fernand Braudel and Claude Ernest Labrousse, *Histoire économique et sociale de la France, Vol. II: 1660–1789* (Paris, 1970).
5 An example of the chronology of the crises can be found in Pierre Goubert, *Beauvais et le Beauvaisis de 1600 à 1730* (Paris, 1960); and a total overview in Marcel Reinhard, André Armengaud, and Jacques Dupaquier, *Histoire générale de la population mondiale* (Paris, 1968; 3rd ed.), 146–270.
6 Jean Meuvret, "Les crises de subsistances et de la démographie de la France d'Ancien Regime," *Population*, I (1946), 643–650.

vagrants. Meuvret also demonstrated that demographic crises were frequently connected with crises in the price of cereals, and perhaps caused by them. He proved, too, that the worst crises, with serious starvation, diminished after 1710, and still further after 1740.

The second group of scholars in this generation, consisting of demographers, appeared quite suddenly with the foundation of the Institut National d'Etudes Démographiques (I.N.E.D.) in 1945—an organization which soon started to publish a journal, *Population*. It is the Institut's good fortune to have as its director Alfred Sauvy, whose skills in this field are unsurpassed in France. But the scholar who has done and is now doing the most essential work in the subject is Louis Henry, who began to publish papers and organize research after 1950.[7]

The first purpose of the Henry group was to calculate correctly the demographic characteristics of pre-Malthusian populations, especially between 1680 and 1790. To do this, they have devised the highly original and powerful method known as family reconstitution. This method is made possible by the exceptional quality and number of French Catholic parish registers, which provide basic information about births, marriages, and deaths. Using these materials, Henry and his group have been able to calculate birth, marriage, and death rates with great accuracy, and to study fertility rates with the same precision. Their first analysis dealt with Crulai, a village in Normandy, whose name is now known by every seventeenth- and eighteenth-century demographic historian.[8] Since then, a number of other monographs have been published.[9] The method has now been accepted, practiced, and imitated in every country, including the United States, where the archives make such research possible.

Such were the beginnings of scientific demographic history in France. Today, twenty years later, what can one say about its condition, its conclusions, and its prospects?

7 The first article by Louis Henry dealing with historical demography was "Une richesse démographique en friche; les registres paroissiaux," *Population*, VIII (1953), 281–290; soon thereafter came the first edition of the famous little manual, *Des registres paroissiaux à l'histoire de la population: manuel de dépouillement et d'exploitation de l'état-civil ancien*, by Michel Fleury and Louis Henry (Paris, 1956).

8 Etienne Gautier and Louis Henry, *La population de Crulai, paroisse normande* (Paris, 1958).

9 Among the best works, all of which appeared among the *cahiers* of the Institut National d'Etudes Démographiques, are: J. Henripin, *La population canadienne au debut du XVIIIe siècle* (Paris, 1954); Jean Ganiage, *Trois villages d'Ile-de-France au 18e siècle* (Paris, 1963); and Jean Valmary, *Familles paysannes au 18e siècle en Bas-Quercy* (Paris, 1965).

During these years, a large quantity of books and articles has been published. Fortunately, they can be surveyed with the aid of general reviews and journals, especially *Population Index* (Princeton), *Population Studies* (London), *Population* (Paris), and, since 1964, *Annales de Démographie Historique* (Paris).

The best papers have dealt with subjects at the parish or regional level, because these rest on the surest foundations. General books and general topics are often hypothetical and hazardous, especially those that must rely upon the crude demographic data available for the years before 1700. To indicate the achievements of the field more clearly, I might discuss two distinct areas: the present state of old questions and the appearance of new problems. I have chosen three "old" problems: demographic crisis; characteristic pre-Malthusian demographic rates; and population growth and economic growth.

DEMOGRAPHIC CRISIS   Two qualifications have been added to Meuvret's conception of a demographic crisis: First, that demographic crises did not occur in large parts of Europe—if they really occurred anywhere. Second, that if they did take place, these crises were caused *not* by the high price of food, nor by any kind of dearth or starvation, but by epidemics.[10]

It should be noted that political and religious prejudices have affected these discussions.[11] Nonetheless, I think that the most reasonable and satisfactory conclusions can be summarized as follows:

1. Genuine short and violent demographic crises occurred in large parts of Europe up to the early eighteenth century.[12]

2. Some crises were substantially the result of the high price of cereals (in Northern and Central France, 1662); others of epidemics

---

10 There is a good summary of these points of view in *Problèmes de mortalité: Actes du Colloque international de démographie historique* (Liège, 1963), 85–89 and 93–97. An example of a sharp attack on the "black" view of demographic crises can be found in Pierre Chaunu, *La civilisation de l'Europe classique* (Paris, 1966), 233–237.

11 The defenders of the old monarchy, still a large group in the French historical tradition, cannot admit that there were famines when the "Grand Roi" reigned. Moreover, many Catholics and Protestants "of the right" regard the mortality crises as God's punishments for human sins, and not as phenomena that resulted from economic, social, or political organization. These prejudices are more often implicit than explicit.

12 See, for example, Reinhard, Armengaud, and Dupaquier, *Population mondiale*, 115 (for the sixteenth century), 217 (for the eighteenth century in Norway), and 261 (for the eighteenth century in western France).

(plague in London, Catalonia, Italy, and Marseille in 1720); and others of both high prices and epidemics (1630).[13]

3. The richest and most important trading countries (England, The Netherlands) did not have real demographic crises (except plagues). Coastal areas, and the Southern and Mediterranean countries, were equally fortunate.[14]

4. An accurate study of a demographic crisis is an excellent way to investigate social structures, because social groups behaved differently during crises. The best-known example is the flight of the rich from misfortune, sickness, and the dangers of contagion. Even clergy and doctors left, the only exceptions being the especially charitable and the particularly well paid (known as "epidemic doctors"). The crisis always struck hardest in the poorest sections, in the poorest families. Epidemics crossed social barriers only when the rich did not flee soon enough.[15]

In sum, demographic crises were one of the characteristics of pre-Malthusian populations. Let us now turn to other characteristics.

CHARACTERISTIC DEMOGRAPHIC RATES   Twenty years ago, demographers thought that the basic demographic characteristics of the whole of France were similar to those of Crulai (the first village studied by Louis Henry): that is, a high marriage rate, late marriages, one birth every second year, an infant mortality rate of less than 20 per cent, an absolute growth in population after 1680, and some emigration from villages to towns or other provinces. More recent family reconstitutions have made it necessary to modify these older conclusions.

13   A crisis of subsistence without an epidemic took place in 1662—see Pierre Goubert, *L'avènement du Roi-Soleil* (Paris, 1967), 281–296. For major mortality crises caused by epidemics of plague, see, for Catalonia and the Mediterranean, Jorge Nadal, *La Población española, siglos XVI a XX* (Barcelona, n.d. but 1966), 53–62. For the famous plague of 1720, see Charles Carrière, M. Courdurié, and F. Rebuffat, *Marseille, ville morte: La peste de 1720* (Marseille, 1968). The mixed crisis of 1630 (scarcity and epidemics) has been studied only in the localities (see, for example, Goubert, *Beauvais, passim.*, and Pierre Deyon, *Amiens, capitale provinciale: Etude sur la Société urbaine au XVII siècle* [Paris, 1967], *passim.*, but especially the first section).

14   The case of England is well known—see, for example, the various works of H. Habbakuk and the precise study by J. D. Chambers, "The Vale of Trent," *Economic History Review*, X (1957), supplement. The favored situation of coastal areas is revealed by Pierre Gouhier, "Port-en-Bessin, 1597–1792," *Cahier des Annales de Normandie* (Caen), I (1962). For the Mediterranean regions see René Baehrel, *Une croissance, la Basse-Provence rurale, fin XVI siècle-1789* (Paris, 1961); and Emmanuel Le Roy Ladurie, *Les Paysans de Languedoc* (Paris, 1966), 2v.

15   See René Baehrel, "La haine de classe en temps d'épidémie," *Annales, Economies, Sociétés, Civilisations*, VII (July–September, 1952), 35ff.; and Carrière, Courdurié, and Rebuffat, *Marseille*, 87.

The first discovery was the variability of death rates, especially those of children. In some places on Normandy's sea shore, the infant mortality rate was as low as 15 per cent; in swampy areas, such as Sologne or Bas-Languedoc, it was as high as 35 or 38 per cent; in the poor and dirty suburbs of industrial towns like Beauvais, Amiens, or Lyon, it was the same or higher. When children were put out to nurse, especially in big towns such as Paris and Lyon, their death-rate exceeded 50 per cent; and it reached 80 per cent among the abandoned children of Paris.[16]

In the last few years differences in female fertility have been emphasized. We used to think, following Henry, that women typically had babies every second year (French-Canadian women being exceptions, with more frequent births). We now know that women in Brittany and in French Flanders gave birth almost *every year*, while in the South-Western provinces, by contrast, it was almost every *third* year.[17] Why? Possibly because of physiological factors, or the beginnings of primitive contraception in the South-West. A very recent thesis by Maurice Garden has demonstrated that in eighteenth-century Lyon women had a Canadian or Breton fertility (but they married late, and their children very often died at the wet nurses' cottages).[18] In a large village near Paris, Argenteuil, my students have found some women with a Breton and others with a South-Western fertility rate.[19] We still have much to learn about fertility.

There is also much to be found out about marriage. Girls generally came very late to marriage (when 25 to 26 years old), and 95 per cent were not pregnant (many more were pregnant in eighteenth-century England).[20] It is difficult to explain these characteristics. We can link them with custom (coming of age at 25), with economic and familial

16 For Beauvais, see Goubert, *Beauvais*; for Amiens, Deyon, *Amiens*; for Normandy, Gouhier, "Port-en-Bessin"; for Lyon, the thesis by Maurice Garden, "Lyon et les Lyonnais au XVIIIᵉ siècle," which will be published in 1970 or 1971; for Paris, the direct work in the archives by two of my students, Charles Delasselle and Paul Galliano, on foundlings and on infants sent to wet-nurses by Parisian hospitals (to be published soon).
17 See, for example, Pierre Goubert, "Legitimate Fecundity and Infant Mortality in France During the Eighteenth Century: A Comparison," *Daedalus*, XCVII (1968), 593–603.
18 Garden, "Lyon."
19 Michel Tyvaert and Jean-Claude Giacchetti, "Argenteuil, 1740–1790: étude de démographie historique," *Annales de Démographie Historique* (Paris, 1969), 40–61.
20 For England, see P. E. H. Hair, "Bridal Pregnancy in Rural England in Earlier Centuries," *Population Studies*, XX (1966), 233–243; "Bridal Pregnancy in Earlier Rural England Further Examined," *ibid.*, XXIV (1970), 59–70. For France, we have the concordant results of the many monographs already cited, which are well summarized in Pierre Chaunu, *La Civilisation de l'Europe classique* (Paris, 1966), 196.

difficulties, with the austerity of the Counter-Reformation, or with the confessor's authority: official Church doctrine stipulated that only in marriage was full sexual activity permitted, and that sexual activity was allowed only in order to produce children. We are also beginning to learn that the average marriage age changed from country to country, and from one century to the next; in particular, we now know that these characteristics changed markedly by the late eighteenth century (more illegitimacy, more pregnant brides).[21] Marriage is the main act of demographic significance that depends on the human will, and it must be considered as a most important historical fact, highly significant for the history of society and of social and religious (or irreligious) mentalities.

What we have learned, above all, is that if we are to reach conclusions about the demographic characteristics of pre-industrial populations, we must emphasize their great variety, and try to explain why the differences arose.

POPULATION GROWTH AND ECONOMIC GROWTH   Here equally wide variations have become apparent. During the eighteenth century, some provinces in Western France did not experience a significant population growth—very likely because they were already fairly densely populated in the seventeenth century—while others (Alsace, Languedoc) grew very quickly and vigorously—very likely because they were sparsely populated before 1715.[22] In some areas, the beginning of the century was marked by demographic difficulties; in others, the end of the century. In addition, the middle of the century was beset by hard times—nevertheless, the general conclusion (though I am a little skeptical) is that French population grew by 30 to 35 per cent between 1720 and 1790, and that this was not a very important growth among European nations.[23] What makes this problematical is that our young economic historians are now denying that there was an agricultural revolution, or indeed any real improvement in French pro-

21 It is difficult to determine age at marriage before 1670, because parish registers are very incomplete. Some information can be obtained from Marcel Lachiver, *La Population de Meulan du XVII au XIX siècle* (Paris, 1969), 138; and from P. Lions, "Un dénombrement de la population de Brueil-en-Vexin en 1625," *Annales de Démographie Historique* (1967), 521–531. For the special case of Touraine, where people married at a younger age, see Gilles Chassier, "Bléré au XVIIIᵉ siècle: étude de démographie historique," *ibid.* (1969).

22 See Reinhard, Armengaud, and Dupaquier, *Population mondiale*, 250, fig. 44, and 252–253.

23 See the recent summary in Braudel and Labrousse, *Histoire économique*, II, 9–84.

duction, during the eighteenth century—or suggesting at most a small improvement of not more than 15 or 18 per cent in agricultural output (industrial production having very little effect).[24] If these historians are right, it becomes rather difficult to explain how six or seven million more Frenchmen could be fed, find work, and appear richer in 1780 than in 1710—but that is another question.

Not only have the old problems been more thoroughly explored, but new questions have been raised by the active demographic research of recent years. The most important is contraception, and I shall also discuss population mobility and the problems of the towns.

CONTRACEPTION   To contraception, or "birth control," a great many articles, speeches, discussions, and passions have been devoted. The major conclusion is that France was the only country to use contraception as early as the last years of the eighteenth century—fifty or one hundred years before any other country. The approximate general birth rate in France stood between 38 and 39 per 1,000 in the decade 1781–1790; it dropped to 35.3 in 1791–1800 and to 31.2 in 1811–1815, and fell to below 30 around 1832. It was below 25 in 1880. *No other country in the known world experienced so early and so rapid a decline.* The tables worked out by the Office of Population Research at Princeton University demonstrate how exceptional the French experience has been.[25] Now we are asking why? exactly when? exactly where? ("how?" is not a difficult question to answer—coitus interruptus).

Some historians have discussed one matter vehemently: did birth control exist as early as the *first* part of the eighteenth century? In some noble or bourgeois families, as among prostitutes, it certainly did. But was contraception practiced in the towns and country in general? Perhaps some form of contraception existed in a few provinces (for

24   There are two new and important articles on this subject: M. Morineau, "Y a-t-il eu une Révolution agricole en France au XVIIIᵉ siècle?," *Revue Historique*, XCII (1968), 299ff.; and Denis Richet, "Croissance et blocages en France du XVᵉ au XVIIIᵉ siècle," *Annales, Economies, Sociétés, Civilisations*, XXXIII (1968), 759ff.

25   The most conclusive local examples can be found in the articles and books already cited by Ganiage (*Trois villages*), Lachiver (*Meulan*), and Tyvaert and Giacchetti ("Argenteuil"), and in Raymond Deniel and Louis Henry, "La population d'un village du Nord de la France, Sainghin-en-Mélantois de 1665 à 1851," *Population*, XX (1965), 563–602. There are good summaries in Reinhard, Armengaud, and Dupaquier, *Population mondiale*, 296 (birth rates, 1791–1815) and 262–267 (eighteenth century). The methods that were used, and some new ideas, are discussed in Jacques Dupaquier and M. Lachiver, "Sur les débuts de la contraception en France, ou les deux malthusianismes," *Annales, Economies, Sociétés, Civilisations*, XXIV (1969), 1391–1406.

instance, in the South-West), but the evidence is not conclusive.[26] Perhaps this was also the case between 1750 and 1770—but it becomes certain that birth control was employed in a number of towns and villages only during the 1780s (around Paris and in the South-West). The practice was propagated from town to country, from South to North, at first very slowly, and then very quickly—except in Western provinces like Brittany.[27] I do not know if the "Révolution de 1789" was a "bourgeois revolution," but I am sure it witnessed a demographic revolution in large areas of the nation.

The reasons for this are not evident, mainly because men (and women) did not write or speak about such behavior. Historical demographers are currently debating possible religious (or irreligious) causes, economic or legal causes (including legal changes in the *code civil*), and changes in the mentality of parents.[28] It seems to me that any interpretation will have to be complex and difficult. It would be useful to separate, on the one hand, the old predispositions toward contraception in certain places and among certain social groups, a practice which accelerated in the 1770s and 1780s, from, on the other hand, the enormous

26 Numerous examples are given in Hélène Bergues, and others, *La prévention des naissances dans la famille* (Paris, 1960). See, too, the various articles on "Histoire biologique et Société" in the special number of *Annales, Economies, Sociétés, Civilisations*, XXIV (1969). For France's dukes and peers, see Louis Henry and Claude Lévy, "Ducs et Pairs sous l'Ancien Régime: caractéristiques démographiques d'une caste," *Population*, XV (1960), 807–830. For the bourgeoisie, see Henry, *Anciennes familles genevoises* (Paris, 1956). For prostitutes, see the first two items cited in this footnote. For the south-west, see Valmary, *Bas-Quercy*, and Anne Zink, *Azereix: La vie d'une communauté rurale à la fin du XVIIIe siècle* (Paris, 1969), 82.

27 The directions in which the practice of contraception spread can be deduced from the many detailed studies, cited above, which have been completed. A number of new ones appeared in *Annales de Démographie Historique* in 1969.

28 The problem of causation has never been studied in depth. It is a most difficult problem, and some attempts to come to grips with it can be found in Reinhard, Armengaud, and Dupaquier, *Population mondiale*; in the works of Chaunu; and in Aries, Bergues, and others, *Prévention des naissances*. Pierre Aries takes his explanation from certain characteristics of family mentality (for example, a concern to do better in raising children); John T. Noonan, *Contraception* (Cambridge, Mass., 1966); Michel Vovelle (in studies of Provence that are soon to appear), J. Dupaquier, and I myself believe that the explanation lies in the decline of religious belief; Pierre Chaunu invokes the long-term consequences of a return to Jansenist asceticism—see, too, Jean-Claude Perrot, "La population du Calvados sous la Révolution et l'Empire," *Contributions à l'histoire démographique de la Révolution et de l'Empire* (Commission d'histoire économique et sociale de la Révolution française, 1965), 115ff. Peasant contraception, especially in the south-west of France, seems to have resulted from the wish to avoid dividing the land, the "family domain," among many children. All these indications emerge from discussions by historical demographers, and should be brought together in a work of synthesis.

(though not general) outbreak of the phenomenon that accompanied the tremendous liberation and social mobility of the French Revolution. Whatever the explanation, it is certain that France was the first birth-controlled nation in the world.

POPULATION MOBILITY   Another problem now under discussion is the mobility of the population. Everybody knows that the French are men who do not move. In the seventeenth and eighteenth centuries, brides and bridegrooms were generally born in the same parish, or in neighboring parishes. Perhaps ten per cent traveled ten miles to become engaged.[29]

But this relative immobility did not last. One of the most impressive discoveries made by recent studies has been that, despite regional variations, during the second half of the eighteenth century, at the very time when contraception was beginning to spread, mobility was multiplying two- or three-fold. People were moving more often, and were traveling farther than before.[30] Once again, this period emerges as a decisive dividing point in demographic history.

Moreover, it is slowly becoming apparent that certain provinces, such as Flanders, Normandy, Dauphiné, and the mountain areas, had a large excess of population, with many more births than deaths. It is clear that their inhabitants were leaving. By contrast, many towns had large deficits (more deaths than births), especially if we add the deaths of foster children to the totals of town deaths. What this implies has been demonstrated by a number of scrupulous local studies, which have recently revealed substantial migration from country regions to a number of towns, particularly to Paris, Rouen, Nantes, Bordeaux, and Lyon.[31] And this raises the demographic problems of town populations, a subject which is still too little understood.

29 All the monographs on villages and regions reveal this low mobility *before* 1750. See, for a start, Goubert, *Beauvais*, 66. The best recent study is Lachiver, *Meulan*, 91–122.
30 This is confirmed by all the local and regional studies cited in the previous footnotes.
31 For Paris, see Louis Henry and Claude Lévy, "Quelques données sur la région autour de Paris au XVIII siècle," *Population*, XVII (1962), 297–326. For Rouen, there are some indications in Chaunu, *Europe classique*, and his *Histoire de Normandie*, which will appear in 1970. For Nantes, see Alain Croix, "La démographie du pays nantais au XVI siècle," *Annales de Démographie Historique* (1967), 63–90, which should be compared with Blayo and Henry, "Données démographiques sur la Bretagne et l'Anjou de 1740 à 1829," *ibid.*, 91ff. For Bordeaux, see the contribution of Poussou to *Histoire de Bordeaux: Bordeaux au XVIII siècle* (1968), 325ff. For Lyon, see the forthcoming book by Garden, cited above.

THE TOWNS   Following the early studies of villages, increasing attention is being given to France's towns. There are many difficulties: the large population that has to be dealt with; the problem of handling the many parishes into which towns are divided—anywhere from ten to forty—especially since their registers are not all equally well preserved; the fact that many infants, sent to wet-nurses, died outside the town; the presence of hospitals, where people both from the town and from the surrounding countryside went for treatment and died; and the very high mobility of the population. It is by no means certain that the sampling techniques worked out by the I.N.E.D. will produce viable results,

Nonetheless, there are young historians at work in many areas. Lyon, in particular, will soon be the most thoroughly studied city in France, when books by Richard Gascon, Natalie Davis, and Maurice Garden appear. Garden's model study of Lyon will soon be published, and he throws fresh light on the whole problem of urban historical demography. His conclusions are striking: more than half of the inhabitants of Lyon were born outside the city; they married very late; and their fertility was extremely high (very often one child a year, which is the highest rate ever observed). Half of the infants were sent away to wet-nurses, and more than half of these died while away. Illegitimacy, pregnant brides, and abortion were not rare—as they were in rural villages.

Cities like Lyon "devoured" the surrounding countryside and occasionally even more distant areas. They rapidly consumed excess populations, and they had to be fed afresh in each generation. But will the picture presented by Lyon hold true for all large cities? It is possible, but we must wait for other books to find out.[32]

The most significant discovery to emerge from the varied studies of recent years is the vast transformation of the late eighteenth century. Some of the elements of that transformation have been mentioned: the spread of contraception and the rise in mobility. But other demographic phenomena also appeared for the first time in this period: an increase in

32   There is a good bibliography of the history of French towns: Philippe Dollinger and Philippe Wolff, *Bibliographie des villes de France* (Paris, 1967). The best town history is the multi-volume *Histoire de Bordeaux* (volumes IV [1966] and V [1968] cover the fifteenth to eighteenth centuries), being produced under the editorship of Charles Higounet. Chapters VIII and IX of Jean Delumeau, *La civilisation de la Renaissance* (Paris, 1967), are very good. Roger Mols, *Introduction à la démographie historique des villes d'Europe* (Gembloux, 1954–1956), 3v., is always useful, but it is already becoming out of date.

illegitimacy, a growth in the percentage of pregnant brides, the beginning of a decline in the infant death rate, and the end of serious demographic crises.[33] Taken together, these changes brought about a revolution in the patterns of French demography.

My conclusion will be optimistic. We have calculated a great many accurate demographic rates for some places and at some dates. We know the differences between one country and another—especially between England and France—and from province to province, from town to village. We can observe evolutions and changes over time. Demographic history is now linked with economic, social, religious, and psychological history. These are remarkable additions to historical knowledge; now we have to explain the rates, their differences and changes. Fortunately, a large group of young historians and demographers are at work. We can hope that they will succeed in explaining what we have detected, but still do not really understand.

---

33 These conclusions are drawn from the various articles and books that have been cited above, and they will be elaborated in the second volume of my book on the Ancien Régime, which is now in press.

Peter Laslett

Age at Menarche in Europe
since the Eighteenth Century

Age at sexual maturation is of obvious interest to historians of the family. It determines the point at which children reach the crisis of adolescence and begin the process of asserting their independence from their parents, and from the family of origin generally. It marks the stage at which they become capable of full sexual intercourse, and, for girls, of experiencing menstruation, both of which stages are often of crucial psychological significance. It introduces the possibility of procreation, which immediately implies stringent social control. For no community at any period, whatever its resources, can ever allow individuals to reproduce at will. In most societies known to me—certainly in all societies belonging to the Christian tradition, and perhaps in almost every other, too—sexual maturation is an essential preliminary to marriage for both sexes.

This is a subject which must affect the historian of social structure generally even more than most of those which concern the family group. If children mature late, then presumably parental supremacy endures longer. This has implications for societies organized on patriarchal lines which are easy to see. Furthermore there are indications that age at sexual maturation may differ between social classes, and this implies a distinction in the fundamental process of personality development between bourgeoisie and workers, or, in the past, between lords and ladies, gentlemen and gentlewomen, as compared to common folk.[1] Yet almost nothing numerical is known about age at sexual maturity for any society before the twentieth century, and what fragments of information we have mostly concern only one of the conspicuous developments which occur at this time to one of the sexes. This is menarche, the onset of menstruation or of the "flowers," as our ancestors more elegantly phrased it. Some statistical information is available on the heights and weights of both sexes in nineteenth century Europe, and it may be that documents will be found which

Peter Laslett is co-founder of the Cambridge Group for the History of Population and Social Structure and is Reader in Politics and the History of Social Structure in the University of Cambridge.

1 See Peter Laslett, *The World we have lost* (London, 1971; 2nd ed.), 89. Interclass differences now appear to be somewhat less than is implied there.

would push our knowledge of these particulars further back. But, for the moment, it looks as if the history of age at menarche—the mean age at which girls become capable of conception—will have to stand for the whole phenomenon of sexual maturation in men and women.

We have to be satisfied, however, with the small things which we can do in historical sociology, and the little insight we have into the secular trend of age at menarche is certainly intriguing. Most of it seems to confirm the tendency toward a progressive decline in the age at which women became mature. Tanner, who is the established authority on this subject, and the only contemporary medical writer who appears to be collecting information on the long-term as well as the short-term trend, estimates that "menarche in Europe has been getting earlier during the last hundred years by between three and four months per decade."[2] To its level in Great Britain in the 1960s of about 13.25 years, it has fallen from about 14.5 in the 1920s, 15.5 in the 1890s, 16.5 in the 1860s, and 17.5 in the 1830s. He prints a series of figures from observations going back over the past 125 years.[3] Though they come from a variety of northern and western European countries (Denmark, Finland, Sweden, Germany, and Great Britain), these observations plot a noticeably regular line.[4] This line slopes downward from an age of a little over 17 for Norway in the 1840s, through the range 15.5–16.2 in the 1880s for Norway, Finland, Sweden, and Germany, down to 14.5–15.0 in the 1920s, and so down to its present level. Starting at 1900, records for the United States show a consistently lower age at menarche, which fell to 12.5–13.0 in 1940–45 (white girls). But the curve is roughly parallel in America, and all series show the same downward tendency for the twentieth century.

The literature provides little critical examination of the sources of these figures, but Tanner has said that the data are sketchy and not entirely reliable for all of the earlier recordings. The Cambridge Group has now begun to collect data for the distribution of age at menarche and some are presented in the Addendum below, with reflections on their accuracy. For all their crudity they constitute the beginnings of a very interesting file, and my object here is to call attention to their value. My object is to call attention to such possibilities as are open to the

2 J. M. Tanner, "The Secular Trend Towards Earlier Physical Maturation," *Tydshrift voor geneeskunde*, XLIV (1966), 531.

3 *Ibid.*, 532. Cf. J. M. Tanner, *Growth at Adolescence* (Oxford, 1962; 2nd ed.), 152.

4 *Ibid.*, 153.

sociological historian, and, particularly, to the historical demographer, for the examination of this important problem. In particular, I use the very imprecise but nevertheless illuminating evidence of an individual document—that of a list of the Christian Orthodox inhabitants of Belgrade, the capital of what was once Serbia, now Yugoslavia, for the year 1733–34. We shall see that estimates of the maximal age at sexual maturity for women recoverable from that document point to a period at which menarche occurred earlier than it apparently did in Norway in the 1840s or in Finland in the 1850s.

Although the evidence of actual observations is difficult to obtain and tricky to use, literary evidence is obtainable and is beginning to be published. It also tends to confirm the probability that age at menarche may have been about fourteen in medieval and early modern times, so that it must have risen later on to reach the ages which have been recorded for the nineteenth century. Tanner himself quotes interestingly from Shakespeare and from an early seventeenth century writer named Quarinonius or Guarinonius. But literary evidence of this kind should be handled with great care, even with some suspicion. [5]

Nevertheless, it is useful to cite the materials from medieval literature collected and discussed in an interesting note by Post.[6] They bear more weight as empirical evidence, being the writings of medieval gynecologists. At their strongest, the statements quoted by Post imply that age at menarche was observed by these physicians to occur in the thirteenth or fourteenth year. Of course, the accuracy of these observations is somewhat impaired by the further claim, which Post quotes from Avicenna and such splendidly entitled works as *Trotula Major* and *Trotula Minor*, that menstruation lasts "until the fiftieth year if the woman is thin; until sixty or sixty-five or fifty-five if she is moist; until thirty-five if moderately fat." Though Post suggests that these absurdities about the cessation of menstruation, the menopause, may be due to the paucity of cases, as few women lived into the higher ages, they seem to me to be unfortunately typical of the literary sources, even when medical. They are

---

5 See Laslett, *The World we have lost*, 57, where I discuss the notorious case of Juliet's marriage age in *Romeo and Juliet* being used as an indication of mean age at marriage for women in Elizabethan England.

6 J. B. Post, "Ages at Menarche and Menopause: Some Medieval Authorities," *Population Studies*, XXV (1971), 83–87.

ordinarily incapable of yielding anything which is, properly speaking, numerical.[7]

The one way to obtain figures would appear to be by working backward from marriage recordings. Since a marriage within the universal Christian church could only be celebrated if both parties were sexually mature, figures for the age at first marriage for women can be taken as figures for *maximal* age at menarche. Care must be taken, however, to distinguish between a promise to marry (a *spousal*), and marriage itself. A person could become engaged at any age, before puberty or after, and the undertaking was regarded as binding by the church like any other promise. This engagement became a valid marriage when sexual intercourse took place, quite apart from a church ceremony. A marriage could exist therefore which had not been celebrated in church, and so, presumably, had never been registered. Nevertheless, both partners to such a union were, by definition, sexually mature at the time it began. But a spousal itself was not a marriage. Indeed, as is well known, inability to copulate in either partner was proper grounds for ending an engagement, or even of annulling a "marriage."[8]

If, therefore, the date of a woman's marriage is known, then it can be assumed that she was sexually mature at the time. But it remains uncertain as to how long she had been mature. Mean age at first marriage is an indication of maximal age at menarche is of little use if it falls above 20. It merely tells us that puberty in that society did not come at a record high age. All of which implies that it is information on *teenage marriage* which is really crucial.

Unfortunately it turns out that women only rarely married before age 20 in Western Europe until the nineteenth century. No mean age at first marriage, as calculated from parish registers by the complex process of family reconstitution,[9] ever falls as low in England, France, or even eighteenth century Canada, where the age was lowest.[10] It seems,

7   *Ibid.* The evidence of family reconstitution may finally establish something like a mean age of cessation of fertility, which would, in its turn, presumably be a firm indicator of the age of menopause. If there is any necessary relationship between menopause and menarche, then it would follow that such a figure could be used to establish the earlier event, too.

8   On spousals, see Laslett, *The World we have lost*, 140–145.

9   See E. A. Wrigley, "Family Reconstitution," in E. A. Wrigley (ed.), *An Introduction to English Historical Demography from the Sixteenth to the Nineteenth Century* (London, 1966), 96–159; *idem.*, "Family Limitation in Pre-Industrial England," *The Economic History Review*, XIX (1966), 82–109; *idem.*, "Mortality in Pre-Industrial England," *Daedalus*, XLVII (1968), 546–577.

10   Jacques Henripin, *La population Canadienne au début du XVIIIe siècle* (Paris, 1954).

after all, that nothing useful can be learned about age at menarche from the study of ecclesiastical marriage registrations in Western Europe—certainly there is nothing to help us decide whether sexual maturity came earlier or later in the eighteenth century than in the nineteenth.

Some women married and had children before twenty, even in England and France. An intense study of the baptismal registers might add to the impression gained from the many miscellaneous sources which bear upon the problem that conception was certainly possible in the teens among the English or French peasantry and townsfolk of earlier times. Little more can be expected of the parochial registers in these countries.[11] Nevertheless, there is an independent documentary source of an "observational" kind in such census-type documents as have survived from before the nineteenth century. If such a list of inhabitants specifies ages and familial relationships, then it is possible to see how many women were married before twenty, and how many at the crucial ages were accompanied by children. This last observation enables us, by subtracting the ages of eldest resident children from those of their mothers, to obtain something like a mean age of first conception for all mothers in the community.[12]

Among the 780 inhabitants of the Warwickshire agricultural and mining village of Chilvers Coton in the year 1684, for example, there were three married women whose ages are given as below twenty. None of these had an accompanying child incontrovertibly her own, though one (aged eighteen) had two present with her who looked as if they belonged to her husband (aged fifty) and had been born to a previous wife. Nevertheless, subtraction shows that one wife living in the village had conceived at fourteen, two at fifteen, one at sixteen,

---

11   It might be thought that information about ages of mothers at the birth of bastards might provide some useful information, and a few such figures are beginning to be available to us from family reconstitution; indeed, one of these appears below. Nevertheless, the first indications are that the proportion of all illegitimate births which took place among women under twenty was low, less than 6 per cent of all those occurring in one English village between the sixteenth and nineteenth centuries, where the women's birth dates are known. This compares with over 35 per cent in the United States in 1959. See Peter Laslett and Karla Oosterveen, *Illegitimacy in England, Sixteenth to Nineteenth Centuries* (forthcoming), for details.

12   See Peter Laslett, "The Work of the Cambridge Group for the History of Population and Social Structure," in Mattei Dogan and Stein Rokkan, *Quantitative Ecological Analysis in the Social Sciences* (Cambridge, Mass., 1969) and the introduction, etc. in Peter Laslett and Richard Wall, eds., *Household and Family in past time* (Cambridge, 1972), for sources of this kind and their exploitation.

two at eighteen, and four at nineteen.[13] Only 31 out of the 229 cases of women with children are described well enough to count, and although it may seem surprising that ten of these women apparently conceived before the age of twenty, it must be remembered that the recently married are the most likely to provide the precise information that makes subtraction possible.

These facts from Chilvers Coton illustrate sufficiently the difficulties of such data. Among the thirty-one whose particulars we can analyze in this way, the mean apparent age at first conception turns out to be well over twenty-two. No estimate for a maximum age of menarche for all women of the village at this time could be based on this handful of cases. If it had been possible to check the census-type document with the parish register, we would at least have had some independently sanctioned dates of first birth, and some reliable marriage ages. But the registers of Chilvers Coton are defective for this period, and, even if we had both good parochial registration and a listing giving ages, the small numbers marrying under twenty in any English village would ensure that no decent maximal figure for age at menarche could be obtained. This is why it is so fortunate that a listing of inhabitants has appeared which clearly belongs to an area and an epoch where mean age at marriage for women was below the age of twenty, and where the possibilities of working out a useful estimate of something like a maximal age at menarche are accordingly much better.

It is true that a much more accurate result would have been obtainable for maximal age at menarche in that region and at that time were there a full and well kept set of Serbian parish registers covering the years from 1650 to 1750 and preferably earlier and later years as well. Family reconstitution based on such a record could yield a mean

13   It is to be expected that the numbers of conceptions below twenty for the whole group of women should be much higher than those for women actually below that age at the time of the count, since the first figure represents those belonging to all the age cohorts present, and the second only to one of them. Nevertheless, in view of the probable loss from the sample of children already dead and those who had left home, which must have been considerable, the difference looks rather large, as it does in Belgrade and in all of the examples we have studied, including official nineteenth-century census documents. The explanation may lie partly in the fact that the very youngest are the least well recorded in all counts of this kind, and in the wish to conceal illegitimate births or births conceived before marriage, a motive which is less important when reporting children's ages later on. More important is the fact that no child born in the year of the count after the date of the count will appear, but all subsequent births which occurred in that year will be referred later on to the year in which the count was made.

age of first marriage for women, and so a maximal age at menarche, for any chosen sub-period of, say, twenty-five, thirty-five or fifty years, depending on the size of the community concerned. It could also yield a mean age of first conception, including pre-marital and extra-marital conceptions, which might suggest a significantly lower age at menarche than the maximum indicated by the mean age at first marriage.[14]

The census-type document from Belgrade which the Cambridge Group for the History of Population and Social Structure has been given the opportunity to work upon is, however, of great interest for many purposes, in addition to the present one. With the expected shortcomings and imperfections, it provides the names, most of the ages and sexes, and indications of relationships within the household, of 1,357 Serbian Orthodox Christians living in Belgrade at a date given by the scholar who had the document printed as being 1733–34. The naming system makes it possible to infer the sexes of nearly all persons and to check the relationship of children to their biological fathers, though not to their mothers.[15]

An examination of the distribution of this population by age, sex, and marital status shows that its marriage habits were very different from those we have found in England and France at the same period, and, in particular, in Chilvers Coton in 1684. Whereas in Belgrade nearly 70 per cent of all women in the age group 15–19 were married or widowed, the proportion at Chilvers Coton was under 10 per cent. Stated a little differently, 87 per cent of all women above the age of fifteen, 96 per cent above twenty, and 98 per cent above twenty-five, were married or widowed in Belgrade. In Chilvers Coton, however, these figures were 54 per cent, 65 per cent, and 77 per cent. In a group of six preindustrial English parishes, the proportion married above the age of fifteen was only 60 per cent, and only a mere six out of the 402 women in these villages aged between fifteen

14 It now seems possible that family reconstitution among a historical population where mean age at marriage was below 20 can be undertaken in Estonia, if not in Serbia. See H. Palli, "Historical demography of Estonia in the seventeenth and eighteenth centuries," J. Kahk and A. Vassar, eds., *Studia historica in honorem Hans Kruus* (Tallihn, 1971), pp. 205–221.

15 See Peter Laslett and Marilyn Clarke, "Houschold and Familial Structure in Belgrade 1733/4," Laslett and Wall, *Household*, pp. 376–400. This rare manuscript appears to have been drawn up by the clergy and was published by D. J. Popović, "Gradja za istoiju Beograda 1711–1739," *Proceedings of the Royal Serbian Academy*, LXXVIII (1935), 59–65. The reference was supplied to the Cambridge Group by Joel Halpern of the University of Massachusetts, and the work of transliteration from the Cyrillic and of translation was done by Stojana Burton.

and nineteen were married at all. Although in the absence of marriage recordings for the women at issue in Belgrade we cannot know their mean age at first marriage, it must have been well below twenty. This in itself is a hint that they reached maturity in the early rather than the late teens.

The high marriage rate among young women is brought out by the first of the three tables printed below, which together present the numerical evidence from the Belgrade list as it bears on the question of the age of sexual maturation. As might be expected in an unsettled population living in a region characterized by a state of military confusion and low material standards, with presumably a modest level of education throughout the community, the figures are approximate in detail and incomplete overall. Sex information is missing for 13.5 per cent of the people, and age information for 11.6 per cent. Some of these persons appear, from their position in their families and the ages of their close kin, to have been eligible for consideration if proper particulars had been present. The peculiarities of the data are plain enough from the figures below, at least in respect of the clustering at various ages.

In Table 1 the numbers and ages of all women up to the age of twenty-one are given with information as to their marital status and the presence of children. In Table 2 mothers only are listed by age from twenty-two upwards. In Table 3 the ages of mothers at the birth of their first child are given. These were obtained by subtracting the number of years given for the eldest resident son or daughter from that of his or her own mother.[16]

The rough and arbitrary character of this series of numbers will convince the reader that very little in the way of reliable detailed inference can be expected of them, though general inferences of a fair probability seem permissible. The figures of Table 3—the ages at the birth of the first child—naturally interest us the most, but some are impossible. Girls of six and eight cannot have had babies. But, before we tackle these and other oddities, let us make what we can of the figures in the first table concerning the number of women married at various ages. They demonstrate that, insofar as women knew their

16   It is not always clear whether a child mentioned after a woman's name is, in fact, her offspring, though in nearly all cases the relationship is made unambiguous by the presence of the words *his* or *her*, or by the naming system which, in Serbian usage, links all offspring to their fathers. The uncertainty is greatest in the case of widows, especially those of more advanced years.

Table 1 Women 10–21, by age, marital status, and presence of offspring

	AGE	NUMBER	MARRIED		WITH CHILDREN	
			NUMBER	%	NUMBER	%
	10	25	0	0	0	0
	11	9	0	0	0	0
	12	19	1	5.3	0	0
	13	16	0	0	0	0
	14	8	0	0	0	0
Totals	10–14	77	1	1.3	0	0
	15	9	3	33.3	0	0
	16	9	5	55.5	0	0
	17	10	8	80.0	1	10.0
	18	15	11	73.2	2	13.3
	19	10	10	100.0	5	50.0
Totals	15–19	53	37	69.8	8	15.1
Totals	10–19	130	38	29.3	8	6.1
	20	31	30[a]	96.6	12	38.7
	21	10	9	90.0	6	60.0
Totals	10–21	171	77[a]	45.0	26	15.2
Totals	15–21	94	76[a]	80.9	26	27.6

a Including one widow.

ages, and had them accurately recorded by the Christian Orthodox priest who seems to have drawn up the census, marriage did in fact come very early. A third of all girls of the age of fifteen, and over half of those of sixteen, already had husbands. These young wives must have been sexually mature if the Christian rules on the point were being observed. Nothing can be said, of course, about the maturation of the six girls of age fifteen, the four aged sixteen, and the two aged seventeen who were not married, and it is possible that their late development was the reason why some of them were still celibate. Nevertheless it would seem out of the question to suppose that their backwardness was the sole reason, or even a major one, for their being spinsters.

For this would imply that sexual maturity was not simply an essential qualification for marriage, but was universally and immediately

Table 2 Mothers, 21 and over, by age

AGE	NUMBERS	AGE	NUMBERS
22	6	40	14
23	4	43	1
24	1	45	2
25	20	46	1
26	11	47	1
27	2	50	15
28	16	55	1
30	38	58	1
31	1	60	8
32	3	63	1
33	1	65	1
34	4	70	2
35	8	78	1
36	6	80	1
37	2	Totals:	22–80 = 177
38	3		0–80 = 203
39	1	Of whom widows =	31

followed by marriage. In the case of Belgrade, where husbands were, on average, nearly ten years older than their wives, such an unlikely rule would present a picture of the men waiting until their late twenties or early thirties to get themselves partners, and then seeking out the youngest nubile girls they could find to marry. Every woman would be offered on the marriage market as soon as she became physiologically capable of mating, and taken up with the shortest possible delay. No market can be as efficient, even with "buyers" and "sellers" as eager as those just described.

Eugene Hammel, of the University of California, Berkeley, a student of present and past Serbian familial life, tells me that nothing in the Serbian social structure or familial custom indicates any tendency toward such extraordinary precipitation. These considerations can be taken to justify the assumption that the non-marriers were not markedly later in maturing than those who did marry, although it is always possible that the really poorly fed and badly developed did follow the others partly because they were still unfit. In general, it would seem that wives in any age group can be taken as representative in these respects of all women in the age group, with some allowance made in the earliest years—say up to sixteen—but none later.

The considerable numbers of cases studied in our own time show

Table 3 Mothers by age at birth of eldest resident child (from subtraction)

	AGE	NUMBERS
	6	1
	8	3
	10	1
	11	1
	12	2
	13	5
	14	10
	15	13
	16	12
	17	16
	18	16
	19	13
	20	20
	21	3
Total	6–21	116
	22	17
	23	9
	24	9
	25	5
	26	5
	27	9
	28	7
	29	3
	30	5
	31	1
	32	3
	33	1
	35	1
	36	1
	37	1
	38	2
	40	4
	42	2
	44	1
	50	1
Total	6–50	203

that ages at menarche are normally distributed and that the range between the earliest and latest ages is relatively short. There does not seem to be much discussion of this range in the literature, nor more than a passing reference to the important possibility that it was greater in the case of the poor and undernourished than in that of the rich and well-fed, the humble not only maturing later, therefore, but over a wider spread of ages. Tanner simply says that a standard deviation of a value of "1.1 years is characteristic of most series studied." [17] If this value of 1.1, or even a somewhat higher one, is applied to the figures in our Table 1, and the assumption of normal distribution is retained for them, then a further and more specific, though still very inexact, numerical indication of the maximal menarcheal age can be obtained. Since over 95 per cent of all cases in a normal distribution will lie within four standard deviations of a value at the extreme, then it follows that practically all girls in Belgrade became fit to marry within four years after the first recorded age at marriage. Since twelve is the lowest age in Table 1, then 12–16 would be a first estimate of the range of ages at issue. This is to place a great deal of weight on a single value, especially as no bride of thirteen or fourteen is present, but the general shape of the distribution certainly implies that the ages between thirteen and fifteen were the years when girls reached marriageability and the years between seventeen and nineteen look very unlikely. [18] This statement is true, even allowing for the possibility of the unmarried being slower developers, and for the half-year which has to be added to the ages in Tables 1 and 2 because they are declared ages, not ages in years and months actually attained.

When we turn finally to the numbers in Table 3 we are at last in a position to work out single numerical estimates for our statistics, but it has to be said that the figures themselves look so haphazard that the ill-defined range just given might be thought of as preferable as a result. Beginning with the whole number of mothers—that is, all women of known age in the sample, accompanied by a child whose age has been subtracted from hers—gives a total of 203 (set out in Tables 2 and 3). The means and medians are as follows:

Mean age at birth of first resident child: 21.40, less 0.75.
Mean age at first conception: 20.65 years.
Median age at birth of first resident child: 20.40, less 0.75.
Estimated maximal median age at first conception: 19.65 years.

17 J. M. Tanner, *Growth at Adolescence*, 154.
18 Some support for the youngest ages being perfectly genuine can be gained even from English evidence, quite apart from Table 3 above. There is the Countess of Leicester who, in 1589, had a child at age thirteen (Laslett, *World we have lost*, 91); a girl at Colyton in Devonshire had a bastard in the eighteenth century when she was thirteen. Though ages at marriage from family reconstitution yield so little, the

The half year does not have to be added here, since the finding of the difference between the ages of the mothers and the eldest resident child has taken care of it, and the 0.75 represents the period of gestation. These ages are absolute maxima for the average number of years lived before first conception, and they accord well enough with the facts already reviewed. But, as must be expected, they add almost nothing in the way of positive information.

For more useful single statistics we must turn to ages below twenty-one years. This is on the assumption that all women must have reached menarche by the beginning of the twenty-second year, and, therefore, first conceptions—or apparent first conceptions—can be disregarded at higher ages.

> Mean age at birth of first resident child of all mothers of twenty-one
>   or under at that birth: 16.69, less 0.75.
> Estimated maximum mean age at first conception: 15.91 ± 0.11 years
>   Median age: 17.66, less 0.75
> Estimated maximum median age at first conception: 16.91 years
>   Interquartile range 13.94–19.20
>   Quartile deviation 2.63.
>   50 per cent of all cases within 2.63 of 16.91 years.

With figures such as those in Table 3, it is obvious that the median is likely to be a better indication of central tendency than the mean, especially with the impossible ages below ten. Our best estimate must therefore be the last set of results given above.

"Best" must here perhaps be read as "least misleading", but this outcome does not correspond to the statistics usually worked out from good data. This estimate is derived from the attributes of the normal distribution, and, for what it is worth, mean age at first conception thus arrived at comes to 16.3 ± 0.11 years, using the standard deviation of 1.1 already referred to. We could allow for the possibility that in the case of this population the spread of ages at menarche might be double what is now usual, and the result would then be 16.7 ± 0.22 years.[19]

---

much rougher ages given in marriage license records for much larger samples are more helpful. Vivien Elliott, working with the Cambridge Group, finds six brides of fifteen, six of sixteen, and nineteen of seventeen among 363 mariners in the London area between 1660 and 1694, and one of twelve, one of fifteen, and three of seventeen among sixty yeomen between 1679 and 1694.

19   Allowance for the proportion of women in the population not married and providing for random variation would raise the figure above seventeen years and perhaps as high as eighteen, but the quality of the data does not warrant such refinements.

In considering these and the other estimates, it must be remembered that they suppose that the interval between becoming mature and conceiving a child within marriage is roughly constant, although that interval is unknown to us. We can only suggest limits for the average time taken for the location of potential partners, court-ship, and marriage in that society, but it seems unlikely that it could be less than a year, and was very probably two years and more. If the age data from the listing from Belgrade in 1733–34 are at all reliable, and if the women in that city were representative of a wider population in that area at that time, it would seem that age at menarche must have been about fifteen years in early eighteenth-century Serbia.

My own impression of the evidence, from Table 1 more par-ticularly than from Table 3, and taking account of the figures in the Addendum, is that the spread of ages at which maturity was attained was wider than that observed in contemporary women. But these suggested inferences would be falsified if it could be shown that the entire distribution of the population by age was seriously distorted by the vagaries in the figures of our tables. They would only be misleading if a downward bias were present, but it must be remembered that the margins are quite narrow. A general shift upward of two years would do much to eliminate the difference which we have tried to establish between the eighteenth-century Balkans and what seems to have been true of samples taken in nineteenth-century Scandinavia.

It would be wearisome in this context to discuss all possible sources of error, and I have preferred to include the full figures. This will per-mit readers to decide whether the pronounced heaping at ages ten and twenty in Table 1 or at twenty-five, thirty, and all higher decennial years in Table 2 results from a rounding downward rather than up-ward. Critical examination would appear to show that some upward effect must be contemplated, but it would affect the measures for the whole population rather than for those under twenty-one, where the revision would at most have to be a month or two.

Some confidence in the age figures for the Belgrade population as a whole can be gained from comparing them with similar distribu-tions for other preindustrial European societies. Mean overall age at Belgrade was 24.5, whereas in the six English communities mentioned above it was 25.73; medians 20.83 and 21.70. For males, the mean at Belgrade was 26.05 (a median of 21.09) and, in the English sample, 25.26 and 20.23; females 23.47 and 20.42 against 26.17 and 22.59. The population was a little younger and the gap is greatest for women, but the discrepancy is no greater than is found between communities in England. The really disconcerting figures come in Table 3, with its impossible ages at birth of the first accompanying child. Though it can be shown that all of these cases were probably the results of a woman marrying a widower with children, and though the errors even in this table offset each other, at least to some extent, the statistics from this set of figures are of problematic value and have been treated as such here.[20]

This rough, preliminary exercise in the numerical study of age at maturity in earlier times may imply two principles. The first is that it cannot be assumed of the persons living in traditional societies, where they were immured for so long in their families of origin and kept under discipline for a good part of their lives, that they were necessarily more likely to be reconciled to their situation for physiological reasons. When we contemplate the patriarchal household in Stuart England, Colonial America, or in France under the *ancien régime*, where marriage was so much later than it was in Belgrade, and where —in England especially but in France, and perhaps the Colonies, as well—so many young people were in subjection as servants (compulsorily celibate like the children), we must think of the long years when young people were capable of fully adult roles, sexual fulfilment, and the direction of a family. If fathers were concerned about the chastity of their daughters, it was because they were probably often quite as capable of producing bastards in their middle teens as they are today. Fathers also faced their teenage sons as grown up persons, as strong as they were themselves in a society where personal, physical violence was more formidable than now.

The second principle is still scarcely established, and it may take many years to decide about it: age at menarche and maturation generally could vary, over time, as well as from social class and place to place. We cannot attempt to go into the reasons for this variation, even if it were within our competence. We may notice that the experts now no longer suppose that climate explains a great deal of the differences in menarcheal age in various parts of the world, so this factor would not account for the contrast between Belgrade and northern Europe.

20 No doubt a difference table of this kind might yield valuable data, given better recordings. No attempt was made to amend these figures because so little was known about the method of registration or the population itself. It may be worth pointing out that the very low and unacceptable values due to remarriage have to be offset in Table 3 against an unknown but assuredly very large proportion of high values which are missing because the child concerned had either died or left home.

Nothing can be said from this haphazard evidence about the extent to which it was due to genetical heritage, just as the body shape of Latin American peoples is different from that of Asian peoples, for reasons of what was once called race. But Frisch and Revelle[21] have recently published evidence that seems finally to bear out the view that "the attainment of a specific body weight at the peak of the adolescent spurt...may be critical for menarche." [22] And such attainment of critical weight is due, as they show, and as Tanner and others have supposed for many years, to nutrition in the early and especially the earliest years. As historical demographers, we know something already about variations in food supply and its effect on demographic rates, its extreme effects in the crisis of subsistence which the French have delineated, and its long term effects in the control of population size. It is interesting to have to recognize that differences in nutrition may have caused variations in the internal balance of the domestic group as well, as it definitely must have influenced the physiological relationships between classes. Moreover, let the American readers of this article reflect on the consequences of the fact that from their very beginnings the American people, and especially American children, have been better fed than Europeans.

Nevertheless, it cannot be correctly claimed that this is the first time that early marriage in areas outside Western Europe has been taken as evidence for age at sexual maturity. In the course of his polemic against the dogma that climate was the determining factor in menarcheal age, and that hot climates caused women to reach maturity earlier, John Roberton contributed to the *Edinburgh Medical and Social Journal* (1843) a title which can only be called warning: "Early marriage so common in oriental countries no proof of early puberty." Examination of that article, which was reprinted in Roberton's book (1851), goes to show that by "oriental" Roberton meant countries further away than Belgrade. He produces no compelling evidence from the European East that the Christian rule about all brides necessarily being mature at marriage was being extensively ignored. There is a tradition

21 Rose Frisch and Roger Revelle, "Variation in Body Weights and the Age of the Adolescent Growth Spurt Among Latin American and Asian Populations in Relation to Calorie Supplies," *Human Biology*, XLI (1969), 185–212, *idem.*, "The Height and Weight of Adolescent Boys and Girls at the Time of Peak Velocity of Growth in Height and Weight: Longitudinal Data," *Ibid.*, 536–559; and especially *idem.*, "Height and Weight at Menarche and a Hypothesis of Menarche," *Archives of Disease in Childhood*, XLVI (1971).
22 *Ibid.*, 558.

in Serbian history that under the Turkish oppression very young males were sometimes "married" for property reasons. But there seems to be no evidence that unions of this kind would have been accepted by the Christian Church as indissoluble matrimony. At the present anyway, the evidence from the Belgrade listing can be accepted as a reliable indicator, rough and ready as it has to be.

ADDENDUM.

Reference to three of the nineteenth-century British medical men who took part in the discussion of this subject confirms Tanner's judgment of the unreliability of their work in detail, but reveals a situation which is of some interest to the subject as a whole. Evidently, age at puberty was a question which engaged the attention of many people at the time. This was because early maturation and early marriage were associated with the degradation of women and with that tendency toward immorality which Europeans of Western Christianity so much deplored in other parts of the world, above all among "savages." There was a deep conviction that climate determined age at puberty, a belief which seems to have originated in an irresponsible remark by Montesquieu in *L'Esprit des Lois*. It was in refutation of this belief that John Roberton, surgeon to the Manchester Lying-In Hospital, undertook his researches, starting in the 1820s and publishing them finally in his *Essays and Notes on the Physiology and Diseases of Women* (London, 1851). James Whitehead, also surgeon to that hospital, held the older view and published his figures in 1847, *On the Causes and Treatment of Abortion and Sterility*. A further set of figures (collected by Graily Hewitt) was published by Walter Rigden in 1869, and the generosity of Rose Frisch of Harvard allows us to add to them two further sets of data. One is a distribution of *age de la première eruption des règles* collected by M. A. Raciborski [*De la puberté*, (Paris, 1844)], and the other a distribution published in the eighth report of the Massachusetts State Board of Health of 1877.[23]

The methods used by the English observers, and presumably by the others too, were to cross-question the women when they came for examination to the Lying-In Hospital as to when they first menstruated, a method which Tanner condemns.[24] These scholars made no record of the exact date of their observations, and the ages which they recorded

23 I am greatly indebted to Frisch both for these references and for discussion of the whole problem in correspondence.
24 Tanner, *Growth*, 154.

are in the form "first menstruated at the age of 11, 12, 13 etc." This presumably means the year attained at last birthday, and so has to be increased by half a year to enter into comparable calculations, though neither these earlier scholars nor Tanner ever mentions that fact.

With all of these points allowed for, there certainly appears to be some tendency toward earlier puberty in women detectable in these figures between the 1820s and the 1840s. Nevertheless it would not be easy to use these distributions to underwrite the claim that menarche in England in the first half of the nineteenth century was as high as it seems to have been in those other parts of Northern and Western Europe for which evidence survives, including the extra six months; Roberton's distribution reveals a mean age of 15.7 years, Whitehead's for the 1830s or 1840s a mean of 15.53 (Whitehead may in fact have added the half year), and Rigden's distribution for the 1860s yields a mean age of 14.96 (15.46?).

2.

Raciborski's French figures for 1844 have a mean of 14.9 (15.4?), and Bowditches American figures of 1877 one of 14.7 (15.5?). All of these statistics contrast with Finnish and Norwegian figures quoted by Tanner for these decades of well over 16 years. It cannot be said to be shown that the secular fall of three months per decade which Tanner quotes does apply to England in the earlier nineteenth century, and in his graph he makes no such claim.

More interesting however is the shape of the distributions, which are printed for convenience at the end of the Addendum. It is obvious at a glance that the spread of the figures is unlikely to be narrow enough to yield a general standard deviation as low as 1.1. Standard deviations for the sets of data are set out below, and in order to be conservative in estimating how much greater the spread might have been in the nineteenth century than it is now, I have calculated values for ages below 20 as well as those for the full distributions. The spread of all five sets of figures is more than half as great again as in contemporary society, even with the extreme values left out at the upper end.

These results are not incompatible with the general proposition that age at menarche is normally distributed, but statistical examination shows that there is some tendency to depart from this curve: it can be suggested that the shape of the figures results from several, presumably normal distributions superimposed. This would lend some further support to the belief that in former times the range of ages was rather greater than it is now. Although it is right to be wary of the higher values, it is difficult to see what could have caused a woman to state that she became mature as late as 20 or even subsequently, especially as she was being questioned before the early 40s. These late ages may, therefore, have some foundation and when they are included the spread of ages at earlier times appears to be greater still. If the effect is genuine, it could be accounted for by greater differences in nutrition and in general well-being in the population, greater class differences in fact.

Mid-nineteenth century distributions of age at menarche

	ENGLAND			FRANCE	MASSACHUSETTS
	Roberton 1820s	Whitehead 1830s–40s	Rigden 1860s	Raciborski 1840s	Bowditch 1870s
9			3		
10	10	9	14	4	4
11	19	26	60	10	26
12	53	136	170	20	49
13	85	332	353	29	107
14	97	638	560	38	142
15	76	761	540	41	112
16	57	967	455	20	83
17	26	499	272	20	14
18	23	393	150	12	20
19	4	148	76		5
20		71	29	4	3
21		9	7		
22		6	3		
23		2	2	2	
24		1			
25		1			
26		1	2		
N	450	4000	2696	200	575

Standard Deviation

	Roberton	Whitehead	Rigden	Raciborski	Bowditch
9–20	1.9	1.7	1.8	1.9	1.7
9–26	1.9	2.2	1.9	2.2	1.7

Edward Shorter

Illegitimacy, Sexual Revolution, and Social Change in Modern Europe

Sexuality in traditional society may be thought of as a great iceberg, frozen by the command of custom, by the need of the surrounding community for stability at the cost of individuality, and by the dismal grind of daily life. Its thawing in England and Western Europe occurred roughly between the middle of the eighteenth and the end of the nineteenth centuries, when a revolution in eroticism took place, specifically among the lower classes, in the direction of libertine sexual behavior. One by one, great chunks—such as premarital sexuality, extra- and intra-marital sexual styles, and the realm of the choice of partners—began falling away from the mass and melting into the swift streams of modern sexuality.

This article considers the crumbling of only a small chunk of the ice: premarital sexuality among young people, studied from the evidence of illegitimacy. However, in other realms of sexuality a liberalization was simultaneously in progress. There is evidence that masturbation was increasing in those years. The first transvestite appears in Berlin police blotters in 1823. Prostitution in Paris tripled in the first half of the nineteenth century. And, between 1830 and 1855, reported rapes in France and England climbed by over 50 per cent.[1] It is not the concern of this paper, however, to pin down qualitatively these other developments. This is a task reserved for future research based upon a

Edward Shorter is Associate Professor of History at the University of Toronto. He is the author of *The Historian and the Computer* (Englewood Cliffs, N.J., 1971) and is working on the large-scale transformation in popular patterns of family life and intimate relationships in modern Europe.

An earlier version of this paper was presented at the 1970 annual meeting of the American Historical Association. The Institute for Advanced Study gave the author the time to write it, and John Gillis, Joan Scott, Charles Tilly, Fred Weinstein, and E. A. Wrigley were kind enough to read it critically. Carolyn Connor and Ann Shorter prepared the graphs at the end.

1 E. H. Hare, "Masturbatory Insanity: The History of an Idea," *Journal of Menta Science*, CVIII (1962), 12 (Hare's explanation for the phenomenon—a sexual outlet imposed by Puritan restrictions on intercourse—strikes me as unlikely); Hans Haustein, "Transvestitismus und Staat am Ende des 18. und im 19. Jahrhundert," *Zeitschrift für Sexualwissenschaft*, XV (1928–29), 116–126 (the man had begun wearing women's clothes in 1797); A.-J.-B. Parent-Duchâtelet, *De la Prostitution dans la ville de Paris* (Paris, 1857), I, 32, 36; Alexander von Öttingen, *Die Moralstatistik in ihrer Bedeutung für eine Socialethik* (Erlangen, 1882; 3rd ed.), 235.

content analysis of pornographic literature and a statistical study of the dossiers of sexual offenders in France and Germany.

What is meant by "liberalization" or "sexual revolution"? With these terms I wish to indicate a change in either, or both, the quantity and quality of sexual activity. Quantity refers to how often people have intercourse and with whom—premarital, extramarital, and marital. By quality I mean to locate the style of activity upon a spectrum running from genital to "polymorphous" sexuality: A genital orientation is the concentration of libidinal gratifications in the genitals alone; polymorphous is the discovery of other areas of the body to be erogenous zones. Liberalization will thus be understood as an increase in the quantity of sexual activity or a shift on the quality spectrum from genital to polymorphous gratification.[2]

Premarital adolescent sexuality, basically a "quantitative" subject, is the easiest portion of the sexual revolution to deal with because reliable statistics pertaining to the behavior of common people may be found and correlated with other indicators of social and economic transformation. Before 1825 data on illegitimacy were accurately preserved in parish registers throughout Europe. And nineteenth-century government statisticians meticulously noted in their annual reports not only the movement of the population, but also the number of illegitimate children born in the various districts of their lands. New insights into the intimate realms of popular life may be gained from these statistics.

Starting around the mid-eighteenth century a dramatic increase in the percentage of illegitimate births commenced all over Europe;[3] illegitimacy further accelerated around the time of the French Revolution, and continued to increase until approximately the mid-nineteenth century. This illegitimacy explosion clearly indicates that a greater number of young people—adults in their early twenties, to go by the statistics on the age of women at the birth of their first illegitimate child—were engaging in premarital sex more often than before.[4] There were slip-ups, and the birth of illegitimate children resulted.

2 This definition permits us to utilize the distinctions Herbert Marcuse first elaborated in *Eros and Civilization: A Philosophical Inquiry into Freud* (Boston, 1955). Paul Robinson has recently reviewed the question in *The Freudian Left: Wilhelm Reich, Gaza Roheim and Herbert Marcuse* (New York, 1969).

3 See the note on the measurement of illegitimacy in the Appendix (259-260).

4 Louis Henry agrees that illegitimacy data are a valid indicator of premarital sexual morality. "L'apport des témoignages et de la statistique," in Institut national d'études démographiques (INED), *La prévention des naissances dans la famille: ses origines dans les temps modernes* (Paris, 1960), 368. When we speak of a sexual revolution, we are not talking

The alternate constructions one might place upon the statistical increase in illegitimacy are, in my view, incorrect. It is impossible to dismiss such a rise as a result of improved procedures for reporting illegitimate births. By all accounts, few bastard children slipped through the net of the baptismal register. In the 1700s, some village pastors of stern morality were inclined to enter all children conceived premaritally as illegitimate, whether born in wedlock or not. To the extent that this practice was abandoned the real proportions of the increase would be masked, but in no event enhanced.[5]

It is also untenable to argue that the illegitimacy explosion stemmed from a "compositional" effect: that, for whatever reason, late in the 1700s more unmarried young women were around than ever before, and so these unmarried women just naturally produced more bastards. To be sure, the percentage of single women in the population did increase all over the continent, but the mentalities of these women, as well as their proportion in the population, were shifting, for the rise in illegitimate fertility, measured by the number of illegitimate births per 1,000 single women, shows that they were behaving more "immorally" than in the past.[6] We are unquestionably confronting a genuine change in popular sexual behavior, not a statistical artifact.

Nor should the illegitimacy explosion be dismissed as the sudden lengthening of the gap between conception and marriage, and as nothing more than that. Some might argue that an increase in illegitimacy was a sign not of changing mentalities but merely of a pregnant girl's increasing difficulty in forcing her seducer to marry her. Or increasing illegitimacy may have stemmed from a couple's greater

---

primarily of teenagers, as may be seen from data on unwed mothers' ages presented by P. E. H. Hair, "Bridal Pregnancy in Earlier Rural England Further Examined," *Population Studies*, XXIV (1970), 65; and by Alain Lottin, "Naissances illégitimes et filles-mères à Lille au XVIIIe siècle," *Revue d'histoire moderne et contemporaine*, XVII (1970), 306. The average age of unwed mothers probably decreased somewhat in the course of the sexual revolution; on nineteenth-century Sweden, see Gustav Sundbärg, *Bevölkerungsstatistik Schwedens, 1750–1900: Einige Hauptresultate* (Stockholm, 1923; 2nd ed.), 126, table 46.

5   See the note on the measurement of illegitimacy in the Appendix (259–260).

6   In few places are time series data available on the number of single unmarried women in the population, the standard denominator for the illegitimate fertility rate. Eighteenth-century Swedish data, presented in the Appendix (264), show that illegitimate fertility was rising at the same time as the illegitimacy ratio, and shorter series found elsewhere confirm this trend. For a sophisticated measurement of illegitimacy, see Joginder Kumar, "Demographic Analysis of Data on Illegitimate Births," *Social Biology*, XVI (1969), 92–107.

willingness to see their first child born out of wedlock. Both arguments account for rising illegitimacy in terms of technical shifts in courtship practices, ignoring changes in attitudes toward sexuality among young people as a whole. Neither argument would demand that the percentage of young people sleeping together before the sealing of a formal engagement had increased.

One piece of evidence forces us to reject both of these arguments: the number of children born within eight months of their parents' marriage. In virtually every community we know about, prenuptial conceptions rose along with illegitimate births. This indicator is charted, where available, in the Appendix (260). The simultaneous upward march of illegitimacy and prenuptial pregnancy means that the rise in illegitimacy itself was *not* merely the result of increasing delay in marriage, with the level of intercourse remaining stable. Rather, if both bastardy and prebridal pregnancy rose, there is an almost complete certainty that the total volume of premarital intercourse was rising.[7] This demonstrates that engaged couples were copulating before marriage more often than before, and that many more casual sexual alliances were being constituted than in the past.

Finally, we should inspect the rough outlines of traditional sexuality. By "traditional" I refer to European rural and small-town society between 1500 and 1700. It was a period of cultural homogeneity in which all popular strata behaved more or less the same, having similar social and sexual values, the same concepts of authority and hierarchy, and an identical appreciation of custom and tradition in their primary social goal, the maintenance of static community life. We have numerous testimonies to the quality of peasant and burgher sex life, but almost none to that of the lower classes (domestic servants, laborers, journeymen, and the industrious poor). But I think it is safe to assume that the comportment of the two strata was similar. Möller has portrayed sex life among the *Kleinbürgertum* in the 1700s: man on top, no foreplay, quick ejaculation, and indifference to partner's orgasm. The gamut seems paper-thin, and the more exotic perversities which delighted the upper classes were doubtless unheard of and unimagined in provincial backwaters. More importantly, people were either chaste before marriage, or began sleeping together only after the

---

7   The certainty is not quite total because a rise in both of these indicators could be due to a drop in infanticide and abortion, or to an increase in fecundity. Yet there is no evidence that the first two lessened at all, to say nothing of decreasing on a scale sufficient to cause the illegitimacy explosion. Nor is there evidence of a change in fecundity.

engagement was sealed.[8] This is the situation from which the great liberalization emerged.

A TYPOLOGY OF ILLEGITIMACY   In order to understand why an increasing number of illegitimate children were born, two questions must be asked: (1) Why did the level of intercourse outside of marriage rise, thereby increasing the incidence of premarital conceptions? (2) Why did a greater percentage of conceptions fail to lead to marriage—why did more of this increased sexual activity result specifically in illegitimacy? To answer the first question one must distinguish, in a general way, among the reasons for having sex; to answer the second requires an understanding of the social situation in which a couple found themselves—for the stability and durability of their own relationship, and the firmness of their integration into the social order about them, would determine whether they would marry before the child was born.

The reader must be warned of the speculative character of my answers to these two questions. The explanations of shifts in sexual mentalities and the typologies of interpersonal relationships from one period to the next are preliminary efforts to make sense of badly fragmented and scattered information on intimate life. The arguments that follow thus are not to be understood as hard statements of fact, but rather as informed guesses about the likely course of events. Only the hope of spurring further research justifies this kind of speculative enterprise, for we are unable to determine what kinds of evidence to seek out until we have arguments that specify exactly what is to be sought.

As a first imprudent step, let us assume that people have intercourse for one of two reasons. They may wish to use their sexuality as a tool for achieving some ulterior external objective, such as obtaining a suitable marriage partner and setting up a home, or avoiding trouble with a superior. If they have such motives in mind as they climb into bed, they are using sex in a *manipulative* fashion. Alternatively, they may be intent upon developing their personalities as fully as possible, upon acquiring self-insight and self-awareness, and, accordingly, think

8   An extensive popular literature on peasant sex practices exists for the nineteenth and twentieth centuries, of which Grassl's "Bäuerliche Liebe," *Zeitschrift für Sexualwissenschaft*, XIII (1926–27), 369–380 is typical. The only scholarly works I have been able to rely on for this picture of premodern sexuality are K. Rob. V. Wikman, *Die Einleitung der Ehe: Eine vergleichend ethno-soziologische Untersuchung über die Vorstufe der Ehe in den Sitten des Schwedischen Volkstums* (Turkü [Finland], 1937), 350–355; Helmut Möller, *Die kleinbürgerliche Familie im 18. Jahrhundert: Verhalten und Gruppenkultur* (Berlin, 1969), 282–301; Peter Laslett, *The World We Have Lost* (New York, 1965), 128–149.

of sex an an integral component of their humanity. For such people, sex is a way of expressing the wish to be free, for the egoism of unconstrained sexuality is a direct assault upon the inhibiting community authority structures about them. I call this *expressive* sexuality. This level of intercourse is higher than that for the manipulative variety because self-expression is an ongoing objective, whereas once the object is attained to which manipulative sexuality was employed, the person may lapse into the unerotic torpor society has ordained as proper. Expressiveness means a lot of sex; manipulativeness means little.

But what about the sex drive? It is always with us, a dark motor of human biology moving men and women to intercourse in all times and all places. Yet its position in the hierarchy of *conscious* needs and impulses is by no means constant, but is rather a function of social and cultural variables which change from one time and place to another. Gagnon and Simon have shown for twentieth-century America that social structure and cultural stances interpose themselves between the steady thrust of the libido and the act of intercourse.[9] My point is that such factors constituted "reasons for intercourse" in nineteenth-century Europe as well. Specifically, there are two: the conscious wish to use sex as a means of manipulating other people to perform non-sexual acts, and the conscious wish to use sex as a spotlight in the introspective search for identity. Changes in these reasons for intercourse suggest that the history of the sexual revolution in Europe may be written as the transformation of lower-class eroticism from manipulation to expression.[10]

But if the social order about the expressive couple remains the same, they will doubtless get married and appear in the records of the statisticians only as contributors to the legitimate birth rate. In order to see why the child whom they conceive is born a bastard, we must look at the stability of their relationship. Instability may result when one of the partners in a relationship (normally the male) is using his social or

9 They summarize their thinking in "Psychosexual Development," reprinted in John Gagnon and William Simon (eds.), *The Sexual Scene* (Chicago, 1970), 23–41.

10 A case study linking romantic love and self-awareness in the eighteenth century is Rudolf Braun, *Industrialisierung und Volksleben: Die Veränderungen der Lebensformen in einem ländlichen Industriegebiet vor 1800* (*Zürcher Oberland*) (Erlenbach-Zurich, 1960), 65–72. On the eighteenth-century diffusion of romantic love, see also Jean-Louis Flandrin, "Contraception, mariage et relations amoureuses dans l'Occident chrétien," *Annales*, XXIV (1969), 1370–1390; Philippe Ariès, "Interprétation pour une histoire des mentalités," in *Prévention des naissances*, 311–327, esp. 323.

economic authority to exploit the other sexually (usually the female). In such a case, marriage is unlikely to follow pregnancy. The likelihood of a subsequent marriage is also reduced when the partners are caught up in a society undergoing rapid flux, so that either the establishment of a family household is impossible, or the male can easily escape the consequences of impregnation by fleeing. The notion of stability in the social situation of the couple therefore incorporates several possibilities.

These two variables—the nature of sexuality (expressive vs. manipulative) and the nature of the couple's social situation (stable vs. unstable)—are strategic in accounting for the illegitimacy explosion in Europe. Because each has its own history (although both must be considered together) we may construct a table which cross-classifies and derives four different situations resulting in the birth of an illegitimate child:

Table 1: The Types of Illegitimacy

	EXPRESSIVE SEXUALITY	MANIPULATIVE SEXUALITY
Stable social situation	True love	Peasant-bundling
Unstable social situation	Hit-and-run	Master–servant exploitation

"Peasant-bundling" illegitimacy lies at the intersection of instrumental sexuality and a stable social situation: persons with things on their mind other than sex whose cohabitation is sanctioned by custom. "Master–servant exploitation" denotes the coercion of women into bed by men who use their power as employers or social superiors to wrest sexual favors from them. Less than rape, the woman consents to being exploited in order to exist in peace with her superiors. There is little question of marriage when pregnancy ensues, a sign of the instability inherent both in the relationship and in the society which permits this kind of illicit exercise of authority. "Hit-and-run" illegitimacy identifies temporary liaisons where the partners articulate romantic sentiments and substantial ego awareness, and thereby are sexually expressive, yet are not inclined to remain together after a conception has taken place, or are prohibited by the force of events from doing so. Finally, in "true love" illegitimacy the psychological orientation of the partners is roughly the same as with the hit-and-run situation (although the couple may come more quickly to think of itself as a domestic unit), yet both their intent and their social environment conspire to permit a swift subsequent wedding and the establishment of a household. The child is technically illegitimate, but, like the offspring of peasant bundlers, is soon enmeshed in orderly family life. Children born of master–servant and of hit-and-run unions are more enduringly illegitimate.

All four types of illegitimacy were present in European society at all stages of historical development, but, in some epochs, some types were more prevalent than others. The explosion of bastardy may be written as the supplanting of peasant-bundling and master–servant exploitation by hit-and-run and true-love illegitimacy as the predominant types. This transition came about because popular premarital sexuality shifted from manipulative to expressive, thus elevating the number of conceptions, and because inconstancy crept into the couples' intentions toward each other, and instability into the structure of the social order in which they found themselves. The result was to make more premarital conceptions into illegitimate births.

These four types represent, in fact, four distinct historical stages in the unfolding of illegitimacy, one giving way to the next in a neat chronological progression.

Stage I Peasant-bundling was the paramount form of illegitimacy in Europe before the eighteenth century. England and Europe had always known some bastardy, on the order of 1 or 2 per cent of all births, and most parish registers turned up an isolated illegitimate child or two in the course of a decade. But these children, when not the offspring of the poor servant girl raped by the village half-wit, stemmed normally from engaged peasant couples who commenced sleeping together before marriage, as was customary, yet delayed the marriage too long. Social authorities in these village and small-town communities put enormous pressure upon hesitant males to wed their swollen fiancées, being persuasive only because the seducer had been, and would continue to be, resident locally and dependent upon the good will of his social betters.

I have not seen data on the legitimation of illegitimate children before 1800, so the characterization cannot be made exactly. Yet excellent information on prenuptial conception and illegitimacy convince me that this portrait must be essentially accurate.[11]

11 The standard work on bundling (*Kiltgang, Freierei*) is Wikman, *Die Einleitung der Ehe*. Parish register investigations now in progress have turned up in most places lots of

Stage II Master–servant exploitation became an ever brighter thread in illegitimacy as the seventeenth century gave way to the eighteenth. Manipulativeness continued paramount in lower-class eroticism; the change seems to have been that people in positions of influence and authority were able, as they had not been before, to take advantage of their exalted stations. We must keep in mind that these little dramas of exploitation happened mostly within the context of lower-class life. At that humble level, the authority of the oldest journeyman of the master tanner, for example, may have been minimal in absolute terms, yet to the girl who swept out of the shop it must have appeared commanding. The abuse of social and economic power to sexual ends doubtless was more difficult in the good old days, with the rest of the community watching vigilantly for disfunctions in the smooth mechanisms of prerogatives and obligations,[12] but the stirrings of social change weakened traditional control over such goings on.

Among the evidence for this characterization is Solé's work on the city of Grenoble in the late seventeenth century. He noted that around half of the illegitimate births (illegitimacy was around 3 per cent of all births) were the work of men who held the mothers of the bastards in some kind of thralldom, as masters of domestic servants or employers of female wage labor. And many of the cases of "rapt" coming before the judiciary of Angoulême in 1643–44 involved the

---

premarital conceptions among traditional peasant populations. In addition to the graphs in the Appendix (265–272), see E. A. Wrigley, *Population and History* (New York, 1969), 88 (a third of all first children in Colyton were baptized within eight months of marriage); P. E. H. Hair, "Bridal Pregnancy in Rural England in Earlier Centuries," *Population Studies*, XX (1966–67), 233–243; Michael Drake, *Population and Society in Norway, 1735–1865* (Cambridge, 1969), 32–40. Oscar Helmuth Werner, *The Unmarried Mother in German Literature with Special Reference to the Period 1770–1800* (New York, 1917), describes the violence of the traditional response to libertine behavior.

12 Chaunu has speculated that in open-field communities, where communal interaction was frequent and controls omnipresent, illegitimacy came from premarital intercourse among youths of the same age. In "bocage" communities, where relative isolation weakened social controls upon the superordinates, illegitimacy came from the masters' sexual exploitation of servants. Open-field morality was, however, more strict. See Pierre Chaunu, *La civilisation de l'Europe classique* (Paris, 1970), 196–197.

master's sexual violation of the servant. "The most common case is that of the farmers (*laboureurs à bœufs*) or village officials who, upon becoming widowers, take as servants a young girl from the parish. They speak to her vaguely of marriage, then when a birth approaches chase her from the house...."[13] In the early 1700s, the illegitimacy ratio in numerous urban communities had just begun to rise, as may be seen from the Appendix (270), whereas that in small rural communities continued at an infinitesimal level, a statistical demonstration of a rise in Stage II illegitimacy. But a detailed study of fathership in parish register data is needed to confirm our picture of master–servant exploitation.

A number of large-scale social changes intervened between Stages II and III, running roughly from 1750, which had the end effect of giving lower-class people a new conception of self and thus an expressive notion of sexuality. The fabric of lower-class life was thus shaken in a way that substantially decreased a pregnant girl's chances of getting married.

Stage III Hit-and-run illegitimacy typified a period when young people swooned romantically through a social landscape of disorder and flux. There was much intercourse, but people were stepping out of their old places en route to new ones, and temporary cohabitations often failed to turn into permanent concubinages. This combination of circumstances raised illegitimacy to historic heights, for the years 1790–1860 were, in virtually every society or community we know about, the peak period of illegitimacy. The graphs in the Appendix (265–272) reveal this conclusion unmistakably.

Time-series data on legitimation demonstrate that only a quarter to a third of all illegitimate children were subsequently legitimated by the *inter*marriage of their parents.[14] The other two-thirds either died, typically a consequence of indifferent care and the lack of a secure home, or remained unlegitimated—by definition outside of a glowing familial

13 Yves-Marie Bercé, "Aspects de la criminalité au XVIIe siècle," *Revue historique*, CCXXXIX (1968), 33–42; Angoulême evidence, 38; Jacques Solé, "Passion charnelle et société urbaine d'Ancien régime: Amour vénal, amour libre et amour fou à Grenoble au milieu du règne de Louis XIV," *Villes de l'Europe méditerranéenne et de l'Europe occidentale du Moyen Age au XIXe siècle: Actes du Colloque de Nice (27–28 Mars 1969)* (Paris, 1970), IX–X (1969), 211–232. In the Norman village of Troarn, Michel Bouvet identified master–servant exploitation as a common source of illegitimacy during the 1700s. "Troarn: Etude de démographie historique (XVIIe–XVIIIe siècles)," *Cahiers des Annales de Normandie*, VI (1968), 53.

14 See the time series on the legitimation of children in the Appendix (260–261).

hearth. Some mothers eventually found husbands other than the fathers of their children; their bastards would then be raised in a domestic atmosphere, but rarely would their new stepfathers adopt them.[15] Legitimation statistics point to an unsettledness in the sexual relations between men and women, hence the sobriquet "hit-and-run."

Stage IV From about 1875, the reintegration of the lower classes into the structure of civil society appears to have removed the transient quality from romantic relationships, leaving their expressive nature unimpaired. Stable communities developed in the sprawling worker quarters of industrial cities; a cohesive lower-class subculture with distinctive values and symbols became elaborated in distinction to the bourgeois society. Outside society accepted placidly the idea of early worker marriage, and, within premarital liaisons themselves, thoughts of subsequent marriage were present at the beginning.[16]

During this stage illegitimacy ratios declined somewhat from their Stage III heights, although they did not return to the low levels of traditional society. And legitimation rates rose steadily during the last third of the century, a sign that couples who coalesced briefly for intercourse were staying together with connubial intent. The modern pattern of cohabitation is between social and economic equals, not between unequals, as in Stage II. The only survey I have been able to find of illegitimate fatherhood late in the century demonstrates that the seducers came from similar social stations as the seduced, which implies a growth of romantic, expressive sexuality in place of the manipulative, instrumental sort.[17]

These portraits of the four stages are meant as ideal types suggesting the sequence of events most places would experience. I do not intend to argue that the infinitely disparate cities and regions of Western

15 In Frankfurt am Main around 1900, only one-fifth of the illegitimate children whose mothers had married another man were actually adopted by their stepfathers (*Namensgebung*). Othmar Spann, *Untersuchungen über die uneheliche Bevölkerung in Frankfurt am Main* (Dresden, 1905), 26.

16 The resiliency of social networks in lower-class neighborhoods around this time has not been a subject of monographic investigation. One occasionally finds in the secondary literature relevant observations, such as Michel Collinet's view that the skilled workers of Paris become "sedentary" after the turn of the twentieth century (*L'Ouvrier français: Essai sur la condition ouvrière* [1900–1950] [Paris, 1951], 114).

17 Theodor Geiger, "Zur Statistik der Unehelichen," *Allgemeines Statistisches Archiv*, XI (1918–19), 212–220. Geiger presents some Norwegian data (1897–98) which show that in 76 per cent of the illegitimate births, both parents were from the same social class; in a further 18 per cent of the cases, a lower-class female had slept with a middle-class male; and, in a final 7 per cent, a middle-class women and a lower-class man (216–218).

Europe marched in lockstep, for the timing of each of these stages would vary from one place to another, depending on events. But the illegitimacy explosion sooner or later came to Breslau and Liverpool, to the Scottish lowlands and the Zurich highlands. Exactly when depended upon the pace of modernization.

SOCIAL CHANGE AND THE WISH TO BE FREE   What touched off the wish to be free—the great drift toward individual innovation and autonomy at the cost of community custom and hierarchy—is one of the most vexing problems of modern scholarship, and a solution to it does not lie within the scope of this paper. Weinstein and Platt state that at the psychoanalytic level, the separation of home and workplace was responsible, for as the father exchanged his continuing presence within the family circle for workaday employment outside, certain emotional connections caused sons to rebel against their fathers' authority. With fathers no longer emotionally nurturant, male children no longer had to obey them.[18] Classical sociology provides other answers: Marx with his insistence upon the capitalist economy as the generator of proletarian rebellion, de Tocqueville with his assertion that equality had proven too much of a good thing. The matter is still unclarified, and my puzzlement is as great as anyone's. But the pattern of takeoff in illegitimacy ratios, and the correlates of illegitimacy with other socioeconomic variables, suggest a partial answer to the question.

It is in the area of changes which enhanced the individual's sense of self and which correspondingly broke down allegiances to custom and to the community that we must seek the motor of the wish to be free. At many levels of social relations and of psychodynamics, sexual freedom threatens the maintenance of community life because of the radical privatism and "egoism" it instills in individuals. (The classic European tradition of conservatism was intensely aware of the nature of this threat, and often damned libertine sexual behavior as "Egois-

18 I have borrowed the phrase from the title of the book by Fred Weinstein and Gerald M. Platt, *The Wish to be Free: Society, Psyche, and Value Change* (Berkeley, 1969). Although I think that the overall argument in Weinstein and Platt is substantially correct, I disagree with their views on the timing of the development of autonomy: (1) The search for autonomy from the family (not just from politics) probably began late in the 1700s, not in the late 1800s, when Freud was writing; (2) Weinstein and Platt argue that women were to acquire a sense of autonomy only in the 1900s, whereas men had liberated themselves from their fathers' authority much earlier. My view is that the shift from manipulative to expressive sexuality happened as much (if not more) among women as among men, and that it occurred late in the 1700s.

mus.") Following accepted practice in the study of modernization, I shall call those areas of the economy and society effecting such changes in individual mentalities the "modern" sector. A case can be made that exposure to the modern sector at least sensitizes the population to the values of individual self-development and precipitates a readiness to experiment with new life styles and personality configurations, which then leads to action, *should all other things be equal*.

Most corrosive of the traditional communitarian order was the modern marketplace economy. This insight into the individualizing impact of capitalism upon the *local* arena is almost as old as the free marketplace itself, and Nisbet, Polanyi, and Wolf have recently reminded us of it again.[19] The notion of the individual as an isolated actor in the economy hell-bent upon maximizing his own profit was the diametric opposite of concepts binding together the traditional local corporation, be it a small-town guild or open-field village. The reality, of course, was quite different from the classical *laissez-faire* model, yet it is likely that the concept was constantly in the thoughts of those involved in wage negotiations, for example, or those who offered their services in a competitive labor market. To be sure, Western Europe had known *export* capitalism, the fabrication of goods for non-local sale, since the Middle Ages, but free markets within the *local* economy date from the eighteenth century in France and England, and from the early nineteenth in Germany.[20]

In the context of sexual history, however, a free market economy meant something a little more precise than the general exchange of goods and services regulated only by the price mechanism. In the countryside it meant agricultural capitalism and the rationalization of husbandry. The laborers and live-in hired hands who worked for improving farmers all over Europe were highly prone to illegitimacy. This is no less true of such English areas of agricultural modernization as Norfolk, Surrey, and Sussex, as it is of French departments—the

19 Robert Nisbet, *Community and Power* (formerly *The Quest for Community*) (New York, 1962), *passim*; Karl Polanyi, *The Great Transformation* (New York, 1944), Chs. 1–4; Eric R. Wolf, *Peasant Wars of the Twentieth Century* (New York, 1969), 276–302.
20 On England see E. A. Wrigley, "A Simple Model of London's Importance in Changing English Society and Economy, 1650–1750," *Past and Present*, XXXVII (1967), 44–70; on France, Louise A. Tilly, "The History of the Grain Riot as a Form of Political Conflict in France," *The Journal of Interdisciplinary History*, II (1971), 23–57. On Germany, Gustav Schmoller, "Die Epochen der Getreidehandelsverfassung und -politik," *Schmollers Jahrbuch*, XX (1896), 695–744, as well as his *Zur Geschichte der deutschen Kleingewerbe* (Halle, 1870) for local markets in non-agricultural goods.

Somme, the Eure, and the Pas-de-Calais—employing numerous rural wage laborers. In Germany, the great farms of Mecklenburg and Niederbayern employed workers among whom illegitimacy flourished.[21] Parish data from the late eighteenth century are still not abundant enough to tell if the accumulation of an agricultural proletariat produced a corresponding initial increase in bastardy, but I suspect that this finding will turn up in the work that E. A. Wrigley and Louis Henry are now directing for England and France.

In towns, a free market economy meant capitalism in the form of factory industry. A distinctive feature of factory worker life in the 1800s was staggering rates of illegitimacy. In France, local studies of industrial towns have established that female factory workers were substantially over-represented among unwed mothers in proportion to the population. In Dresden and Munich, an illegitimate child often accompanied worker parents to the altar.[22] Yet these are only examples; the systematic statistical analysis required to demonstrate such hypotheses is inordinately difficult to obtain because: (1) as noted, we simply do not know about the development of illegitimacy over time in a sufficient number of municipalities to permit us to isolate the impact of factory industrialization; and (2) what appears to be the effect of factory industry may, in fact, be the effect of residence in a city.

The fact that the single group most prone to illegitimacy was urban domestic servants gives pause to attaching too much importance to factories and to the modern economy.[23] I have argued elsewhere that urbanity itself constitutes an important independent variable in

21 A glance at maps of illegitimacy in any of these countries shows that counties, departments, or Regierungsbezirke with a high concentration of landownership in the hands of a few have, by and large, high levels of bastardy. I examined the statistical relationship between engrossment and illegitimacy in Bavaria in "Sexual Change and Illegitimacy: The European Experience," in Robert Bezucha (ed.), Modern European Social History (Lexington, Mass., 1972), pp. 231–269.

22 Jules Michelet suggested that factory workers sought out sex as a compensation for the ghastliness of shop floor life. Cited in Georges Duveau, La Vie ouvrière en France sous le Second Empire (Paris, 1946), 423. See Ernest Bertrand, "Essai sur la moralité des classes ouvrières dans leur vie privée," Journal de la Société de Statistique de Paris, XIII (1872), 86–95 for occupations of illegitimate mothers in Châlons-sur-Marne, Troyes, and Reims.

23 Othmar Spann was preoccupied with this problem. See his "Die geschlechtlich-sittlichen Verhältnisse in Dienstboten- und Arbeiterinnenstande, gemessen an der Erscheinung der unehelichen Geburten," Zeitschrift für Socialwissenschaft, VII (1904), 287–303, and his Uneheliche Bevölkerung, 170–171. Illegitimacy rates of factory women and domestic servants in Berlin in 1907 were twice as high as for those groups in Prussia on the whole (measured as the number of illegitimate births per 1,000 single women of

accounting for the distribution of illegitimacy, but I was unable then, and still cannot now, fit the impact of the city into a neat theoretical structure. We can see the city accelerating illegitimacy by reducing the chances that an impregnation will eventuate in marriage. But does urban residence by itself shift lower-class mentalities from manipulativeness to expressiveness? What difference the city makes is one of the big questions in modern social science, and another unresolved puzzle in this paper.

Among the empirical evidence I can offer on this subject is that illegitimacy began to turn upward in the cities first, spreading to the villages only later. In every city in England and the continent for which data are available, the upsurge in illegitimacy commenced around 1750 or before, as may be seen from the Appendix (267–268). Second, except in England cities had much higher illegitimacy ratios than surrounding rural areas. Yet such illegitimacy may have been solely due to the fact that there were more single women in the cities than in the countryside. And, because of all of these urban maidservants, seamstresses, and the like, a higher proportion of all urban births were illegitimate than in the countryside. But that does not mean that the typical urban girl would be more likely than the typical country girl to behave immorally and produce illegitimate children. Maybe no differences existed in the morality of young women in the city and the country. Further research will clarify this question.[24]

---

childbearing age), even though overall illegitimate fertility in Berlin was only fractionally higher than in Prussia as a whole. L. Berger, "Untersuchungen über den Zusammenhang zwischen Beruf und Fruchtbarkeit unter besonderer Berücksichtigung des Königreichs Preussen," *Zeitschrift des königlich preussischen statistischen Landesamts,* LII. (1912), 231–232. I am grateful to John Knodel for calling this article to my attention.

Robert Michels wrote about illegitimacy among "isolated" groups within the population, such as urban domestics and seamstresses, in *Sittlichkeit in Ziffern? Kritik der Moralstatistik* (Munich, 1928), 172–180. Abel Châtelain has been working on the entire question of maidservant migration. "Migrations et domesticité feminine urbaine en France, XVIIIe siècle–XXe siècle," *Revue d'histoire économique et sociale,* XLIV (1969), 506–528.

24 The urban-rural distinction is standard in illegitimacy discussions, and the interested reader may consult A. Legoyt, "Les Naissances naturelles," *Journal de la Société de Statistique de Paris,* VIII (1867), 62–77; Karl Seutemann, "Die Legitimationen unehelicher Kinder nach dem Berufe und der Berufsstellung der Eltern in Oesterreich," *Statistische Monatschrift,* V (1900), 13–68; Öttingen, *Moralstatistik,* and other works cited in the Appendix. Some, such as Möller in *Kleinbürgerliche Familie,* say the bigger the city, the greater the illegitimacy (289). F. G. Dreyfus talks of an urban "masse de population flottante, très mal enracinée et intégrée," *Sociétés et mentalités à Mayence dans la seconde moitié du XVIIIe siècle* (Paris, 1968), 254.

English cities are a puzzling case apart, for their illegitimacy *ratios* were often beneath those of the surrounding countryside. In London, for example, illegitimacy in 1859 was an unbelievably low 4 per cent of all births. (In Vienna in 1864, illegitimate births exceeded the legitimate.) Either something about English cities, such as their great prostitution, made them remarkably different from their continental counterparts, or many births were not being registered as bastards (something that could easily have happened in English vital statistics registration).[25]

The final sensitizing variable crucial in value change appears to be exposure to primary education. Formal education, if only of a rudimentary sort, is calculated precisely to give the individual a sense of self by teaching logical thought. Learning to read requires the acquisition of linear logic, which mode of thought then surely spreads to other intellectual processes and levels of perception, to say nothing of the logical capacities instilled by other kinds of formal education. Logic and rationality are just other words for ego control, the psychostructural state of mind whence expressive sexuality flows. It is surely significant that the illegitimacy explosion coincided closely in time with the spread of primary education, and in space with the diffusion of literacy among the population.[26]

To review a provisional reconstruction of the psychodynamics of the sexual revolution: It appears that liberal sexual attitudes probably flowed from heightened ego awareness and from weakened superego controls. Traditional European society internalized anti-sexual values which commanded repression. But, when new values began to replace old ones, the superego restrictions on gratification gave way to the demands of the ego for individual self-fulfillment, and it was but a short logical step to see sexual fulfillment as integral to this larger personality objective. I do not mean that people became "sexualized" human beings; instead they became pluralized, seeing sex as an intrinsic part of

25 The English statistical service thought prostitution a likely explanation of low urban illegitimacy. Anon., "Illegitimacy in England and Wales, 1879," *Journal of the Statistical Society*, XLIV (1881), 397.

26 W. G. Lumley, "Observations upon the Statistics of Illegitimacy," *Journal of the Statistical Society of London*, XXV (1862), 219–274, raises the possibility of a positive correlation among bastardy and the level of education in Scotland, although he is uncertain about England (234, 260). There are strong theoretical reasons for suspecting a causal relationship between illegitimacy and primary education, but no evidence is available in published sources to permit verification. I am reluctant to put much faith in correlations among census data because so many other factors among a literate population could account for illegitimacy. The case history method seems most promising for checking this linkage in my model.

their humanity. This makes the sexual revolution an integrated movement of self-awareness, not a turbulent unleashing of carnality. If my argument is correct, behind this wish to be free lay the market economy, evoking ego orientation from those caught up in it, and primary education, stressing logical thought and control of the external world.

SOCIAL CHANGES DECREASE THE LIKELIHOOD THAT CONCEPTION LEADS TO MARRIAGE   Let us imagine a young girl has just told her suitor that she is pregnant. He has three possible responses, in the event that he does not wish to propose marriage in short order:

(1) "I love you but we can't get married until I inherit the shoe shop at age 42."
(2) "I love you but the authorities won't let us get married because they're afraid we might go on welfare."
(3) "So long, honey."

Which of these responses hundreds of thousands of young men selected is the key to the second strategic variable in accounting for illegitimacy: the chances of conception resulting in marriage before the child was born. The response was determined by the presence or absence of three principal social conditions, and our understanding of the sources of illegitimacy will be incomplete without a quick glance at them.

Response (1), the need to delay marriage until the man could establish an independent livelihood, was doubtless spoken most often in areas of lagging artisanal economy and impartible agricultural inheritance, late in the eighteenth and early in the nineteenth centuries. Age-old custom in Europe stipulated that the ability to support a family was a precondition of marriage, and, customarily, young men would not take brides until a master craftsman's license was in the offing or until the parents declared themselves ready to abandon farming and let the son take over the big house. In the 1700s, however, population grew so rapidly that the vacant positions which would allow for economic independence were soon filled up. Though other jobs entailing economic dependence were always available (witness the howls over a shortage of rural wage laborers), these positions were not thought suitable for establishing a "bürgerliche Existenz." A hesitancy to subdivide the fields and the stranglehold of the guilds upon the expansion of the artisanal sector saw to it that these economic backwaters did not expand with the growth of population. Hence there were rising ages at marriage and cries of "overpopulation"—and illegitimacy.

This model of population growth, rising ages at marriage, and illegitimacy works best for the areas of Europe not permeated by cottage industry. Where the domestic system was found, people married earlier, yet *also* produced more illegitimate children. (I do not wish to argue a direct positive correlation between age at marriage and illegitimacy. Too many other variables intervened: such as strength of familial controls and the mentalities of the population.) But in a cottage industrial area the delay in marriage was more likely due to abandonment of the mother by her seducer (response 3), rather than to a need for patience arising from economic exigencies (response 1).[27]

Response (2) is a special Central European variant of response (1), for in most German-speaking areas from Austria to Pomerania legal restrictions on marriage were reinforced in the nineteenth century. These laws were the bureaucratic elaboration of traditional community bars upon the marriage of the indigent, and were promulgated in the first half of the century at the behest of municipal governments. Town councils all over Germany feared that permitting the lower classes to marry freely would result in the swamping of local poor-relief funds by the children of the poor. Had things been as before, with no value changes underway among the lower classes, this calculation might have proved rewarding. Yet the lower classes had by now (as we have seen) abandoned their traditional chastity before marriage, and proceeded to saddle these anxious municipalities with hordes of illegitimate children. This is why Central European illegitimacy ratios in the first two-thirds of the century were so strikingly high. In the late 1860s these laws were repealed, and, in the space of a year or two, illegitimacy ratios all over Germany sagged.[28] It must be borne in mind that these laws were not

27   For population dynamics in a society with ossified guilds and nonpartible farms, I have drawn on the case most familiar to me: the state of Bavaria. See Edward Shorter, "Social Policy and Social Change in Bavaria, 1800–1860" unpub. Ph.D. thesis (Harvard, 1968). On long-term trends in the distribution of property in rural areas, see Günther Franz, *Geschichte des deutschen Bauernstandes vom frühen Mittelalter bis zum 19. Jahrhundert* (Stuttgart, 1970), 210–227.

28   On these marriage and settlement laws, see Karl Braun, "Das ZwangsZölibat für Mittellose in Deutschland," *Vierteljahrschrift für Volkswirtschaft und Kulturgeschichte*, XX (1867), 1–80; Eduard Schübler, *Die Gesetze über Niederlassung und Verehelichung in den verschiedenen deutschen Staaten* (Stuttgart, 1855); John Knodel, "Law, Marriage and Illegitimacy in Nineteenth-Century Germany," *Population Studies*, XX (1966–67), 279–294; Mack Walker, "Home Towns and State Administrators: South German Politics, 1815–30," *Political Science Quarterly*, LXXXII (1967), 35–60. Illegitimacy *rates*, however, were much less affected by the abolition of marriage laws.

responsible for the initial take off of illegitimacy, postdating that explosion by several decades. Other factors were behind central European illegitimacy as well, for even in the absence of such legislation several German states experienced the highest incidence of bastardy on the continent.

Under different circumstances than in responses (1) and (2), the man might refuse to marry the girl altogether (response 3), and, after obliging her by "recognizing" the child at its birth, he would disassociate himself entirely from his foundering family.[29] Chronologically, the period of most frequent absconding was the first half of the nineteenth century (when the other two responses were also most often heard), yet refusals to stay by the fallen woman probably happened most in the modern sector—factory industry and the city—rather than in the small towns of traditional society. All statistics point to the city as a place where conception out of wedlock meant abandonment by one's lover, as seen by the numbers of foundlings, of single women in lying-in hospitals (a sign, in the eyes of some, that the unwed mother was alone), and of single women on relief. In Austria, a negative correlation turns up in communes larger than 2,000 between the percentage of bastard children legitimated and the size of place, indicating the relative impermanence of sexual liaisons in the metropolis. Some of this dismal showing of urban places was due to the pregnant country girls who would come to the city to bear their illegitimate children, and then return home. But, even after they have been discounted, the mid-nineteenth century city remained a place of dislocation.[30]

29 Recognition in French and Belgian law meant that the father conceded to the child some inheritance rights and support obligations, but this did not constitute either a legitimation or an adoption of the bastard. In Paris during 1880–84, more children were recognized (20.5 per cent) than legitimated (18.6 per cent), a sign of great instability in relationships between the sexes. Keep in mind that some of those recognized also turn up in the legitimation statistics, which means that we cannot add the two figures together to determine the total proportion of illegitimate children brought into the charmed circle of family life.

30 Seutemann, "Legitimation unehelicher Kinder," 42, for Austrian urban legitimation. The Dresden illegitimacy ratio in 1873–79 was around 20 per cent with non-local mothers included, 16 per cent with them excluded, indicating that urban ratios were high for reasons other than the "fleeing pregnant peasant" effect. Öttingen, *Moralstatistik*, 317.

A sad little literature on child mortality, foundlings, and unwed mothers on relief shows in a way that most cold demographic statistics do not the human cost of illegitimacy. The historian must span a long emotional distance between all of this expressive sexuality and the thousands of small tragedies behind the astonishingly high rate of illegitimate infant mortality. See William Acton, "Observations on Illegitimacy in the London Parishes of St. Marylebone, St. Pancras . . . during the Year 1857," *Journal of the Statistical Society of London*, XXII (1859), 491–505; Ed. Ducpetiaux, "Du sort des

Illegitimacy reached its absolute height during the first half of the nineteenth century simply because these three kinds of responses to the announcement of a pregnancy happened to coincide. Illegitimacy declined when such social conditions ceased to obtain.

SEXUAL BEHAVIOR AND FAMILY PATTERNS   At the end, we must resolve a paradox which has emerged from the uneven distribution among the social classes of the contagion of libertine sexual behavior. The middle classes, as the lower, were exposed to marketplace mentalities and education, yet their sexual attitudes throughout the 1800s remained defiantly puritanical; indeed, the evidence of Victorianism would have it that the more one were educated, the more prudish and moralistic one became.[31] How ironical that those middle-class types who preached the gospel of autonomy—liberalism, *laissez-faire* capitalism, and universal suffrage—were the most repressive people sexually. In class terms, they were the movers and doers, the *bourgeoisie d'affaires*. Yet those who favored economic collectivism and political community were the most liberated sexually, with a high degree of personal control and autonomy. In class terms, they comprised the proletariat.[32]

If the argument about exposure to modernity and education is correct, one would expect the middle classes, rather than the lower classes, to have been in the vanguard of the sexual revolution. Other variables must have intervened to leap the gap between thinking about "the real me" and actually climbing into bed for intercourse. That is where the family enters. The lower classes were able to respond to the priming of the pump only because the family ceased for them to be an agency of social control. To go by existing evidence, it was the middle-class family which maintained the restrictive sexual taboos of traditional society, and which continued to demand chastity before marriage throughout the 1800s. For the family, sexuality and marriage went hand-in-hand. Intercourse before marriage would harm the family

enfants trouvés et abandonnés en Belgique," *Bulletin de la Commission Centrale de Statistique* (of Belgium), I (1843), 207–271; René Lafabrègue, "Des enfants trouvés à Paris," *Annales de démographie internationale*, II (1878), 226–299; Othmar Spann "Die Lage und das Schicksal der unehelichen Kinder," *Mutterschutz. Zeitschrift zur Reform der Sexuellen Ethik*, III (1907), 345–358; H. Neumann, "Die jugendlichen Berliner unehelicher Herkunft," *Jährbucher für Nationalökonomie und Statistik*, VIII (1894), 536–549.
31   See Steven Marcus, *The Other Victorians: A Study of Sexuality and Pornography in Mid-Nineteenth-Century England* (New York, 1966).
32   This paradox was pointed out to me by Fred Weinstein.

by (1) sullying the daughter and ruining her prospects of an advantageous marriage, and (2) threatening the continuation of the family name and property from generation to generation.

But even beyond this calculus of familial interest, the concept of *Ehrbarkeit* has always been a lynch pin in the ideology of the petty-bourgeois family. The quickest way to make oneself dishonorable was by sexual transgression. This notion of honor had disseminated from the master craftsmen of the guild system to all bourgeois family circles, but lower-class persons by definition were not master artisans, and, although formerly they had been willing respectfully to look on as the burghers exhorted one another to be honorable, for them this social ideology had become meaningless by the nineteenth century.[33]

One might plausibly argue that in the course of the eighteenth century population growth decapitated the authority of the lower-class family by creating so many children that parents had nothing to pass on to their extra-numerous offspring, and hence no control over their behavior. And cottage industry created alternate sources of employment to enable children to escape the authority of the family by physically removing themselves or otherwise acquiring economic independence. Once children decided to exchange the old internalized values of abstinence for new ones of self-fulfillment, parents were powerless to stop them. The petty-bourgeois family did not undergo this fate because it managed to control its fertility[34] and to preserve the sense of family tradition which said that children would follow in the footsteps of the father. To be sure, young men of middle-class origin responded to a new *Zeitgeist* of gratification by sleeping with prostitutes; but these liaisons posed no threat to the family. What we know about middle-class daughters suggests that they stayed pure before marriage. Thus the authority of the middle-class family over its offspring remained inviolate, and, as a result, middle-class youth, however sensitized by change, did not actually break out of the web of familial custom and control. But the youth of the lower classes did, which resolves the apparent paradox.

---

33 For this discussion of the traditional petty-bourgeois family, I rely on Möller, *Kleinbürgerliche Familie.*

34 There is now a mass of evidence, both literary and statistical, that middle-class French families had consciously adopted family limitation by about 1775. See *Prévention des naissances*; on birth control, see the most recent in a chain of local studies, Marcel Lachiver, *La Population de Meulan du XVIIe au XIXe siècle (vers 1600–1870)* (Paris, 1969), 210. The question is still unclarified for Germany.

Thus in a long chain of argumentation we get from rising illegitimacy to the emergence of class differences in family structure. The chain has a number of linkages, the solidity of which may be verified by the test of quantitative data. These may be time-series data relating the change from year to year in some possible causative factor, such as an increase in literacy, to some such index of sexual behavior as prenuptial conceptions. Or the testing may be done with "ecological" data, using census information to spot a statistical relationship between the number of factory workers in an area and the number of young people living away from home, or the number of illegitimate children in the population. I have tried to cast the argument of this paper to permit precisely this kind of verification with statistical procedures.

If the propositions presented here about sexual behavior, family structure, and social change are correct, we may expect future work to turn up the following kinds of regularities:

1. If the proposition is true that illegitimacy stemmed from a change in mentalities (rather than from some purely "compositional" effect, such as an increase in the number of single women), we should expect to find the incidence of shotgun weddings increasing in the same places and at the same times as illegitimacy. This simultaneity would indicate that the percentage of all young people practicing premarital intercourse was climbing, ruling out explanations of bastardy which fixed solely upon courtship practices.

2. If the proposition is right that exposure to primary education effected a liberalization of sexual values, we should expect parish register data to point to a higher level of illegitimacy among young women with some rudiments of education than among those without. If the hypothesis is accurate that involvement in marketplace situations brought about libertine sexual behavior, we should expect female servants within the rationalized sector of capitalist agriculture to evidence higher illegitimacy rates than servants on traditional seigneurial estates.

3. If the proposition is true that the passage from Stage III illegitimacy (hit-and-run) to Stage IV (true love) came in consequence of greater residential stability, we should expect strong areal correlations between territorial mobility and illegitimacy, taken district by district. Likewise, the notion of a transition from stage II illegitimacy (master-servant exploitation) to the subsequent romantic-love stages may be critically inspected through parish register data: Did a tendency emerge over the years for premarital lovers to come from the same social class?

If all of the correlations turn out in the predicted direction, we may smile and use our footing on this tiny base of confidence for better leverage on other vexing questions. If the correlations turn out to be zero, or, worse yet, the reverse of what the argument had anticipated, we shall have to return to the drawing board.

Yet this is an agenda for the future. As a starting point in the unraveling of European sexual history this paper has attempted: (1) to verify with exact quantitative data the existence of a late eighteenth-century revolution in premarital sexual behavior, and (2) to speculate, with arguments about social change and psychodynamics at many removes from the actual data, why this revolution took place. Future work will doubtless modify substantially the speculative elements of this argument. Future work will probably not, however, dispute that there is something to be explained. The evidence of illegitimacy and of prebridal pregnancy point inescapably to a drastic change in the sexual experience of the European lower classes in the course of modernization.

APPENDIX

A NOTE ON THE MEASUREMENT OF ILLEGITIMACY   To avoid confusion in the terminology of measurement, I refer to the percentage of illegitimate births among all births (illegitimate births/100 total births) as the illegitimacy *ratio*; and to the number of illegitimate births per 1,000 unmarried women in the population of childbearing age as the illegitimacy *rate*. The latter measure is clearly preferable to the former as an indicator of relative illegitimacy because the ratio is dependent upon the number of legitimate births. If, for example, the number of legitimate births in a place dropped, the illegitimacy ratio would appear to rise, for fewer legitimate births in the denominator would make the illegitimate births in the numerator appear more important, even though, in fact, illegitimacy had not changed at all. Another peril one encounters in using the ratio is the possibility that differences from one place to another (or one time to another) in illegitimacy may be solely attributable to differences in the distribution of single women from one place or time to another. If there are more single women in a town, more illegitimacy may be found there, all else being equal. Yet the single women in a town with a high illegitimacy ratio may not be more immoral, or find themselves abandoned at the altar more often, than the women in another town with a lower illegitimacy ratio. The illegitimacy rate would indicate that both towns were the same.

Experienced researchers, such as the INED scholars in France, are generally convinced of the accuracy, or at least of the constancy over time, in the biases of parish register data. The only major collapse of illegitimacy reporting of which I am aware came with English civil registration of births in 1838. The Act (Statute 6 and 7 Will. IV, cap. 86) made no mention of illegitimacy, and statisticians were able to determine if a child were a bastard only if the space for the father's name were left blank. Needless to say, an unwed mother could easily invent something, or take the name of her suitor, if the man were agreeable, and no one would be the wiser. See Lumley, "Observations upon the Statistics of Illegitimacy," esp. 220–221; *Sixth Annual Report of the Registrar General of Births, Deaths, and Marriages in England* (London, 1845), xxx–xxxix. Some deficiencies also crop up in seventeenth-century English parish register data, and it is possible that an apparent early seventeenth-century peak in illegitimacy may be an artifact caused by a late seventeenth-century tendency not to register the children of common-law unions as illegitimate. I have this information from E. A. Wrigley, who says that of the genuineness of the eighteenth-century explosion there can be no doubt. For an instance of the registration of legitimate but prenuptially conceived children as *illegitimate*, see Julius Gmelin, "Bevölkerungsbewegung im Hällischen seit Mitte des 16. Jahrhunderts," *Allgemeines Statistisches Archiv,* VI (I) (1902), 248.

Hélin noted some improvement in the accuracy of illegitimacy statistics in Liège, nonetheless attributing the great rise in bastardy there to a "relâchement de contraintes sociales devenues traditionnelles depuis la Contre Réforme" (209–210). Although I an suspicious of Hélin's explanation, I think the data he reports are of excellent quality. Etienne Hélin, *La démographie de Liège aux XVIIe et XVIIIe siècles* (Brussels, 1963).

TIME SERIES ON THE LEGITIMATION OF ILLEGITIMATE CHILDREN   I have been able to obtain only two time series on legitimation: statistics for the city of Paris and for the Kingdom of Belgium. The figures represent the total number of children legitimated in a given bloc of years per 100 illegitimate children born in that time, not the illegitimate children born in a given period who were subsequently legitimated.

PARIS		BELGIUM	
Percent legitimated		Percent legitimated	
1822	7.2	1851–60	34.7
1881–84	18.6	1861–70	38.7
1885–89	20.1	1871–80	43.1
1890–94	23.2	1881–90	46.9
1895–99	25.6	1891–1900	57.5
1900–04	27.1	1901–10	65.2
1905–09	31.3	1911–13	61.1
1910–14	35.3		

Sources for Paris: *Recherches statistiques sur la Ville de Paris et la département de la Seine* (Paris, 1826), tables 23 and 24. *Annuaire statistique de la Ville de Paris*, yearly after 1880. Sources for Belgium: *Annuaire statistique de la Belgique et du Congo Belge*, XXXIV (1903), 109–111, and XLIV (1913), 129–131.

The standard treatments of legitimation are Moriz Ertl, "Uneheliche Geburt und Legitimation. Ein Beitrag zur Beurtheilung der 'unehelichen Geburtenziffer,'" *Statistische Monatschrift* (Austria), XIII (1887), 393–438, which reviews available statistics throughout Europe; Seutemann, "Die Legitimationen unehelicher Kinder," 13–68. Analysis of Swiss conditions may be found in yearly volumes of the *Zeitschrift für Schweizerische Statistik*, for example, XLIV (1908), 168–173, and XLIX (1913), 122–128, which yield a short time series. France is discussed in Legoyt, "Les Naissances naturelles," 71–72. Three studies trace legitimation among cohorts of illegitimate births after allowing for mortality: Eugen Würzburger, "Zur Statistik der Legitimationen unehelicher Kinder," *Jahrbücher für Nationalökonomie und Statistik*, XVIII (1899), 94–98; Othmar Spann, "Die Legitimation der unehelichen Kinder in Österreich unter Berucksichtigung der Sterblichkeit nach Gebieten," *Statistische Monatschrift*, XIV (1909), 129–138; "Legitimirung unehelicher Kinder," *Statistisches Jahrbuch der Stadt Berlin*, XXII (1895), 55–57.

SOURCES OF DATA FOR GRAPHS ON ILLEGITIMACY   The years indicated on the horizontal scale represent the endpoints of the blocs of years for which the average illegitimacy figure has been computed. The lines for prenuptial conception represent the percentage of all first births born within eight months (or thereabouts) of the wedding.

The inclusion of stillbirths in the illegitimacy statistics varies from one source to another; I have made no effort to note their presence or absence, partly because the inclusion of stillbirths elevates the illegitimacy ratios only minimally, partly because that information is missing for many places.

1.   *France*. Wesley D. Camp, *Marriage and the Family in France since the Revolution* (New York, 1961), 108.

2.   *Paris*. Data on *enfants trouvés* (1670–1800) and illegitimate births (1806–20) are from E. Charlot and J. Dupaquier. "Mouvement annuel de la population de la Ville de Paris de 1670 à 1821," *Annales de Démographie Historique*, 1967, 512–515. Data for 1831–1900 are from *Annuaire Statistique de la Ville de Paris*, 53–54 (1932–34), 107–108. No illegitimacy data are available for 1821–30.

3. *Brittany and Anjou (selected villages)*. Yves Blayo and Louis Henry, "Données démographiques sur la Bretagne et l'Anjou de 1740 à 1829," *Annales de Démographie Historique, 1967*, 107.

4. *Lille*. Alain Lottin, "Naissances illégitimes et filles-mères à Lille," 292.

5. *Bordeaux*. Review of B. Saint-Jours, *La Population de Bordeaux depuis le XVIe siècle* (1911) in *Annales de Démographie Historique, 1968*, 182.

6. *Tamerville (Normandy)*. Philippe Wiel, "Une grosse paroisse Cotentin aux XVIIe et XVIIIe siècles," *Annales de Démographie Historique, 1969*, 161.

7. *Villedieu-les-Poëles (Normandy)*. Marie-Hélène Jouan, "Un bourg artisanal normand au XVIIIe siècle: Villedieu-les-Poëles, 1711-1790," *Annales de Démographie Historique, 1969*, 122.

8. *Sainghin-en-Mélantois (Nord)*. Raymond Deniel and Louis Henry, "La Population d'un village du Nord de la France: Sainghin-en-Mélantois, de 1665 à 1851," *Population*, XX (1965), 582. (1) means the prenuptial conceptions of peasants and artisans, (2) those of farm laborers and weavers.

9. *Meulan (near Paris)*. Lachiver, *La Population de Meulan*, 67.

10. *Boulay (Moselle)*. Jacques Houdaille, "La Population de Boulay (Moselle) avant 1850," *Population*, XXII (1967), 1060.

11. *Troarn (Normandy)*. Bouvet, "Troarn: Etude de démographie historique," 122-123. Bouvet's published yearly data are not convertible into ratios over blocs of time; my graph is therefore an approximate representation of the illegitimacy ratio.

12. *Leipzig*. W. Hanauer, "Historisch-statistische Untersuchungen über uneheliche Geburten," *Zeitschrift für Hygiene*, CVIII (1927-28), 663.

13. *Chemnitz. Ibid.*

14. *Frankfurt am Main. Ibid.*, 660-662.

15-18. *Freiberg, Lychen, Stroppen, Stuttgart, Durlach, Weiden, and Northeim.* Möller, *Kleinbürgerliche Familie*, 290.

19. *Hamburg.* Hanauer, "Historisch-statistische Untersuchungen," 663.

20. *Husum (Schleswig-Holstein)*. Ingwer Ernst Momsen, *Die Bevölkerung der Stadt Husum von 1769 bis 1860* (Kiel, 1969), 382-383.

21. *Halle.* Hanauer, "Historisch-statistische Untersuchungen," 662.

22. *Seven parishes near Tölz (Bavaria)*. Stephan Glonner, "Bevölkerungsbewegung von sieben Pfarreien im Kgl. Bayerischen Bezirksamte Tölz seit Ende des XVI. Jahrhunderts," *Allgemeines Statistisches Archiv*, IV (1896), 263–279.

23. *An Oldenburg town* (no name given). Erich Meyer, "Beiträge zum Sexualleben de Landjugend," *Zeitschrift für Sexualwissenschaft*, XVI (1929–30), 108.

24–26. *Boitin (Mecklenburg), Volkhardinghaüsen (Hesse), and Kreüth (Bavaria)*. Jacques Houdaille, "Quelques résultats sur la démographie de trois villages d'Allemagne de 1750 à 1879," *Population*, XXV (1970), 649–654.

27. *Steiermark*. Otto von Zwiedineck-Südenhorst, "Die Illegitimität in Steiermark," *Statistische Monatschrift*, XXI (1895), 160.

28. *Sixteen Oberbayern villages 1760–1830*, courtesy Michael Phayer. Data for the *Kingdom of Bavaria, 1825–95* from Lindner, *Die unehelichen Geburten als Sozialphänomen*, 20. The Palatinate is included.

29. *Seventeen parishes around Hall in Württemburg*. Gmelin, "Bevölkerungsbewegung im Hällischen," 248.

30. *Göttelfingen (Württemberg)*. Ilse Müller, "Bevölkerungsgeschichtliche Untersuchungen in drei Gemeinden des württembergischen Schwarzwaldes," *Archiv für Bevölkerungswissenschaft*, IX (1939), 193.

31. *Böhringen (Württemberg)*. G. Heckh, "Bevölkerungsgeschichte und Bevölkerungsbewegung des Kirchspiels Böhringen auf der Uracher Alb vom 16. Jahrhundert bis zur Gegenwart," *Archiv für Rassen- und Gesellschaftshygiene*, XXXIII (1939–40), 134. I am indebted to John Knodel for the references to Böhringen and Göttelfingen.

32. *Anhausen (Bavaria)*. John Knodel, "Two and a Half Centuries of Demographic History in a Bavarian Village," *Population Studies*, XXIV (1970), 367.

33. *Tirol and Vorarlberg*. Vinc. Goehlert, "Die Entwickelung der Bevölkerung von Tirol and Vorarlberg," *Statistische Monatschrift*, VI (1880), 63–64.

34. *Eibesthal (Lower Austria)*. Franz Riedling, "Bevölkerungsbewegung im Orte Eibesthal in Nieder-Oesterreich in den Jahren 1683–1890," *Statistische Monatschrift*, IV (1899), 262.

35. *Canton of Neuchâtel*. Guillaume, "Recherches sur le mouvement de la population dans le canton de Neuchâtel de 1760 à 1875," *Zeitschrift für Schweizerische Statistik*, XIII (1877), 38.

36. *Belgium. Annuaire Statistique de la Belgique et du Congo Belge,* XXXIV (1903), 109–111.

37. *Liège.* Hélin, *Démographie de Liège,* 256–258.

38. *Rotterdam.* A. M. Van der Woude and G. J. Mentink, "La Population de Rotterdam au XVIIe et au XVIIIe siècle," *Population,* XXI (1966), 1180.

39. *Sweden.* Gustav Sundbärg, *Bevölkerungsstatistik Schwedens,* 117, 129.

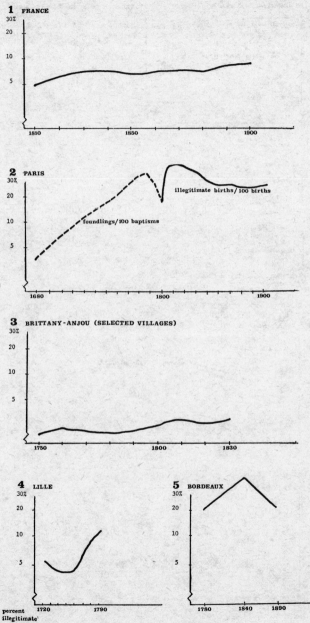

1 FRANCE

2 PARIS

illegitimate births/100 births

foundlings/100 baptisms

3 BRITTANY-ANJOU (SELECTED VILLAGES)

4 LILLE

5 BORDEAUX

percent
illegitimate

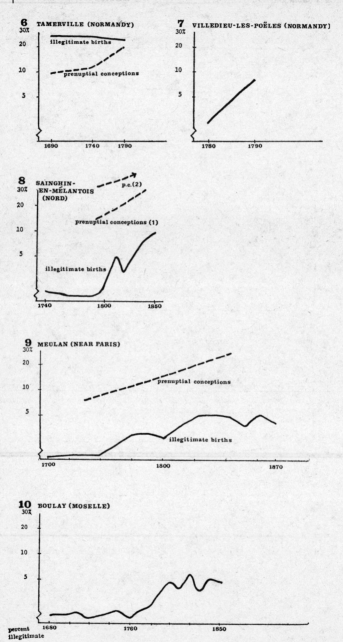

6 TAMERVILLE (NORMANDY)

30%

20

illegitimate births

10

prenuptial conceptions

5

1690   1740   1790

7 VILLEDIEU-LES-POÊLES (NORMANDY)

30%

20

10

5

1780   1790

8 SAINGHIN-EN-MÉLANTOIS (NORD)

30%

p.c.(2)

20

10

prenuptial conceptions (1)

5

illegitimate births

1740   1800   1850

9 MEULAN (NEAR PARIS)

30%

20

prenuptial conceptions

10

5

illegitimate births

1700   1800   1870

10 BOULAY (MOSELLE)

30%

20

10

5

percent illegitimate   1680   1760   1850

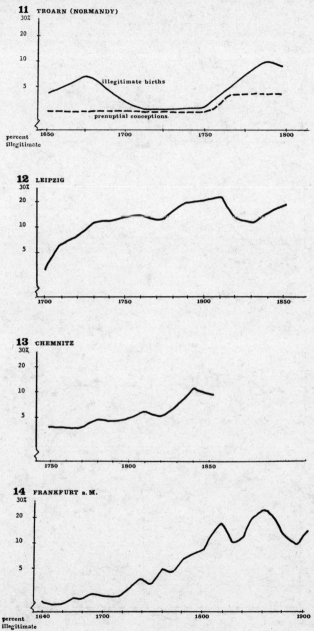

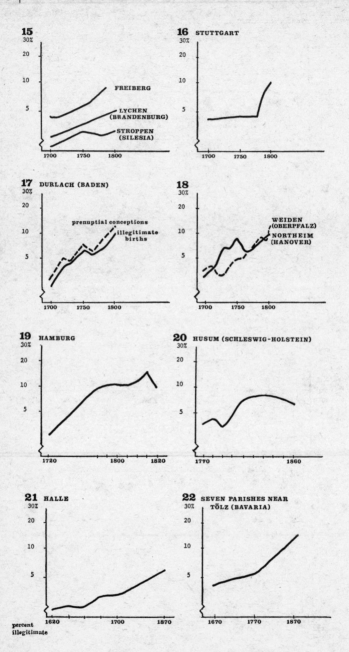

15

16 STUTTGART

FREIBERG

LYCHEN (BRANDENBURG)

STROPPEN (SILESIA)

17 DURLACH (BADEN)

prenuptial conceptions

illegitimate births

18

WEIDEN (OBERPFALZ)

NORTHEIM (HANOVER)

19 HAMBURG

20 HUSUM (SCHLESWIG-HOLSTEIN)

21 HALLE

22 SEVEN PARISHES NEAR TÖLZ (BAVARIA)

percent illegitimate

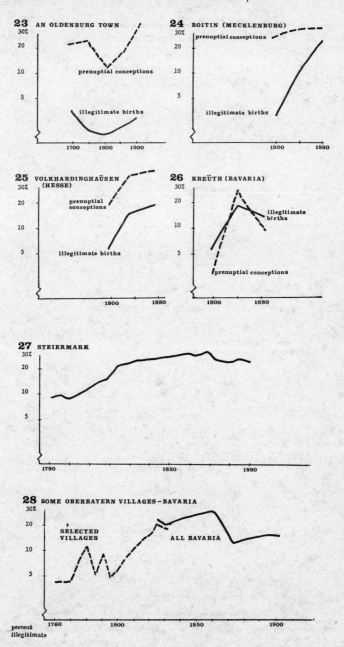

23 AN OLDENBURG TOWN

prenuptial conceptions

illegitimate births

24 BOITIN (MECKLENBURG)

prenuptial conceptions

illegitimate births

25 VOLKHARDINGHAÜSEN (HESSE)

prenuptial conceptions

illegitimate births

26 KREÜTH (BAVARIA)

illegitimate births

prenuptial conceptions

27 STEIERMARK

28 SOME OBERBAYERN VILLAGES – BAVARIA

SELECTED VILLAGES

ALL BAVARIA

percent illegitimate

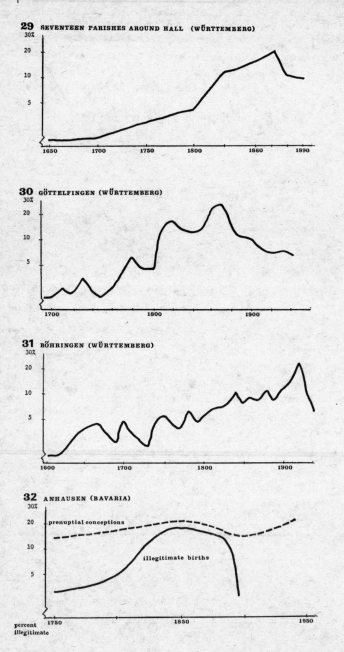

29 SEVENTEEN PARISHES AROUND HALL (WÜRTTEMBERG)

30 GÖTTELFINGEN (WÜRTTEMBERG)

31 BÖHRINGEN (WÜRTTEMBERG)

32 ANHAUSEN (BAVARIA)

prenuptial conceptions

illegitimate births

percent
illegitimate

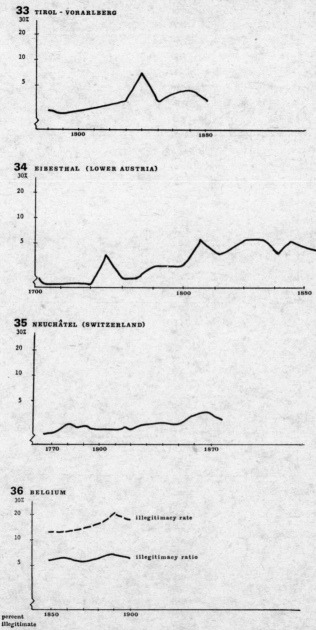

33 TIROL - VORARLBERG

34 EIBESTHAL (LOWER AUSTRIA)

35 NEUCHÂTEL (SWITZERLAND)

36 BELGIUM

illegitimacy rate

illegitimacy ratio

percent
illegitimate

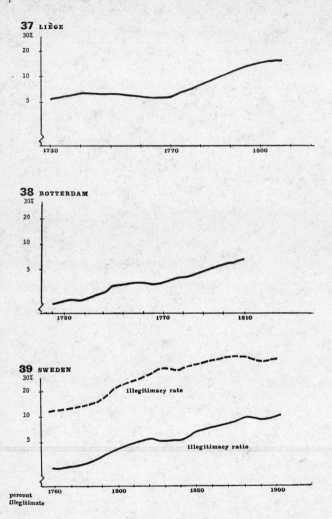

37 LIÈGE

38 ROTTERDAM

39 SWEDEN

illegitimacy rate

illegitimacy ratio

percent
illegitimate

Robert V. Wells

Demographic Change and the Life Cycle of American Families

Between the eighteenth and the twentieth centuries, major changes occurred in the patterns of birth and death of the American population. The birth rate declined by over 50 per cent, from around 50 per 1,000 in 1800 to less than 20 per 1,000 today.[1] Although the evidence on mortality is less clear, there can be no doubt that substantial improvements in life expectancy occurred during this period. The best estimates indicate that life expectancy at birth came close to doubling between about 1800 and 1970.[2] In view of the magnitude of these changes, it is surprising to find that so little is known of their impact on American social institutions.

How did these major demographic changes affect one of the fundamental parts of our society—the family? In particular, how did the decline in both fertility and mortality alter the life cycle of the American family in the two centuries since the American Revolution?[3]

Glick, who has played an important role in the study of American families in the twentieth century, has described the life cycle of the family:

Between formation and dissolution, families go through a series of characteristic stages which lend themselves to demographic analysis. These stages include marriage, the establishment of a household, bearing and rearing children, marriage of the children, and the later years before the family is finally dissolved. Successive readjustments of behavior patterns are required as the adult members shift their roles from

Robert V. Wells is Assistant Professor of History at Union College. He is the author of "Family Size and Fertility Control in Eighteenth Century America: A Study of Quaker Families," *Population Studies*, XXV (1971). An earlier version of this paper was delivered at the 1971 meeting of the Population Association of America.

1 For estimates of the birth rate in 1800, see Ansley J. Coale and Melvin Zelnik, *New Estimates of Fertility and Population in the United States* (Princeton, 1963), 39; W. S. Thompson and P. K. Whelpton, *Population Trends in the United States* (New York, 1933), 263.

2 The standard estimate for life expectancy at birth for before 1800 is about 35 years; see Thompson and Whelpton, *Population Trends*, 239. My own work has indicated that this figure may be slightly low, but not by more than five years.

3 Compare the approach and findings of this study with Peter R. Uhlenberg, "A Study of Cohort Life Cycles: Cohorts of Native Born Massachusetts Women, 1830–1920," *Population Studies*, XXIII (1969), 407–420.

newly wedded persons to parents of small children, parents of older children, older couples without children at home, and surviving widows or widowers.[4]

By comparing the patterns of marriage, childbearing, and death of adults of the eighteenth and twentieth centuries, it should be possible to determine those aspects of family life which have remained relatively stable over time, as well as the ways in which the life of the family has changed in the last 200 years.

Two studies provide the basic evidence for this paper. My own work provides data on 276 Quaker families in which the wife was born before 1786. These families lived in New York, New Jersey, and Pennsylvania in the eighteenth and early nineteenth centuries. As most of the data come from before 1800, these will be referred to as eighteenth-century families. These Quakers cannot be assumed to represent the American population as a whole before 1800, but there is evidence to suggest that their life cycle was much the same as that of their contemporaries. Figures for American families in general in the nineteenth and twentieth centuries have been taken from the study by Glick and Parke, "New Approaches in Studying the Life Cycle of the Family."[5] This study was the first attempt to examine the family life cycle by cohort analysis, and, as such, is more comparable to the Quaker data than Glick's earlier work.[6] In all, Glick and Parke consider the family life cycle of six different cohorts of women (defined by the year of birth), but only two of these groups have been selected for consideration here. The first includes families in which the wives were born between 1880 and 1889; this is the earliest group for which the authors present data. The second group of families is defined by wives born between 1920 and 1929; they are selected for study here

---

4 Paul C. Glick, *American Families* (New York, 1957), 53.

5 See Paul C. Glick and Robert Parke, Jr., *Demography*, II (1965), 187–202; for a listing of Glick's earlier writings, see 187. It should be noted that, although the subjects of Glick's figures are still alive, he has predicted aggregate demographic characteristics on the basis of current mortality trends. Historians who wish to incorporate the family life cycle concept into their own work should consult the article by John B. Lansing and Leslie Kish, "Family Life Cycle as an Independent Variable," *American Sociological Review*, XXII (1957), 512–519. The importance of this study lies in the suggestion that behavior patterns of adults are likely to change as people move from one stage of the life cycle of the family to another.

6 Cohort analysis groups persons under study by events which they all experience at the same time. The two most common events used to define a group (i.e., a cohort) are the year of birth and the year of marriage. The cohorts are then followed over time, for as long as the study requires, to see when, or at what age, other events occur.

because they are the most recent group for which the figures are relatively complete.

Three other points need to be mentioned before proceeding to the analysis of change in family life cycles. First, the following information is for first marriages only. It raises several questions which will be considered at the end of the paper. Second, the discussion concentrates on the experience of the wives. In part this is because the data for the Quaker women of this study are better than that for their husbands, but it is also true that the figures for the men are virtually the same except for the fact that they married later than the women, and hence reached each successive stage of the family at a correspondingly older age. Third, this study concentrates on the experience of the adult members of a family. It would be of obvious interest to know how children were affected by changing fertility and mortality, but the lack of both data and space prevent an exploration of this subject here.

Since the life of a family begins with marriage, let us look first at the changes in the age at first marriage between the eighteenth and twentieth centuries. As seen in my study of the Quakers, the median age at first marriage was 20.5 for the women.[7] Studies of genealogies and New England town records suggest that, in this regard, they were much like other eighteenth-century Americans.[8] Among wives born between 1880 and 1889, however, families were formed somewhat later in the life of the bride as the median age at first marriage had increased to 21.6 among women. This increase is not surprising, for the age at first marriage among women appears to have been on the rise throughout the eighteenth century.[9] The twentieth century brought a reversal to this long-term trend, for women born between 1920 and 1929 were marrying at a median age of 20.8 years, much the same as in the colonial period. Certainly marriage patterns varied, but the difference between the highest and the lowest figures of just over one year among the women suggests that marriages were formed at much the same point in life throughout the last two centuries.

In most cases, marriage was followed within a year or two by a first child, whether the couple lived in the eighteenth or twentieth

7 These figures, and those which follow, have been summarized in Tables 1 and 2 in the Appendix. The sources for the data and the way in which the figures were calculated are described there.

8 This evidence has been collected in Robert V. Wells, "Quaker Marriage Patterns in a Colonial Perspective," unpublished paper.

9 *Ibid.*

centuries. But there the similarity in childbearing patterns ends. According to Glick and Parke, the median age of mothers at the birth of their last child was 30.5 for women born in the 1920s. Thus, for these wives, the median length of time spent between marriage and the end of the childbearing stage of life was only 9.7 years. This figure contrasts sharply with the 17.4 years which one of the Quaker women of the eighteenth century might expect to spend bearing children. Among the Friends studied here, the median age of mothers at the birth of the last child was 37.9 years.[10] I have suggested elsewhere that these Quakers were among the first Americans deliberately to limit the size of their families.[11] As a result, their families were, in all probability, smaller than the average for eighteenth-century America, and their childbearing presumably ended at an earlier age. Thus, if anything, the decline in length of the childbearing period between the late-eighteenth and the mid-twentieth centuries is understated. It is of interest to note that among wives born between 1880 and 1889, the median length of the childbearing period was 11.3 years, considerably shorter than that of the eighteenth-century families. Apparently, the decline in fertility was well underway by the end of the nineteenth century and, among groups like these Quakers, this trend may date back to the era of the American Revolution.

Because of the longer time spent in childbearing, parents of the eighteenth century also spent more of their life rearing their children than did parents in later years. Among the Quakers of this study, the last child married and left home when the mother was of a median age of 60.2. Wives born between 1880 and 1889 were of a median age of 56.2 when their last child left home. They were only slightly younger than the eighteenth-century women in this regard, because the rise in the age at marriage had partially offset the effects of the reduced childbearing period. But, by the mid-twentieth century, earlier marriages and a shorter time spent bearing children combined to free parents of their children at an earlier age. The median age among the last group of wives when their children were finally married and gone was 52.0, almost ten years less than the corresponding figure among the Quakers. Almost forty years passed between the formation of an eighteenth-century family and the time when child-rearing was finished. By the end of the nineteenth century, however, the effects of the

10 This figure is for all women married before the age of forty-five.
11 Robert V. Wells, "Family Size and Fertility Control in Eighteenth Century America: A Study of Quaker Families," *Population Studies*, XXV (1971), 173–182.

gradual decline in fertility were beginning to show. Families in which the wife was born between 1880 and 1889, and whose childbearing held to the average, were spending only thirty-five years in the child-rearing stage; among couples where the wife was born between 1920 and 1929, the median interval between the formation of a family and the departure of the last child was only thirty-one years.

In addition to spending less of their life rearing children, the evidence suggests that parents in the twentieth century experienced a more stable family situation. As Glick has pointed out, once modern parents stopped childbearing, their family was normally of a constant size until their children began to marry and leave home.[12] Families of the late eighteenth century, however, were subjected to growth for a much longer period and high mortality continually threatened the family with the death of parents and children. The stability of twentieth-century families is emphasized by the fact that only 31 per cent of the total time spent rearing children was devoted to childbearing by wives born between 1920 and 1929. The comparable figures are 33 per cent for wives born between 1880 and 1889, and 44 per cent for the wives born before 1786. Undoubtedly women benefited from this change, not only because they had fewer children to raise, but also because the burden of pregnancy less frequently interfered with their ability to rear their children.

In addition to the changes in the life cycle of the family introduced by the long-term decline in fertility, improving conditions of mortality also had a recognizable impact on the family. However, the effects of increased life expectancy were felt predominantly in the twentieth century, for, until about 1890, conditions of mortality improved slowly, if at all.

The most fundamental change wrought by the decline in mortality has been an increase in the length of marriage. Among the Quakers studied here, the median duration of marriage was 30.4 years. Although other information on mortality before 1800 is scarce, studies of Andover and Plymouth in Massachusetts suggest that the life chances of these Quakers were not unusually good in the context of the colonial period.[13] It is important to note, however, that the median duration of marriage is somewhat deceptive regarding mortality conditions. A

---

12 Glick, *American Families*, 67.
13 Philip J. Greven, Jr., *Four Generations: Population, Land, and Family in Colonial Andover, Massachusetts* (Ithaca, 1970), 192, 195; John Demos, *A Little Commonwealth: Family Life in Plymouth Colony* (New York, 1970), 192–193.

surprisingly high proportion of these Quaker unions ended relatively quickly. Although only 1.9 per cent of the marriages lasted less than a year, almost a fifth (18.8 per cent) had been dissolved by the death of one partner before the fifteenth anniversary had been reached; after twenty-five years, 38.4 per cent of the unions once formed no longer existed. Couples who lived at the end of the 1800s could hope for but a little more time together than had these Quakers. Wives born between 1880 and 1889 had a median duration of marriage of 35.4 years, an increase of just over five years in about a century. In the next forty years, however, medical and sanitary improvements had a striking effect on the family, the median length of married life increasing to 43.6 years among the last group of wives.[14]

The fact that husbands and wives could expect a longer life together after about 1900 is, in itself, important. It is especially important, however, when one recalls the reduction in the length of child-rearing which had occurred by that period. Couples who married in the twentieth century were among the first who could reasonably expect a life together after their children had left home. By subtracting the median figure for the length of the child-rearing stage of life from that of the duration of marriage, it is apparent that couples in which the wife was born between 1920 and 1929 could expect 12.4 years of married life after their children had left home. In contrast, half of the marriages involving a wife born between 1880 and 1889 were broken by the death of one partner less than a year after the last child departed. Even more startling is the situation among the families of the eighteenth century. Fully 69 per cent of all the Quaker marriages studied were of shorter duration than the median length of child-rearing among that group. In fact, a Quaker widow or widower, whose experience held to the median, could expect to have children to take care of for 9.3 years after the death of his or her first spouse. Thus, by the twentieth century, longer marriages combined with a continuing decline in fertility to produce a situation in which, for the first time, couples could *expect* a life together after their children were gone. Companionship was beginning to join reproduction as an important expectation of marriage.

The relative decrease in the importance of children in the life of twentieth-century families is further illustrated by the increased duration between the marriage of the last child and the death of the last

14 This figure is based on the estimates of mortality trends among the cohort born between 1920 and 1929 in Glick and Parke, "New Approaches," 194–195, and Table 1.

parent to die. Among the Quakers who lived in the late 1700s, marriage was virtually synonymous with children. We have already seen that one spouse could expect to die before the children were completely reared; of equal importance is the fact that the surviving partner could expect to die less than five years after the last child married. Old age, without family, was not common before 1800. This situation had clearly changed by the twentieth century, as the experience of the wives born from 1880 to 1889 indicates. Among this group of families, wives who outlived their husbands died almost twenty years after their last child had left home; among the men of this group who survived their wives, the corresponding figure was fifteen years. Obviously, similar figures for the families in which the wife was born between 1920 and 1929 are not available. But unless life chances are sharply reduced, the trend toward a longer life after the children have left home should continue. Apparently, old age with no children present is largely a phenomenon of the modern world; the nation's founders seldom had to face the problem.

The last stage of the life cycle of the family which concerns us here is the length of widowhood, that is, the time between the death of one spouse and the death of the second. Here, too, improvements in life expectancy have had their effects. The Quaker widows of the 1700s survived for an average of 13.7 years after the death of their husbands. This figure is considerably below the median length of widowhood of 18.7 years for the wives born between 1880 and 1889. The corresponding increase in the length of widowhood among the men was much less. While the Quaker widowers of this study lived for 12.5 years after their wives had died, the figure for men whose wives were born between 1880 and 1889 was 14.2, an increase of almost two years. In addition to living longer after their children have left home, parents of the twentieth century are faced with an increased amount of time in their old age with none of their family around. In a very real sense, the reductions in fertility and mortality have increased the possibility of loneliness in old age.

This analysis of changes in the life cycle of the family has been carried out on first marriages only. It is, therefore, desirable to examine how typical these patterns are of the experience of all families in the various periods under consideration. Among the Quakers studied here, fully 88 per cent of all marriages were the first for both partners. Furthermore, of the wives, 97.5 per cent had never been married before; among the husbands, the proportion marrying for the first time was 88.8 per cent. Remarriage among these Quakers was rare, and there is evidence to suggest that other eighteenth-century American populations shared this pattern of behavior.[15] While the proportion of first marriages to all marriages is rather high, a surprisingly large number of these Quakers never wed. Perhaps as many as half of the Quaker children born before 1800 never married at all. Of course, most of those who did not marry died before they had the opportunity to wed. But, between 12 and 15 per cent of these Quakers who lived to the age of fifty died without marrying.

Depending upon one's perspective, first marriages were both more and less typical in 1950 than they were before 1800. The proportion of marriages which were the first for both husband and wife had fallen from 88 per cent before 1800 to 67 per cent by 1950.[16] Likewise, while 97.5 per cent of the Quaker wives were marrying for the first time, only 74.4 per cent of the brides in 1950 had never been married before. The corresponding figures for the men show a decline in the proportion marrying for the first time from 88.8 per cent to 75.5 per cent. While first marriages were less typical of all marriages in the twentieth century than they had been earlier, there can be little doubt that a higher proportion of the population took a spouse at least once. The proportion never married in 1950 of 7 to 8 per cent was approximately half that found among the Quakers. The percentage of children who died before marrying was clearly less, too. Perhaps 80 to 85 per cent of all children born in the middle of the twentieth century could expect to marry, compared to about 50 per cent among these Quakers.[17]

One last difference between the Quaker families of the eighteenth century and those of Americans in the mid-twentieth century deserves mention. Once a Quaker couple married they remained united until one spouse died. Divorce was extremely rare among the Friends, and among their contemporaries as well.[18] Among Americans in 1950, however, about 16 per cent of all marriages involved one partner who had been married, but who had divorced his previous spouse.[19] In fact, much of the increase in remarriage between 1800 and 1950 may

15 See Wells, "Quaker Marriage Patterns."
16 Glick, *American Families*, 142.
17 *Ibid.*, 140.
18 George E. Howard, *A History of Matrimonial Institutions* (Chicago, 1904), II, last part.
19 Glick, *American Families*, 142.

be the result of a rising number of divorces which were followed by a new marriage for one or both partners. From the point of view of the children, the increased family stability which resulted from parents being assured of a longer life together has been offset, to some extent, by a willingness of couples voluntarily to end their unions.

When the life cycle of these Quaker families (who do not seem to have been greatly different from their contemporaries) is compared to that of modern families, it seems apparent that, in the course of the last two centuries, the life cycle of most American families has become significantly more complex. From an almost exclusive concern with childbearing and child-rearing before 1800, the emphasis within a family has gradually shifted until now the life of the parents after their children have left home has become a major part of family living. This change can only partially be explained by the improved mortality conditions in modern America. The long-term decline in fertility, which may have started about the time of the American Revolution, also reduced the emphasis on the childbearing aspects of marriage. Thus, the life cycle of the family in the mid-twentieth century reflects both an intimate relationship to the modern world, and has roots which extend back to the founding of the nation.

APPENDIX

Table 1   Median Age of Wives at Stages of the Life Cycle of the Family

STAGE OF THE LIFE CYCLE OF THE FAMILY	WIVES BORN		
	BEFORE 1786 (QUAKERS)	1880–1889	1920–1929
A. First marriage	20.5[a]	21.6	20.8
B. Birth of last child	37.9	32.9	30.5
C. Marriage of last child	60.2	56.2	52.0
D. Death of first spouse to die	50.9	57.0	64.4

a As measured by the interquartile range, the distribution around the median of the age at first marriage, the age of the mother at the birth of her last child, and the duration of marriage seem to have been much the same from one group to another.

Sources: The data for wives born before 1786 are my own. The information for the other wives is from Glick and Parke, "New Approaches", 190, Table 1.

Table 2 *Median Length of Selected Stages of the Life Cycle of the Family (in Years)*

STAGE OF THE LIFE CYCLE OF THE FAMILY	WIVES BORN		
	BEFORE 1786 (QUAKERS)	1880–1889	1920–1929
1. Childbearing	17.4	11.3	9.7
2. Child-rearing	39.7	34.6	31.2
3. Duration of Marriage	30.4	35.4	43.6
4. Old Age Together	− 9.3	0.8	12.4
5. Widowhood			
Female	13.7	18.7	—
Male	12.5	14.2	—
6. Marriage of last child to death of last spouse, when last is			
Female	4.4	19.5	—
Male	3.2	15.0	—

Source: The above table was derived as follows:

Table 2

Line 1 = Line B − Line A ⎫
Line 2 = Line C − Line A ⎪ From Table 1
Line 3 = Line D − Line A ⎬
Line 4 = Line D − Line C ⎭

Line 5 = The figures for the husbands and wives born before 1786 were calculated directly from my data. For the others, see Glick and Parke, "New Approaches," 195.

Line 6 = Line 4 + Line 5

Joseph F. Kett

Adolescence and Youth
in Nineteenth-Century America

The modern concept of adolescence was created by Hall and his colleagues at Clark University in the 1890s and given full expression in Hall's two volume *Adolescence.*[1] Hall described adolescence as a second birth, marked by a sudden rise of moral idealism, chivalry, and religious enthusiasm. In the context of Hall's celebrated theory of recapitulation—the idea that the child passes in succession through the various historical epochs already traversed by man—the adolescent became a kind of noble savage. His activities were inevitable reflections of psychic echoes out of a distant past.[2] Weird and pseudo-scientific in retrospect, Hall's concept had a profound impact in his day. A parade of books on the teen years, the "awkward age," the high school, and the juvenile delinquent followed, while a virtual profession of advisers on the tribulations of youth emerged.[3]

One can also argue that adolescence has become a unique topic of interest in the twentieth century because of social conditions peculiar to our own time—specifically, the emergence of a yawning time gap between the onset of sexual maturity and the full incorporation of young people into the economic life of the adult world. Before we can rest content with this explanation, however, we have to confront the historical fact of numerous references to adolescence or youth long before Hall's time.

In the Middle Ages speculations about the "ages of man" had usually included a stage of youth or adolescence, and, at times, two separate stages. Such speculation had often centered more on the

Joseph F. Kett is Associate Professor of History at the University of Virginia. He is the author of *The formation of the American Medical Profession* (New Haven, 1968), and of articles on social and scientific history.

1 G. Stanley Hall, *Adolescence: Its Psychology and Its Relations to Physiology, Anthropology, Sociology, Sex, Crime, Religion, and Education* (New York), 1904, 2v.
2 *Ibid.*, I, viii–x; II, Chs. 11, 12.
3 Hall's influence was vast, but a representative sample of the literature on adolescence after 1900 would include: Irving King, *The High School Age* (Indianapolis, 1914); Jane Addams, *The Spirit of Youth and the City Streets* (New York, 1909); Michael V. O'Shea, *Social Development in Education* (Boston, 1909). O'Shea was a good example of the entrepreneur of adolescence; his papers (Wisconsin Historical Society) consist mainly of correspondence with publishers in connection with his editing of various series on the problems of youth.

exact number of the ages than on their moral or psychological content, however. Indeed, the fascination with dividing the life cycle by whole or magical numbers survived into the early 1800s.[4] Humanists and philosophers—Elyot and Ascham in the sixteenth century, Comenius in the seventeenth century, and Rousseau in the eighteenth century—had also located moral as well as physical changes at adolescence.[5] Of these, Rousseau was assuredly the most emphatic, and the direction of both European and American medical literature in the late eighteenth and early nineteenth centuries paralleled his insistence on a profound change at puberty. One indication was the rise of a scientific literature on masturbatory insanity, touched off by the publication of the Swiss physician Samuel A. Tissot's *Onania, or a Treatise upon the Disorders Produced by Masturbation* (Lausanne, 1758). A popularization of this species of literature took place in early nineteenth-century America in the form of innumerable "candid talks with youth" books and pamphlets.[6]

Writers on physiology displayed another side of the growing interest in adolescence. Dunglison, in his influential physiology text, found at puberty a freshening of the external senses, a rise of idealism, a qualitative leap in intellectual capacity, and the dawn of a tender modesty.[7] Like Hall, Dunglison insisted that adolescence was a moral and psychological stage of life which began with puberty and terminated with the end of physical growth in the early twenties. There was, indeed, a connection between the two sides of the emerging concept

4 Philippe Ariès (trans. Robert Baldick), *Centuries of Childhood: A Social History of Family Life* (New York, 1962), 21; Charles Sayle, *The Ages of Man* (London, 1916), xv; "The Stages of Human Life," *Boston Medical and Surgical Journal*, IV (1831), 289–291; E. G. Wheeler, "The Periods of Human Life," *ibid.*, XXII (1840), 395–396.

5 Thomas Elyot, *The Boke Named the Governour* (London, 1907), Bk. I, Ch. 14; Roger Ascham, *The Schoolmaster*, in J. A. Giles (ed.), *The Whole Works of Roger Ascham* (London, 1864), III, 147; M. W. Keatinge (ed.), *The Great Didactic of John Amos Comenius, Now for the First Time Englished* (London, 1896), 409, *passim*; Jean Jacques Rousseau, *Émile* (London, 1911; Everyman ed.), Bk. IV. Like Hall, Rousseau described adolescence as a second birth.

6 E. H. Hare, "Masturbatory Insanity: The History of an Idea," *Journal of Mental Science*, CVIII (1962), 1–25; Christopher W. Hufeland, *The Art of Prolonging Life* (London, 1797), II, 55–62; [Anon.], *An Hour's Conference with Fathers and Sons, in Relation to A Common and Fatal Indulgence of Youth* (Boston, 1840).

7 Robley Dunglison, *Human Physiology, Illustrated by Numerous Engravings* (Philadelphia, 1832), II, 398–404. See also Alm. Lepelletier, *Traité de Physiologie Médicale et Philosophique* (Paris, 1833), IV, 473–478; Peter M. Roget, *Treatise on Physiology and Phrenology* (Edinburgh, 1838), II, 204, 208; James Copeland, *A Dictionary of Practical Medicine* (Boston, 1834), I, 41–43; Amariah Brigham, *Remarks on the Influence of Mental Cultivation Upon Health* (Hartford, 1832), 56–59, 93, 46–47.

of adolescence, for the more writers celebrated the idealism of adolescents, the more befoulment they saw in masturbation.

Simply to note scientific and medical references to adolescence before the work of Hall tells us little, however, about the origin of popular ideas about adolescence. To revert specifically to the American context, we may well ask whether a writer such as Dunglison was simply giving scientific expression to long-standing popular assumptions or whether he stood at the end of a relatively short line of development. This is, for many reasons, a more difficult question to answer. An abundant and systematic literature on adolescent guidance did not exist in America before 1900. The word "adolescence" appeared only rarely outside of scientific literature prior to the twentieth century. But the absence of an elaborate literature on adolescent guidance before 1900 does not mean that ideas about adolescence did not exist or that they were of only marginal concern. It indicates merely that adolescence was not the public, official concern prior to 1900 that it has since become.

The evolution of popular, as opposed to strictly scientific, ideas about adolescence can be understood by studying the changing usage of "youth," the word usually employed before 1900 to denote the intermediate stage of development. Numerous references to "youth" can be found as early as the seventeenth century. New England Puritans, Cotton Mather in particular, published numerous sermons on the rising generation. Yet one is left with a feeling that Puritans used "youth" more as a noun than as a concept. Their sermons routinely mixed up children, youth, young people, and young men. This slippery use of designations in turn reflected various aspects of the mentality and social experience of seventeenth-century New England Puritans. As Demos has suggested, adolescence scarcely existed as a private issue in seventeenth-century New England. In a stable agrarian society, the range of occupational and religious choices open to young people was so narrow as to preclude a period of doubt and indecision. One generation passed quietly into the next. But even if adolescence had existed as a social experience in seventeenth-century New England, Puritans would have had difficulty in coming to terms with it. They hardly believed that individuals moved through stages of life. To take their favorite analogy, life was a highway. There were various signposts along the way, and older individuals had a greater physical and mental capacity that younger ones. But the sum of forces at one point on the highway did not necessarily determine direction at the next.

Childhood was the beginning of the continuum of life, but the course of childhood did not necessarily determine later development.[8]

Verbal distinctions between childhood and youth, practically nonexistent in the seventeenth century and still rare in the eighteenth, became much more common after 1800. A growing conceptual segregation of childhood and youth paralleled the sharpening of terminology. If the favorite analogy in the 1600s was the comparison of life to a highway, the darling metaphor of the 1800s was the comparison of human life to the cycle of the seasons. One illustration of the new understanding of human development was the changing nature of biography and autobiography. Biographers and autobiographers in the seventeenth and eighteenth centuries either ignored the childhood of their subjects or treated the events of childhood simply as indications of later development. The focus was more on remarkable instances—close scrapes with death, providential good fortune, and the like—than on organic growth. After 1800, in contrast, chapters on childhood increasingly replaced the family tree as the introduction to the subject's life, and the tendency now was to concentrate on a recounting of the unexceptional events of childhood. Finally, after roughly 1830, more and more biographies and autobiographies emphasized that the early years provided a positive thrust for, rather than merely an indication of, later development.[9]

The heightened awareness of childhood in early nineteenth-century America involved not only a recognition of the organic character of human growth, but also a tendency toward preserving juvenile innocence rather than stimulating children to imitate adults. The celebration of juvenile innocence, in turn, produced the fear of precocity so pervasive in nineteenth-century thought. Since Puritans had

8 Cotton Mather, *The Best Ornaments of Youth* (Boston, 1707), 25. See the following works by Mather: *Repeated Warnings: Another Essay to Warn Young People Against Rebellions That Must Be Repented Of* (Boston, 1712); *Things That Young People Should Think Upon* (Boston, 1700); *The Young Man's Preservative* (London, 1702). See also Samuel Moody, *The Vain Youth Summoned* (Boston, 1707); John Demos, *A Little Commonwealth: Family Life in Plymouth Colony* (New York, 1970), Ch. 10; Philip J. Greven, Jr., *Four Generations: Population, Land, and Family in Colonial Andover, Massachusetts* (Ithaca, 1970).
9 Paul Delany, *British Autobiography in the Seventeenth Century* (London, 1969); Daniel B. Shea, Jr., *Spiritual Autobiography in Early America* (Princeton, 1969), 91, *passim*; David Humphreys, *An Essay on the Life of the Honorable Major General Israel Putnam* (Boston, 1818); Mason L. Weems, *The Life of Benjamin Franklin; with Many Choice Anecdotes and Admirable Sayings of this Great Man* (Philadelphia, 1829), 11–12; Jason Whitman, *A Memoir of the Rev. Bernard Whitman* (Boston, 1837), 16; [Eliza B. Lee], *Sketches of a New England Village in the Last Century* (Boston, 1838).

viewed childhood as a condition to be worked off with all due speed, they tended to applaud children who acted like adults. The different direction of nineteenth-century thought can be traced in the emphasis placed in biographies after 1800 on the ability of subjects to get along with their peers in childhood. It was illustrated also in the immense importance which common school reformers attached to the location of schoolhouses away from the busy scenes of secular life and to the gradual conversion of the school into "an asylum for the preservation and culture of childhood." [10] Inevitably, the fear of precocity in children was carried over to a concern with the premature development of adolescents, an anxiety which pervaded the popular literature of the nineteenth century on masturbatory insanity. In the popular image, the precocious lad and the compulsive masturbator had so much in common—a stooping gait, a shifting eye, a sunken chest—that one is entitled to view many references to precocity as euphemisms for masturbation. Here again the break with tradition was profound. Samuel Danforth's sermon of 1674, *The Cry of Sodom Enquired into ... Together with Solemn Exhortations to Tremble at God's Judgements and to Abandon Youthful Lusts*, condemned "self-pollution" along with other sexual indulgences, but never suggested that masturbation threatened psychological or even physical stability. [11] The more sentimentalized became the image of early childhood in the nineteenth century, the more threatening became the onset of youth. The preoccupation of nineteenth-century writers with masturbatory insanity thus reflected a keen, if often quackish, sensitivity to the psychological dangers of adolescence.

The disposition to view the life cycle as divided into a series of disparate stages, the tendency to sentimentalize childhood, and the rising fear of precocity, all had the effect of throwing youth, the intermediate stage of development, into sharper relief. For the first time a class of books aimed specifically at youth appeared. Addressed to those who had recently left the security of Protestant homesteads for life in urban countinghouses, the "advice to youth" books celebrated the idealism of youth but warned incessantly of the dangers of fast living and rash judgment. [12]

10 "Honor Due to Aged Teachers," *American Annals of Education*, VII (1837), 118.
11 Cambridge, Mass., 1674; see also Stephen Marcus, *The Other Victorians: A Study in Sexuality and Pornography in Mid-Nineteenth-Century England* (New York, 1966), 19–20.
12 Joel Hawes, *Lectures to Young Men* (Boston, 1832); A. B. Muzzey, *The Young Man's*

To unravel the intricate web of social and attitudinal changes which lay behind this conceptual segregation of childhood and youth is not easy. Broadly speaking, the changes can be correlated with the rise of romanticism. But romanticism is a vague term; reference to it illuminates but does not explain historical change. Yet to be more specific is risky. A heightened awareness of childhood and youth emerged at different places in the Western world after the middle of the eighteenth century, amidst widely differing social conditions.[13] Population concentration in America after 1800 probably gave children a new degree of conspicuousness. As the Demoses have noted, the decline of the family as a working unit in an urban setting gave rise to "an important 'discontinuity of age groups.' Children and adults are much more obviously separated from each other than is ever the case in a rural environment."[14] But it is also true that many were led to an appreciation of the innocence of smaller children by personal experiences of a religious rather than a social nature. We can see this connection in the life and thought of Catherine E. Beecher. Like any daughter of Lyman Beecher, she was expected to experience a religious conversion, was told that it was her own fault if she did not, and yet was told that there was nothing that she could do to bring about her own salvation. She initially despaired and ultimately rebelled, turning toward liberal religion and a belief that the instincts of the small child were a truer guide to morality than the solemn syllogisms of New England orthodoxy.[15]

Friend (Boston, 1838; 2nd ed.); John Austin, A Voice to Youth (New York, 1847). These tracts were usually written by evangelical Protestant ministers.

13 Peter Coveney, The Image of Childhood. The Individual and Society: A Study of the Theme in English Literature (Baltimore, 1967; rev. ed.; originally published as Poor Monkey), Chs. 1–3; F. Musgrove, Youth and the Social Order (London, 1964), 49, 53; Bernard Wishy, The Child and the Republic: The Dawn of Modern American Child Nurture (Philadelphia, 1968); John and Virginia Demos, "Adolescence in Historical Perspective," Journal of Marriage and the Family, XXXI (1969), 632–633.

14 Ibid., 637. They also note that in an urban setting young people "have the opportunity to form numerous contacts among their own peers." This is a useful insight, but we should be wary of equating "urban" with city, for there is an abundance of evidence pointing to the existence of such peer groups in the small towns of early nineteenth-century New England; see, for example, William Stickney (ed.), The Autobiography of Amos Kendall (Boston, 1872), 3, 39, passim. There are also many references in the literature of religious revivalism to bands of young people roaming about at camp meetings in the early 1800s.

15 Catherine E. Beecher, Common Sense Applied to Religion: or the Bible and the People (New York, 1857), xx–xxii; and Religious Training of Children in the School, the Family, and

While the sentimentalization of childhood in early nineteenth-century America owed something to urban liberalism, a fresh focus on both children and youth grew contemporaneously out of the very opposite source, rural and village Calvinism and the revivals of the Second Great Awakening—that massive outpouring of religious enthusiasm which swept first one and then another section of the nation from the 1790s onward. Teenagers became truly conspicuous for the first time in American history, and evangelicals involved in the Awakening noted time and again the singularly important role of children and youth, especially the latter, in the revivals. This role had been foreshadowed in the Great Awakening of the 1740s but, as the Great Awakening waned, there was a general return to the pattern of aged church membership. During the Second Awakening, in contrast, teenage conversion became the norm.[16]

The frequency of teenage conversions in the Second Awakening is significant for a number of reasons. First of all, it was a reflection of increasing pressures on young people for choice and commitment. The spread of commercialization, pressure on the land in older sections of the nation, and internal migrations—all fundamental aspects of American social life after 1800—altered both the opportunities and life patterns of young people. The rise of new religious denominations, such as Methodism, Universalism, and Unitarianism, was no less important and more directly relevant to the religious experience of young people. Religious diversity had always characterized American life, but in the colonial period dissenters could always be sealed off in water-tight compartments like Rhode Island. By 1820 the various denominations were competing for converts in the same towns and villages. Religious alternatives were at the parental door.[17]

The argument is often advanced that the choices available to young people are greater today than in former times and, hence, that in our day generations more quickly become strangers to each other

the Church (New York, 1864); C. P. C., "Every Child a Unitarian," Western Messenger, IV (1837), 248–249.
16 Joshua Bradley (ed.), Accounts of Religious Revivals in Many Parts of the United States from 1815 to 1818 (Albany, N.Y., 1819), 25, 29, 33, 39, 43, 132–133; William W. Woodward, Surprising Accounts of the Revival of Religion in the United States of America, in Different Parts of the World, and among Different Denominations of Christians (n.p., 1802); [Anon.], "Revival of Religion in Washington City," Methodist Magazine, V (1822), 436.
17 Joseph F. Kett, "Growing Up in Rural New England, 1800–1840," in Tamara K. Hareven (ed.), Anonymous Americans: Explorations in Nineteenth-Century Social History (Englewood Cliffs, N.J., 1971), 1–16.

than in the past.[18] But social change is as much a subjective as an objective phenomenon. It exists not only in reality but also in the eye of the beholder. Boys subjected to the traditional modes of child-rearing, in which an absolute value was placed on submission to adult norms, found the appearance of even a small degree of social change profoundly unsettling. For many, religious conversion in the teen years proved to be at least a temporary therapy for doubt and uncertainty.

While the pattern of teenage conversion reflected social change, the phenomenon of teenage conversion became a subject of inquiry and speculation on the part of the evangelical ministry, the group with the most consistent institutional and intellectual concern with young people throughout the nineteenth century. The principal by-product of this interest was the emergence of a conviction among evangelicals that adolescence was the ideal time to induce a religious conversion. By 1820 there was a disposition among evangelicals to argue that something in the nature of youth, a combination of idealism, plasticity, and emotional enthusiasm, rendered it especially suited to conversion. By all accounts the youth involved in the Second Awakening ranged in age from five to twenty or twenty-five, but the majority of references were to young people between twelve and twenty. Prior to the 1830s, few viewed conversions under twelve with any enthusiasm; at the same time, few were eager to put off conversion until after a youth had left home to make his way in the world. Partly by this negative process of addition and subtraction, and partly by the positive affirmation of the idealism of youth, evangelicals came to embrace the ideal of teenage conversion.

Although the practice of calling up teenagers to give testimonials of a conversion experience survived into the late nineteenth century, it had lost much of its significance by the Gilded Age. Hall himself, born in 1844, belonged to one of the last generations of New England boys expected to go through an elaborate ritual of conversion during adolescence.[19] When he and his co-workers at Clark University in the 1890s were developing the modern concept of adolescence, they resurrected the old adolescent-conversion nexus by establishing a practically automatic connection between puberty and a kind of ultimate concern

18 Margaret Mead, *Culture and Commitment: A Study of the Generation Gap* (New York, 1970).
19 For Hall's religious experiences, see G. Stanley Hall, *Life and Confessions of a Psychologist* (New York, 1924), 163, 137.

which manifested itself specifically in religious conversion.[20] The connection had never been so neatly fixed in practice, but Hall and his colleagues paid homage to a nineteenth-century initiation rite which had affected millions of boys. Only if we grasp the profound roots of adolescent conversion in nineteenth-century America can we comprehend why so many of the writers on adolescence between 1890 and 1905 came into the field not by way of social reform and the juvenile courts, as the later history of the concept might suggest, but from religious psychology.

The pattern of teenage conversion which, as a matter of both expectation and reality, grew out of the Second Awakening, had the effect of forcing people to clarify the traditionally nebulous distinction between childhood and youth and of riveting attention on the psychological reactions as well as on the physical growth of youth. If religion were to be a matter of the heart as well as of the head, and if youth were the time for religious conversion, then youth had to be characterized by a rise of emotional sensibility. Indeed, the evangelical clergymen who wrote the "advice to youth" books were often led to a concern with the problems of youth after personal experience with young people during revivals. So, too, if some conversions were authentic, others, everyone conceded, were spurious—the products of mere "sympathetic enthusiasm."[21] The inevitable implication was that the emotional reactions of young people were at times unreliable and, specifically, that some adolescents, especially girls, were prone to insanity. The propensity of youths toward mental instability—melancholy for males and hysteria for females—was set down by medical writers from the 1830s onward under the rubric "pubertal insanity."[22] In a sense, youthfulness had acquired a psychological as well as a chronological content.

20 Hall, *Adolescence*, II, Ch. 14; Arthur H. Daniels, "The New Life: A Study in Regeneration," *American Journal of Psychology*, VI (1893), 61–106; Edwin D. Starbuck, *The Psychology of Religion: An Empirical Study of the Growth of Religious Consciousness* (New York, 1906).

21 For an example of the connection between the revival and the advice book, see Edward A. Lawrence, *The Life of Rev. Joel Hawes, D.D., Twelfth Pastor of the First Church, Hartford, Conn.* (Boston, 1881; 2nd ed.), 106–120. On "sympathetic enthusiasm" see "Early Piety," *American Sunday School Magazine*, IV (1837), 79.

22 Edward H. Dixon, *Women and Her Diseases, from the Cradle to the Grave* (Philadelphia, 1864); Joseph Parrish, "The Change of Life in Women, with Remarks on the Periods Usually Called 'Critical,'" *Boston Medical and Surgical Journal*, XLIX (1854) 54–57, 350; C. B. Burr, "The Insanity of Pubescence," *American Journal of Insanity*, XLII (1887), 328–339.

The new concern for distinguishing childhood and youth had a variety of institutional effects. In the war against the rum demon and the grog shop, for example, both the Cold Water Army, designed for younger children, and the Cadets of Temperance, designed for teen-agers, grew rapidly in the 1840s.[23] In Sunday Schools the holding of special classes for those in their middle teens indicated the importance attached to those years by evangelicals. It is indeed worth noting that evangelical Sunday Schools were often more carefully age-graded than were most secular schools.[24]

By the 1830s, however, demands for separating boys and youths affected secular education as well. In the late eighteenth and early nineteenth centuries, schools at any level were rarely graded by numer-ical age. One could meet pupils from four to twenty-three in district schools, from eight to twenty-five in academies, and from thirteen to thirty in colleges. By the 1830s school promoters were showing visible concern over these jagged fluctuations. Their agitation hardly resulted in the quick establishment of a graded school system. The en-tire process of gradation had a jerky quality which left many areas unaffected until the late nineteenth century. Prior to 1850, moreover, few educational writers showed much interest in setting age ceilings; in 1860 one could still find twenty-five-year-old academy students and thirty-year-old college students. But age floors were under con-struction in the 1820s and 1830s, especially in the colleges. Conditions in colonial colleges had never been altogether orderly, but, after a series of unusually violent college riots in the early 1800s, the situation grew desperate at many institutions. The disposition of students to view their horizontal ties to their peers more seriously than their ver-tical ties to adults not only indicated an emerging solidarity among students, but also focused public attention on the need to reform col-lege discipline. Two ideas were common to most of the proposals for reform. First, an increasing number of writers on education recog-nized that the older method of detecting offences by tutorial espionage had no future and that faculty "weasels" who peeked over transoms and through keyholes were only exacerbating the problem. The sole

23 Charles H. Miller, "The Order of Cadets of Temperance," in *One Hundred Years of Temperance Work: A Memorial Volume of the Centennial Temperance Conference held in Philadelphia, Pa., Sept., 1886* (New York, 1886), 527; Julia Colman, "The Cold Water Army," *ibid.*, 262–263.

24 "Elder Scholars," *American Sunday School Magazine*, II (1825), 38; *Fourth Annual Report of the Massachusetts Sabbath School Society, . . . 1836* (Boston, 1836), 29, 40.

recourse was to make a direct appeal to the honor and good sense of youth. Second, such appeals would be fruitless, many felt, as long as colleges continued to accept "mere boys" of thirteen or fourteen. Ideally, then, the colleges were to become institutions for young men rather than for children.[25]

It is easier to note the existence of a concept of youth in early nineteenth-century America than to delineate its scope. There is a temptation to argue that references to youth in the 1830s meant the same thing as Hall implied by adolescence. Certainly the differences between medical definitions of adolescence in the 1830s and Hall's later formulation of it were slight. But significant differences do exist between popular references to youth in the early nineteenth century and the connotation of adolescence in our century. For adolescence is now applied mainly to teenagers, while the early nineteenth-century concept of youth extended over a broader span of years from the middle teens to the middle twenties. Hall himself insisted that adolescence embraced the long period from puberty to the end of physical growth in the twenties, but he was running against the tide even in his own day. From the 1870s, there was a growing disposition to define youth narrowly as the years from fourteen to nineteen, and virtually all of the writers on adolescence who followed in Hall's wake equated adolescence with the teen years. Paradoxically, while we think of prolonged adolescence as a twentieth-century phenomenon, the definition of youth in the early 1800s was broader than the generally accepted meaning of adolescence in the twentieth century.[26]

The concept of youth was not only more extensive in the early nineteenth century, but the focus was primarily on those in their late teens and early twenties. The famous Currier and Ives sequence dating from the 1860s—"The Four Seasons of Life"—is indicative. Childhood is symbolized by a group of tiny tots at play in a field, youth by a sober twenty-year-old walking down a country lane arm in arm with his inamorata. So, too, the youth of the "advice to youth"

25 *Journal of the Proceedings of a Convention of Literary and Scientific Gentlemen, Held in the Common Council Chamber of the City of New-York, Oct., 1830* (New York, 1831), *passim*; "College Instruction and Discipline," *American Quarterly Review*, IX (1831), 302–304; "College Education," *Democratic Review*, XX (1847), 129–130.

26 For an example of the post-Civil War tendency to equate youth with the teen years, see Edward E. Hale, *How To Do It* (Boston, 1871), 27, 12. At the other extreme, some traditional religious sects did not describe a boy as a youth until he had reached the age of eighteen. See Adelaide L. Fries (ed.), *Records of the Moravians of North Carolina* (Raleigh, 1922), I, 420–421.

books were closer to manhood than to childhood: They comprised those who had recently left Protestant homes for life in the city. In a word, the youth of the 1830s and 1840s was more of a burgeoning independent than a frustrated dependent.

There were frustrated dependents in the 1830s and the concept of youth did extend downward to include boys at puberty. But, for a variety of reasons, few either chose to focus on the crisis around puberty or thought it more significant than later crises.

First of all, in the early 1800s it was difficult to formulate horizontal concepts about juveniles, especially about those in their middle teens, because teenage experiences in preindustrial American society were not graded in any precise way by numerical age. There was no set age for leaving school or for starting work. Fourteen was the usual age for apprenticeship, but there were so many exceptions in practice, especially in the case of farm boys, that no one could draw an automatic connection between arrival at the age of fourteen and the commencement of work. Even those boys who entered apprenticeships at fourteen had frequently started to do chores or farm tasks years earlier. The relationship between school and work, moreover, was far less definite than it has since become. Today we assume that entry into the labor market follows education, but, in the 1830s, education and labor were interwoven. Most boys worked for part of the year and then attended school. The structure of educational institutions complemented this process. Academy students, for example, usually attended only one or two terms a year, after harvest and before planting. District schools were divided into summer sessions, taught by women and intended for girls and very young boys, and winter sessions, taught by men and attended by farm boys of all ages. Seasonal education thus complemented seasonal labor. The nature of education and labor combined made it difficult to say whether a fifteen-year-old boy was dependent or semi-dependent, a child or a youth, for at different times of the year he was likely to be each.

The onset of male puberty failed to coincide with any fundamentally new life experience. Boys at puberty simply were not conspicuous in the way they later became. In contrast, by Hall's day, school gradation had reached the point where at fourteen the great majority of boys left elementary school and had to choose between high school and the job market. It is not surprising that Hall's theory of adolescence, and virtually all of the popular literature on adolescence between 1900 and 1915, assigned overriding importance to puberty. The twentieth century has argued that no matter where the boy is, what he is doing, or what he has been through, with the onset of puberty he becomes an adolescent. In the 1830s, in contrast, popular definitions of youth took their cue more from social status than from physiology. If a sixteen-year-old boy were in district school, he was called a child, and for the most part treated like one. If in college, he was usually described as a youth. Strictly speaking, the same boy could be a child for part of the year and a youth for the remainder. Or, again, one could meet seventeen-year-old children and fifteen-year-old youths.

A second reason for the relative emphasis on later adolescence was simply that the kind of perils which confronted youths in their late teens were of more absorbing interest than those of the early teens. One such peril, that of leaving home, has already been noted. As the image of home became more sentimentalized in the nineteenth century, one's entry into the world of affairs appeared more threatening. Or, we can argue, the more menacing the world became, the greater the disposition to drench home and family in sentiment. Whatever the priority, by the 1840s more and more individuals were inclined to view the first few years after the break with home as critical ones. But other events of the late teens and early twenties gave rise to equally pertinent anxieties. Individuals so diverse as Orestes Brownson, John Humphrey Noyes, and Horace Bushnell, for example, all experienced a pattern of religious drifting in their twenties after premature, teenage conversions, and a clear tone of anxiety in the "advice to youth" literature suggests that such vacillations were widespread. Alongside these crises, those of the early and middle teens seemed less significant.[27]

There was one notable exception to the lack of interest in the middle teens; paradoxically, the years around puberty were thought to be extremely critical for girls. The description of the tribulations of adolescent girls was a standard feature of sentimental novels from Susanna Rowson's *Charlotte Temple* (published as *Charlotte, A Tale of Truth* [Philadelphia, 1794]) through James Fenimore Cooper's *Tales for Fifteen* (New York, 1823), just as the tendency of racy tales of love and seduction to induce hysteria in teenage girls was a principal

27   On leaving home, see Samuel G. Goodrich, *Recollections of a Lifetime, or Men and Things I Have Seen* (New York, 1857), I, 409. See also Orestes A. Brownson, *The Convert: or, Leaves from My Experience* (New York, 1857), 13; George W. Noyes, *Religious Experience of John Humphrey Noyes, Founder of the Oneida Community* (New York, 1923), 9, 16, Ch. 5; H. Shelton Smith (ed.), *Horace Bushnell* (New York, 1964), 376.

argument against the novel as a literary genre.[28] The paradox arose from the fact that girls were not really viewed as having, like boys, a period of youth. A society which failed to provide a significant social role for women outside of marriage had difficulty envisioning girls passing through a protracted period of adjustment to responsibility, but no trouble recognizing the threat to female virtue posed by the sudden onset of sexual maturity. Stated another way, girls were seen as experiencing a wrenching adolescence between fourteen and sixteen, but not as having a stage of youth; boys went through a relatively painless physical adolescence, but followed it with a critical period of youth. This helps to explain why one scarcely meets any male versions of Charlotte Temple in antebellum literature, that is, with fourteen- or fifteen-year-old boys. In contrast, a considerable number of youths of eighteen to twenty, from Brown's Arthur Mervyn to Simms' Ralph Colleton (in *Guy Rivers*) to Melville's Pierre Glendenning, appeared in the same literature as central figures.[29]

In all of this, was there any sense in antebellum America that youth should be prolonged—that pressures for achievement or choice should be removed or relaxed in youth? We usually assume that the prolongation of adolescence is a relatively recent idea. It was certainly the central message of Hall's work, and, in one form or another, it has pervaded most twentieth-century literature on youth. But was the idea present even before Hall wrote?

In some respects, the desirability of prolonging adolescence was a nineteenth-century discovery. In the 1840s, Fowler had pleaded for a reduction of academic pressures during adolescence and had lauded the value of a late ripening of the faculties.[30] So, too, school reformers

28 Susanna H. Rowson, *Charlotte Temple, A Tale of Truth* (New York, 1905); James F. Beard (ed.), *Tales for Fifteen (1823) by James Fenimore Cooper: A Facsimile Reproduction* (Gainesville, Fla., 1959); Terence Martin, *The Instructed Vision: Scottish Common Sense Philosophy and the Origins of American Fiction* (Bloomington, Ind., 1961), 64–68.

29 Charles Brockden Brown, *Arthur Mervyn; or Memoirs of the Year 1793* (Philadelphia, 1799), 2v.; William G. Simms, *Guy Rivers; A Tale of Georgia* (New York, 1834); Herman Melville, *Pierre; or the Ambiguities* (New York, 1852). Prior to 1860, social conventions prohibited public discussions of the sexual faculties. It is not until the Gilded Age that one encounters a full treatment of the painfulness of female puberty in comparison with male puberty. See Edward H. Clarke, *Sex in Education; or a Fair Chance for the Girls* (Boston, 1873); E. S. Duffey, *No Sex in Education; or An Equal Chance for both Girls and Boys* (Philadelphia, 1874); Julia W. Howe (ed.), *Sex in Education: A Reply to Dr. E. H. Clarke's Sex in Education* (Boston, 1874).

30 Orson S. Fowler, *Physiology, Animal and Mental: Applied to the Preservation and Restoration of Health of Body and Power of Mind* (New York, 1848; 5th ed.), 270–289.

in the 1830s and 1840s often spoke of the need to preserve adolescents from premature knowledge of the world.[31] Yet such declarations were not equivalent to Hall's defense of a moratorium on career and intellectual commitment during adolescence. It was one thing to complain about excess study or premature sophistication, and another to say that young people should be indulged in their doubt and allowed time to reflect on life's possibilities and choices.

The idea of prolonging adolescence by encouraging a postponement of choice was not prominent before 1860, at least partly because of the kind of institutions that middle-class boys encountered, which permitted a certain amount of stumbling about before one was settled in a calling. The loose and informal character of the academies, and the ease with which those over twenty-five could start their college education, allowed a number of false starts. The feebleness of licensing requirements made it possible to switch from occupations to professions, or from occupation to occupation. Occupations simply did not have the rigid quality that they later acquired, and, in practice, many people had more than one occupation. Characteristically, antebellum books of advice aimed at mechanics usually assumed that the reader had already settled in a line of work and needed only to improve his competence.

Although the problem of career choice did not arise before 1860 with its later intensity, young people could still be confronted by agonizing decisions, especially in religion. Yet, despite the many declarations in the 1830s and 1840s about the desirability of reducing academic pressures on young people, there was a widespread reluctance to allow young people a period of doubt and indecision even on religious matters. There was a sense that if young people were given time to choose, they would make the wrong choices. As the nineteenth century wore on, the need to fix religious character early in life became nearly an obsession among Protestants. By the 1850s many Protestants were committed to the ideal that religious growth should be so gradual and steady that the Christian would be unable to say exactly when the change of heart had come.

Voiced early in the century by Unitarians, fully articulated by

See also Andrew Combe, *The Principles of Physiology, Applied to the Preservation of Health and to the Improvement of Physical and Mental Education* (New York, 1838), 204.

31 "Educating Children to Death," *American Annals of Education*, VII (1837), 15; "The Proper Time for Sending Children to School," *Common School Journal*, XIII (1851), 270.

Horace Bushnell in *Views of Christian Nurture* (1847), and adopted increasingly by most Protestants after mid-century, the ideal of linear human development challenged longstanding Calvinist assumptions about the need for a radical regeneration of the soul.[32] Even evangelical Calvinists, who could never accept Bushnell's liberalism, were, by mid-century, placing more emphasis on inducing early religious decisions, on bringing down the age of conversion from eighteen or nineteen to fourteen or fifteen. By the 1850s religious conversion had ceased to be a resolution of religious doubts in late adolescence and had become, instead, a kind of Victorian initiation rite, a capstone of childhood and a prelude to youth.[33]

Whether liberal or Calvinist, American Protestant thought about juveniles was increasingly marked not by declarations of the need for a regimen of prolonged doubt followed by conversion, but by a veritable culture of early conversions, teenage temperance pledges, and institutionalized revivals for young people, all aimed at fixing character so firmly that no amount of jarring in later youth could drive the individual off course. Thus the ultimate paradox of nineteenth-century thought about youth was that it viewed the postponement of choice and fixed purpose as inconsistent with the protection of young people from worldliness, while in the twentieth century we have come to view the prolongation of adolescence as a corollary of protectiveness.

32 See, for example, Joseph Ware, *Memoir of Henry Ware, Jr.* (Boston, 1848).

33 An illustration to the tendency of earlier conversion can be found in the records of the Essex County North [Massachusetts] Ministerial Association, for its official history contains brief biographical and autobiographical conversion narratives for its candidates in the first half of the nineteenth century. The average age of conversion for candidates born between 1774 and 1798 was 19.5 years. For those born between 1799 and 1812 it was 17.2 years, while for those born between 1813 and 1833 it was only 15.8 years. See *Contributions to the Ecclesiastical History of Essex County, Massachusetts* (Boston, 1865). See also Joseph Packard (ed. Thomas J. Packard), *Recollections of a Long Life* (Washington, D.C., 1902), 48.

Virginia Yans McLaughlin

Patterns of Work and Family Organization:

Buffalo's Italians
In their discussions of industrialization and urbanization, some social scientists have described the family as a dependent variable. Implicitly or explicitly, they view technical and economic organization as the prime determinant of family organization.[1] Not surprisingly, power relationships within the family are also frequently considered to be dependent upon economic roles within the larger society. A common assumption, for example, is that because the industrial city offers work opportunities to women, they can become less reliant upon their husbands and fathers, especially if the latter are unemployed. And so, the argument continues, female employment outside the home encourages the decline of "traditional" family relationships in which the chief power and control reside with the male. In extreme cases, the unemployed male deserts his family altogether and female-headed households result.

Not all social scientists, of course, agree with this interpretation. Historians have a specific task in this dispute—to seek empirical evidence which will sustain or weaken generalizations concerning the dependent and causal relationships between the family, urbanization, and industrialization. As Goode put it, one of our difficulties is a "simple lack of information about the past history of family systems under varying conditions of urbanization and industrialization."[2]

In line with Goode's suggestion, this paper attempts to add to our knowledge of family history by examining the relationship between female occupational patterns and family organization among south Italians in Buffalo from about 1900 to 1930. It questions the idea that the family should be viewed simply as a dependent variable

Virginia Yans McLaughlin is Assistant Professor of History at Princeton University. She is revising her dissertation, "Like the Fingers of the Hand: The Family and Community Life of First-Generation Italian-Americans in Buffalo, New York," for publication. This paper was originally presented before the American Historical Association, Boston, 1970. The author would like to thank Allen F. Davis and J. Stanley Lemons for their criticisms.

1 For a discussion of the relationship between the family, urbanization, and industrialization, see William J. Goode, *The Family* (Englewood Cliffs, N.J., 1964), 110; Sidney M. Greenfield, "Industrialization and the Family in Sociological Theory," *American Journal of Sociology*, LXVII (1961), 312–314.
2 William J. Goode, "The Process of Role Bargaining in the Impact of Urbanization and Industrialization on Family Systems," *Current Sociology*, XII (1963–64), 1.

by demonstrating that female assumption of new economic functions did not necessarily alter family power arrangements or disrupt the "traditional" family.

Any historian attempting to deal with working-class families immediately confronts the problem of documentation. Until recently, scholars have relied upon the reports of reformers and social workers for evidence concerning "the inarticulate." Thus, we have viewed working-class history through a filter of middle-class values. In order to overcome this problem, as well as the scarcity of literary sources concerning the family, historians have increasingly relied upon manuscript censuses and other statistical data. Much, but not all, of the argument presented in this paper is based upon such evidence, and I should caution the reader concerning its limitations. With the help of census materials, we can inform ourselves about the percentage of husbandless families, of unemployed males, and of employed wives. On the basis of these formal indices, inferences can be drawn regarding possible power relationships within the family. Statistics concerning household organization, however, cannot tell us to what degree traditional arrangements were being strained without actually being eliminated, nor can they describe the quality and "normal" tensions of family life. The picture that emerges tends to be static: If the family were broken, we can assume conflicts occurred. But if a family remained together, we cannot conversely assume that it did so free of tension. This is a problem, especially with relatively stable groups such as Buffalo's south Italians, who did not exhibit extreme family pathology in the process of becoming assimilated into American society. Statistics simply do not permit absolute conclusions concerning conflict and change among Italian families remaining together. But female occupational arrangements can tell something about family power alignments. Buffalo's south Italians favored conservative female employment patterns, patterns which usually kept women working at home or under relatives' supervision despite possibilities of better pay and opportunities elsewhere. These occupational styles, it will be argued, are a strong indication that patriarchal control continued.

An examination of south Italian families within the context of one city, Buffalo, makes one thing abundantly clear. The usual question—"What is the impact of 'urban-industrial life' upon the family?" —is much too general, too imprecise. The class and ethnic identity of the families in question, as well as the type of city and range of industrial development existing in the communities under consideration, must be specified because each can play a critical part in determining the family's relationship to the social order. First, in some cases, ethnic background and associated cultural ideals had an important impact upon the way immigrant families responded to their new environment. Buffalo's south Italian women, for example, expressed, and acted upon, a decided preference for occupations which permitted minimal strain upon their traditional familial arrangements. In this way, Old World family values could continue to operate effectively even within an advanced industrial city such as Buffalo. Other options were available, and other ethnic groups took them. This clearly suggests that south Italian values played an important part in determining family work patterns; in other words, the family acted as an independent variable. Some may wish to argue that immigrant family values, not the family itself, were the prime determinant here. Such an argument makes a strict distinction between the family as a formal structure and the system of values, norms, rights, and obligations associated with it. Although such a distinction is useful in some cases, in this paper values and organization are considered together as parts of the family as a social institution.

In discussing the relationships between economic and familial organization, it should also be noted that actually available work opportunities define the perimeters of behavior. In a small city dominated by one industry, the relationships between family and economy should be relatively clear. In the early twentieth century, for example, Homestead, Pennsylvania was a typical steel mill town, offering work to men on a fairly regular basis. Women could find employment only occasionally. Therefore, the possibilities for varying family occupational patterns were obviously limited: In Homestead, the overwhelming majority of working-class families adopted the attitude that men should be the breadwinners and that women should contribute to the family economy through their housekeeping skills, and not by leaving the home to work.[3] In a cotton mill town, another type of one-industry city, we would expect to find women from needy families working; ethnic or cultural biases against female employment would probably be modified to meet the family's economic needs. In short, in one-industry towns, family occupational patterns would ultimately be determined by that industry regardless of cultural preferences. In larger, highly diversified manufacturing centers

3 Margaret F. Byington, "The Family in a Typical Mill Town," *American Journal of Sociology*, XIV (1909), 648–659.

such as Buffalo, a variety of economic opportunities for both men and women existed; despite the city's emphasis on heavy industry women could, and did, find work. In such cities, the relationship between occupational patterns and family organization was, as we shall see, correspondingly much more complex. The nature of work opportunities permitted freer expression of cultural preferences concerning women's work role, and Old World family values could operate easily despite the urban-industrial context.

Finally, it should be emphasized that the subjects being considered, south Italian immigrants, were "working-class." I use that term here to refer not only to their occupational status as an unskilled, frequently unemployed group, but also to their relatively stable life style and culture, much of which represented a survival from traditional European peasant life.[4] In such families, the occupational positions of husband and wife are frequently related to family structure. Hence, our original question regarding the family's status as a dependent or an independent variable is raised once again. Most social scientists argue that working-class and lower-class family structures are dependent upon occupational arrangements. They frequently cite unusual work patterns, for example, as a cause for family disorganization. The Moynihan report is a case in point. It stressed male employment difficulties in conjunction with more stable female employment as a key cause for male desertion and consequent female control of the family.[5] Some historians similarly suggest that disrupted preindustrial work patterns upset family stability among first-generation immigrants. The move to industrial America supposedly caused radical changes in the traditional male-dominated family economy and hence forced a restructuring in family roles and relationships.[6]

Although this model appears logical enough, it is not in agreement with historical fact. Buffalo's south Italians provide a fine example.

4 Herbert Gans, *The Urban Villagers: Group and Class in the Life of Italian-Americans* (Glencoe, 1962), 250, views working-class culture as a "continuation of European peasant culture." S. M. Miller and Frank Riessman, "The Working Class Subculture: A New View," *Social Problems*, IX (1961), 90, 95, correctly emphasize the distinction between working- and lower-class culture, a distinction of which the author is aware. Although white immigrants shared many of the hardships which today's urban poor experience, I think it is best to place them in the working-class category because of their traditional peasant background, much of which survived immigration.

5 Daniel P. Moynihan, "The Negro Family: The Case for National Action," in Lee Rainwater and William L. Yancey (eds.), *The Moynihan Report and the Politics of Controversy* (Cambridge, Mass., 1967), 41–124.

6 Oscar Handlin, *The Uprooted* (New York, 1951), 228ff., 239 takes this position.

Because tradition bestowed upon the mother great prestige, authority, and power (frequently including control of the household budget), south Italian peasant family organization was not purely patriarchal. Male superiority and paternal control, however, were the norm. To this degree at least, the south Italian family resembled the traditional peasant form described by Handlin in *The Uprooted*.[7] The New World's industrial work patterns, however, did not destroy it. Specifically, women leaving the home to work did not necessarily cause an erosion of male control. This was true throughout the decades under consideration, despite the existence of certain female prerogatives in south Italian familial culture which could have emerged during times of family crisis, such as periods of male unemployment.

In southern Italy economic functions and family functions were closely integrated. Tradition required Italian men, the majority of them poor peasants without farms of their own, to support their families; children contributed their work in the fields or at home; wives ran their households, and, from this area, most of their rights derived. But the basis for each person's status within the family was *not* purely economic. Thus, strong cultural traditions sustained male authority despite seasonal or year-round unemployment. Although wife and children worked outside the home at harvest time in Sicily and more often elsewhere, the father's domination over family affairs remained unchallenged. Apparently this "family constellation" was strong enough to endure periods of male unemployment in America when women worked.[8] Consequently, family disorganization among Italians (measured by male desertion and non-support, at least) remained relatively rare, and female-controlled families were unusual. This appears more remarkable given the existence of certain female privileges in south Italian culture.[9] The point is that male authority

7 *Ibid.*; Leonard Moss and Walter Thomson, "The South Italian Family: Literature and Observation," *Human Organization*, XVIII (1959), 38, quote an old Italian proverb testifying to the mother's importance: "If the father should die, the family would suffer; if the mother should die, the family ceases to exist." Although the two sources of authority were constantly clashing, the father was generally able to assert himself, "receiving his main support," according to Covello, "from the elevated status of the male in general." See Leonard Covello, "The Social Background of the Italo-American School Child: A Study of the Southern Italian Family Mores and Their Effect on the School Situation in Italy and America," unpub. Ph.D. thesis (New York University, 1944), 347.

8 Gans, *The Urban Villagers*, 240–241.

9 Covello, "Italo-American School Child," 328ff., 336, 378. See also Phyllis Williams, *South Italian Folkways in Europe and America* (New Haven, 1938), 76–77.

did not depend entirely upon fulfillment of economic obligations; therefore, when a woman co-opted the male's economic function in whole or in part by becoming a wage-earner, she did not necessarily obtain greater bargaining power and so tip the balance of family authority in her favor.

Despite a potentially disruptive work situation, Buffalo's Italian men performed exceedingly well as husbands and fathers. Until the 1920s brought slightly improved conditions, the majority worked in low-paying construction, railroad, and other seasonal outdoor occupations; most were unemployed six or more months a year. This condition was not peculiar only to Buffalo Italians. Outdoor laborers all over the nation faced similar difficulties.[10] Frequently, construction work drew Italians away from the city and their families. In addition, the immigration process itself had caused temporary separations for many. Buffalo Italians, then, endured two conditions commonly associated with family breakdown and female domination—irregular male employment and temporary absence of the father from the household[11] —but the proportion of husbandless or female-headed families among them remained surprisingly low. Calculations based upon the 1905 New York State manuscript census reveal that only 4 per cent of more than 2,000 first-generation families were headed by women with no spouse present.[12] And some of these were widows, not deserted wives. In 1908–09 Italians were the least likely Buffalo ethnic group to obtain welfare because of neglect or desertion by a family head. And, although the proportion applying for welfare had increased by the 1920s, the percentage giving desertion or non-support as their justification actually declined from 6 per cent in 1908 to 4 per cent in 1926.[13]

10 Amy Bernardy, "L'Emigrazione delle donne e dei fanciulli italiana," *Bolletino dell'Emigrazione* (1909), 17. Bernardy toured several eastern cities, including Buffalo, and noted the seasonal unemployment of Italian men. See also U.S. Department of Commerce, *Seasonal Operation in the Construction Industries: Summary of Report and Recommendations of a Committee of the President's Conference on Unemployment* (Washington, D.C., 1924).

11 Gans, *The Urban Villagers*, 240–241.

12 All figures cited are either from the New York State manuscript censuses of 1905 (Buffalo, 1905) and 1925 (unpublished census schedules) unless otherwise indicated. For a discussion of the accuracy of these censuses, see Virginia Yans McLaughlin, "Like the Fingers of the Hand: The Family and Community Life of First-Generation Italian-Americans in Buffalo, New York, 1880–1930," unpub. Ph.D. thesis. (State University of New York at Buffalo, 1970), 450–455. A 10 per cent sample check revealed that in no case did coding and key-punching errors exceed the reasonable range of 5 per cent in any one variable; in most cases it remained well below that figure.

13 The 1908–09 figures are from United States Senate, *Reports of the Immigration Commission*, XXXIV, 61st Cong., 3rd Sess., *Immigrants as Charity Seekers*, I (Washington,

These figures dispute the notion that male unemployment or contact with industrial city life disrupted immigrant working-class families; they also invite comparison with other urban groups who did not fare as well. How can the south Italian family's relative stability be explained? Undoubtedly inherited ethnic traditions supporting male authority helped, but let us look elsewhere before coming to definite conclusions. The answer resides, at least partially, in long-term female employment patterns, for they, and not male unemployment, distinguished Italians from less stable working-class families.

The south Italian family's traditional work patterns and economic roles were not seriously disturbed after immigration to a modern industrial city. Most important of all, women's work roles were adapted to the new industrial situation. This resulted to some extent from Buffalo's peculiar occupational structure. Unlike other upstate cities, heavy industry and transportation dominated its economy. The city offered comparatively little in the way of light industrial production for unskilled women. But it should be emphasized that even though alternatives were available, Italians *preferred* specific types of labor— occupations on the fringes of Buffalo's industrial structure—where customary family relationships could be and were effectively maintained. This preference helps to explain why Italian immigrant families remained stable. There was for them a period of transition, a time of adjustment, rather than rapid family disorganization or reorganization. Thus there was a lot of room in some late nineteenth- and early twentieth-century cities for immigrant families who wished to avoid a head-on collision with the new way of life. It was not simply a case of occupational arrangements determining family organization; cultural preferences also played a part in determining patterns of work. In short, traditional family values acted as an independent variable, and the occupational opportunities of industrial cities provided enough variation for individual families to find work arrangements appropriate for their cultural needs.

D.C., 1911), 137. The 1926 figures were computed by the author from City of Buffalo Department of Public Welfare, *Annual Report of the Bureau of Public Welfare for Fiscal Year Ending June 30, 1927* (Buffalo, 1927). The Charity Organization Society did not aid persons of the Jewish faith, and, therefore, they are not included in the 1907–08 figures. The author is well aware that welfare agency statistics do not necessarily give the most accurate picture of family life. Nevertheless, it is not necessary to rely upon these alone. Other sources confirm family stability among Italians. See McLaughlin, "Like the Fingers of the Hand," 121ff.

Let us first turn to the occupational patterns of Buffalo's first-generation Italian women in the period preceding World War I. In 1905, for example, less than 2 per cent of more than 2,000 wives reported to census-takers full-time employment which could have taken them from domestic concerns; some involved themselves in family enterprises which did not draw them permanently from the home or give them the status of independent wage earners. Only three women worked because their husbands were unemployed; only 1 per cent of the working women had children. Clearly, in 1905 Italian women did not sacrifice child-rearing responsibilities for work and no trend toward female assumption of the role of chief provider existed. Most women who contributed to the family budget in this year did so by providing housekeeping services to roomers and boarders residing with their families. Twelve per cent of all first-generation wives belonged to this category. The remaining 86 per cent reported no occupation at all, but we know that several hundred women engaged in part-time work as part of family groups. They did so most commonly as migrant laborers in northwestern New York's canneries and vineyards during the summer. A smaller number worked in Buffalo's domestic industries.

Italian women and girls rarely left their homes unsupervised by relatives or friends to work either as housekeepers or as factory laborers. Buffalo's Irish, Polish, Swedish, and German women commonly sought employment as domestics in middle-class homes, but jealous Italian men would not permit their wives to work under another man's roof, no matter how serious the family's economic circumstances. For example, efforts of various organizations in Buffalo and elsewhere to interest Italian women in such positions failed to erode this Mediterranean attitude toward female honor. The women themselves preferred employment which would not separate them from their families; even second-generation Italians failed to find service occupations as agreeable as did those of other ethnic groups.[14] Italian husbands and fathers apparently appreciated the dangers of female employment outside the home. A National Federation of Settlements survey, noting that Italian parents tended to be more careful than most

14 This was a common attitude among Italians all over the United States. See, for example, Williams, *South Italian Folkways*, 36; Bernardy, "L'Emigrazione," 8. For efforts to interest Italian women in domestic service, see "Uncle Sam's Debt to the Italians," Utica *Pensiero Italiano* (Sept. 26, 1914), which discusses an Italian baroness who attempted to work with organizations and individuals in several cities, including Buffalo, to place Italian women in such positions.

regarding their daughters' place of employment, cited parental concern for their children's morality as a reason.[15]

Buffalo Italians responded to economic need by removing male children from school and sending them to work so that the women could remain in a sheltered environment. The 1905 manuscript census reveals that sons and daughters under fifteen, for example, had an equal chance to remain in school. From the ages of fifteen to nineteen, they dropped out of school at the same rate—79 per cent of the sons and 82 per cent of the daughters left school or were not attending. But the sons generally entered the labor force, while the daughters remained at home. Boys withdrawn from school had to pay the price of restricted occupational mobility, which helps to explain the Italians' slow rise up the social ladder. Considerations of female honor restricted the girls' freedom and achievement. As a result, Italian women almost always worked within the confines of their homes or as part of a family group, especially before World War I. Most who labored did so only part-time or by the season. This continued to be true throughout the 1920s. If these occupational patterns are examined in detail, it becomes clear that they minimized strain upon the traditional family system.

An examination of the homework industry indicates that Italians were especially noted for their preference for this type of occupation, which also acted as a kind of shock absorber for other ethnic groups including, for example, Russians and Germans. There are a number of ways in which homework did not challenge Old World family organization. The mother's roles as arbiter of household organization and tasks and as disciplinarian and child-rearer were reinforced by her economic position as manager of the domestic undertaking, be it artificial flower-making, basting, or sewing. Because she still had not become, in the strict sense of the term, a wage-earner, she presented no clear threat to her husband's authority and power. The basic unit of homework industries continued to be just as it had been in the Old World—the family, not the individual. The seasonal nature of most homework industry meant that the wife and child were only sporadically occupied. Finally, and critically, the wife did not leave the home, and therefore did not abandon her important roles of childbearing and child-rearing. These two responsibilities clearly exceeded in importance any economic obligation, for homework wages were lower than

15 Robert A. Woods and Robert J. Kennedy, *Young Working Girls: A Summary of Evidence from Two Thousand Social Workers* (Boston, 1913), 59, 23.

those a woman could earn working full- or even part-time away from home. The similarity between the family as a working productive unit in preindustrial southern Italy and in America under the home-work system is striking.

Although some domestic manufacture existed in Buffalo and Italians worked in it, the women and their children earned better pay as migrant laborers on farms and processing sheds near Buffalo. The canneries, which also utilized the family as the basic work unit, permitted the same sort of easing of family members into a poten-tially disruptive work situation. Due to the immigrants' handling of the situation and the industry's special character, the Italian family was able to maintain its Old World complexion. Once again, although Italians preferred this kind of work, other ethnic groups in different parts of the nation engaged in it, probably for similar reasons.[16]

At first glance it seems surprising that conservative south Italian men would sometimes permit women and children to leave their Buffalo homes without husbands and fathers. The men sought and often obtained city construction jobs during the summer. South Italian mores, after all, required a husband to guard his wife with a jealous eye. In Italy, moreover, the wife who left home to work was viewed disapprovingly. But was going to the cannery really such a radical departure? In the first place, seasonal migration had not been an un-usual experience for south Italian families. Laborers frequently fol-lowed harvests throughout the *Mezzogiorno*. Second, though many fathers remained in Buffalo, some found employment with their families as harvesters or as canning factory mechanics.[17] Third, the women and children did not drift as separate family members into the labor mar-ket. They were recruited, lived, and worked as a family under the close scrutiny of the Italian-American community of migrant workers, many of whom were close associates, *paesani*, and kin. Fourth, as was the case in Italy, the seasonal income earned by wives and children who ventured into migrant labor camps was never understood as a replacement of the father's wages, as earlier figures on low desertion and non-support rates indicated, but as a supplement. The Italian father

16   Alexander Cance, "Immigrant Rural Communities," *The Survey*, XXV (1911), 588; United States Senate, *Reports of the Immigration Commission*, III, 61st Cong., 2nd Sess., *Immigrants in Industries, Recent Immigrants in Agriculture*, II (Washington, D.C., 1911), 489–490, 801.
17   Maria Maddalena de Rossi, "Le donne ed i fanciulli italiani a Buffalo e ad Albion," in Segretariato femminile per la tutela delle donne e dei fanciulli emigranti, *Relazione* (Rome, 1913), 14.

did not relinquish his obligation to support his family; likewise, he did not forfeit his control and authority over it. Finally, like the domestic industries, the migrant labor camp permitted close integration of living and working quarters and therefore did not separate the family's productive from its child-rearing capacities. Here a close integration of economic and family functions, similar to those which existed in Italy, prevailed. In short, the initiation of women into the factory system did not necessarily cause disruption of the traditional south Italian family.

The seasonal and part-time character of female employment patterns also prevented disruption. In the pre-World War I era, when Italian males were most likely to be chronically unemployed, their wives were also likely to be unemployed for at least as long. If women contributed to the family budget the year round, they generally did so by keeping boarders, an activity which did not contribute to their social or financial independence. Rarely did the Italian wife provide greater financial stability than her husband. Cultural tradition prevented her from taking the one suitable readily available job for unskilled women which would have guaranteed more steady employment than her husband—work as a maid or domestic. The contrast with black women who continue to depend upon this important source of income is striking. Equally striking are the contrasting attitudes between Italian and Polish families toward women entering the work world. Unfortunately, none of the evidence presented in the following pages allows for class distinctions between ethnic groups. (Because the overwhelming majority of both Italians and Poles were unskilled laborers, the difficulty is not a serious one.)

Buffalo's Polish women eagerly sought work in factories and as domestics.[18] According to a 1910 survey of 146 Buffalo firms employing almost 11,000 individuals of Polish background, two Polish women found employment in the city's manufacturing and industrial establishments for every eight Polish men. If *all* Italian women who worked in all occupations—excluding those in cannery work and those with boarders in their households—are considered, the ratio for 1905 was only one to twenty.[19] Even granting a higher proportion of Polish

18 United States Senate, *Recent Immigrants in Agriculture*, II, 491; John Daniels, "Polish Laborers and Their Needs," Buffalo *Express* (March 13, 1910), 7.
19 John Daniels, "Polish Wage Earners in Buffalo," Buffalo *Express* (March 6, 1910), 3, contains information on the Polish population. The Buffalo Italian data are based upon the New York State manuscript census for 1905.

women to men, these differences are significant. They were not peculiar to Buffalo alone. Butler, noting the relative unimportance of
Italian women in Pittsburgh's industrial life, also emphasized cultural
differences between Italian and Polish women. "The Polish women,"
she wrote in 1910, "have not the conservatism which keeps the Italian
girl at home. They have not the same standard of close-knit family
relations. There is a flexibility in their attitude toward life and toward
their part in it."[20] In 1909 Tobenkin compared Chicago's Italian, Polish, Jewish, and Lithuanian girls and came to similar conclusions regarding the Italians' conservatism.[21] In New York City, Italian girls left
domestic and personal service work to other ethnic groups and entered
the factory. Still, they viewed factory work chiefly as an opportunity
to learn a skill such as sewing, which they might keep up at home after
marriage.[22]

During the war and pre-depression years when more Italian
women began to leave their homes to work, Italian men were also more
likely to be employed, or at least more likely to be earning higher in-
comes. Hence female employment did not represent a serious challenge
to male authority at this time. Even after World War I female employment patterns had not changed radically, at least insofar as first-generation wives were concerned. An analysis of fifteen densely populated
blocks in the Buffalo ward most heavily settled by Italians in 1925 indicated that although daughters had gone to work in silk factories,
clothing trades, or offices, not one mother or wife in this district had
left her home to work. Very few households in these blocks, moreover,
contained boarders or lodgers, so the number of women contributing
to family income in this way had actually declined.[23] Italian women
continued to work in the canneries during the summer after the war,
but, as I have argued, this work tended to sustain, not challenge, traditional family relationships.

Italians retained a cultural bias against female employment even
among the second generation. A survey of all second-generation families in sixteen wards, once again including those most heavily populated
by Italians, revealed that in 1925 only 12 per cent had working wives

20 Elizabeth Beardsley Butler, "The Working Women of Pittsburgh," *The Survey*,
XXIII (1910), 573.
21 Elias Tobenkin, "The Immigrant Girl in Chicago," *The Survey*, XXIII (1909),
190.
22 Mary Van Kleeck, *Artificial Flower Makers* (New York, 1913), 32, 38.
23 New York State manuscript census, 1925.

(120 of 1,022). Moreover, these women were not forced to work because their spouses were unemployed or had deserted their families. Only one had no husband, and she may have been a widow. The remaining wives had employed husbands.[24] The evidence produced by the 1905 data and suggested by the 1925 samples is amply substantiated by other local and national sources.[25] In some cities, especially those with significant light industry, Italian women worked more often than they did in Buffalo, but even in these cases they tended to enter occupations which, like the canneries, assured the security and protection of working closely with fellow Italians or at least within Little Italy's confines.

Even if women entered factories in greater numbers, they could not have been the family's chief support. Italian female factory laborers, like most women in industry, tended to be irregularly employed. For example, in 1909 Odencrantz, known for her studies of women wage earners, found that one-half of a group of 1,000 New York City working girls held their jobs for less than six months, chiefly because most had seasonal occupations and their employers frequently discharged them.[26] Most of the light industries to which women flocked for employment, such as clothing, textiles, food, candy, and paper box manufacturing, responded to irregular seasonal demand. Employers in these trades could not afford to maintain a year-round labor force if they wished to maximize profits. The situation was worst in cities like Buffalo where heavy industry predominated.[27] Thus, even if other working-class

24 *Ibid.*, Wards 12–27. Second-generation families were defined here as a family with an Italian name in which both spouses were born in the United States, in which the wife was born in the United States and the husband in Italy, or in which the husband was born in the United States and the wife in Italy. In every case, of course, in which the wife was born in the United States, she could have been of either non-Italian or Italian descent.

25 The following support the description of female employment: For the pre-war period, the infrequency of Italian female employment outside of the home is observed in Walter Goodale, "Children of Sunny Italy," Buffalo *Express* (Oct. 15, 1915), 1. Post-war sources on Italian female employment include: H. E. Burber, *Industrial Analysis of Buffalo* (Buffalo, n.d.), no p.; Eleanor G. Coit, "An Industrial Study, Buffalo, New York" (unpub. paper, Business and Industrial Department, Young Women's Christian Association, 1922), 44; Young Women's Christian Association (Business and Industrial Department), "Further Data from the Industrial Study," *Buffalo Foundation Forum* (Nov., 1922), 12. For a national perspective, see Bernardy, "L'Emigrazione," 12, 50; Butler, "The Working Women of Pittsburgh," 571–572.

26 Louise Odencrantz, "The Irregularity of Employment of Women Factory Workers," *The Survey*, XXII (1909), 200.

27 Coit, "Industrial Study," 49; Business and Industrial Department, YWCA, "Some Facts Concerning Women in Buffalo Industries, A Study Bringing up to Date Certain

ethnics took a more open-minded approach toward female labor than did Buffalo's south Italians, the nature of work opportunities for unskilled females in early twentieth-century America made it possible, albeit difficult, for them to supplant their husbands as chief breadwinners.

Why was family disorganization minimal and why were female-headed families rare among Italian-Americans? First, Italians had strong cultural and historical traditions regarding their women's role which survived long after emigration. The male continued to dominate in spite of his own unemployment and despite the existence of certain matriarchal privileges within the south Italian family. The conservatism of female employment patterns is clear evidence for continuing male domination. Male unemployment, furthermore, was not an entirely new experience for this group of former peasants any more than it was for other agricultural laborers, and the Italians withstood it as well in America as they did in Italy. Once in the United States, the peculiar occupational patterns of Italian women permitted the traditional family system to survive. Rather than permit their wives to leave the home, men who needed money resigned themselves "rather painfully" to daughters working in factories. The general disposition toward women's work, however, remained one of disapproval.[28] This attitude persisted well into the 1920s, and it had a considerable influence upon second-generation families, which looked unfavorably upon female employment.

More Italian women entered the labor force after World War I, but generally these were daughters, not mothers. By contributing to the family income, they merely fulfilled the proper function of children, and hence represented no challenge to their fathers' prestige and control. In any case, because daughters and sons—not wives and mothers—left the home to work, the latter had little opportunity to enhance their bargaining power within the family by way of significant economic contributions.

Figures on the Employment of Women in 200 Industries" (unpub. paper, Buffalo, 1925), 6–7; Burber, *Industrial Analysis of Buffalo*. Each of the above indicate some of the major companies which employed women, most of which had highly seasonal employment cycles. Thomas W. Triller, "The History of the Development of the International Institute in Buffalo, New York," unpub. M.A. thesis (University of Buffalo School of Social Work, 1952), 4, quoting a report of Miss Ely (Nov. 1, 1919) to the International Institute for Women, notes that Buffalo's industry simply did not provide enough work for women.

28 Bernardy, "L'Emigrazione," 13.

Although Buffalo's Italians differed in some ways from other working-class groups, on the basis of their experience it is possible to offer a few speculations regarding the white working-class of late nineteenth- and early twentieth-century America. Single and unmarried sons and daughters, not wives and mothers, were the most likely candidates in these families to supplement the male head's earnings. Most were not occupied full-time or year-round. The white working-class male family head, though poor and unemployed, therefore probably found himself in a stronger familial position than does today's urban unemployed male, who is forced to depend upon his wife's wages. In the case of blacks, of course, wives and mothers supposedly assumed year-round employment or at least significantly more stable positions than their husbands and so challenged male control and authority within the family. Further studies of white working class families, especially those in which wives worked year-round and husbands remained unemployed, and of ethnic groups with strong matriarchal tendencies, are required to determine the relative importance of ethnicity, the slavery heritage, and employment patterns. The findings of this paper, however, caution against assuming, as Moynihan and others have, that partial or total female control of the economic function necessarily predicts family power arrangements. Furthermore, before applying Moynihan's matriarchal model to the past, we should examine historical evidence to see if matriarchal families existed. As TenHouten suggests, conceptual muddling has caused many scholars to confuse matriarchies with female-headed families, a structure in which no male is present.[29]

In conclusion, contrary to general descriptions of European immigrant adjustment, Buffalo's Italians suffered no immediate or radical disruption in family life. Although the Italian family had its share of poverty and unemployment, it did not develop a characteristic frequently associated today with lower-class life—a female-headed family system. In fact, there is little evidence of family disorganization among Buffalo's Italians. This is not to suggest that these Italians and their contemporaries were superior or more adaptable than today's urban minorities. First-generation European immigrants entered an industrializing economy and responded to it with the equipment of a traditional peasant background. Their historical experience as a class was strikingly different from today's urban workers.

29 Warren TenHouten, "The Black Family Myth and Reality," *Psychiatry*, XXXIII (1970), 154.

We have moved throughout this discussion from the narrow focus of women's history to the broader realm of women, the family, and working-class culture. The seasonal, part-time, sporadic work patterns of wage-earning women stemmed partly from their sexual peculiarities, for most women dropped out of the labor market during the childbearing and child-rearing years. But the demands of a developing capitalist industrial economy for a cheap labor force which could be discharged periodically with a minimum of difficulty also explains their position. In this case the demands of employers and working-class cultural priorities coincided. The traditional, conservative character of this era's working-class culture advocated keeping women at home in order to avoid familial tensions, and in this manner worked toward providing the part-time labor force which employers sought.

We are now in a position to question clichés concerning the impact of industrialization and employment upon the family and woman's role. Probably no one generalization will hold for all women in all families everywhere. One can only plead for careful examination of women within the context of family life by class, ethnic group, region, city, and perhaps by religious background.

John Demos

Developmental Perspectives
on the History of Childhood   Among the shifting cur-
rents of scholarly inquiry it is possible to discern a growing interest in
the study of childhood in times past. A number of historians have
undertaken detailed research into particular aspects of this subject;
some of their projects are now complete, others are still in progress.[1]
The major professional organizations have recently included such
work in the programs of their annual meetings, and, in March 1970,
the first conference devoted entirely to the investigation of "childhood
and youth in history" was held at Clark University in Worcester,
Massachusetts.

The sources of this trend are many and complex. But, as often
happens in such cases, a single book seems to have exerted a very special influence. I refer to the seminal work of Ariès.[2] Few recent studies
are better known, and there is no need to summarize the contents here.
Nor is there space to enter the controversy that has arisen over some
particular parts of the book. But it may be worthwhile to examine
briefly the kind of approach to the study of childhood that Ariès so
brilliantly seems to represent.

In analyzing childhood across a span of nearly a millennium,
Ariès illuminated a vast territory of social and intellectual history. He
examined with great imagination portraits of children, medical treatises on the care of infants, pedagogical tracts, toys and games, and a
variety of other materials, in order to reveal certain core elements of
medieval and early modern society, and of the transition between the
two. It is clear, however, that he has concentrated not so much on the
actual life-experience of children in the past as on the prevalent attitudes *toward* and *about* these children. His work is founded on the important and incontrovertible assumption that much can be learned
about a culture by investigating the way it regards its young. In this
sense, *Centuries of Childhood* is primarily about adults—those who

John Demos is Associate Professor of History at Brandeis University. He is the author
of *A Little Commonwealth: Family Life in Plymouth Colony* (New York, 1970).
1 See, for example, David Hunt, *Parents and Children in History: The Psychology of
Family Life in Early Modern France* (New York, 1970); Bernard Wishy, *The Child and
the Republic: The Dawn of Modern American Child Nurture* (Philadelphia, 1967); Robert
H. Bremner, *et al.*, *Childhood and Youth in America* (Cambridge, Mass., 1970–71), I–II.
2 Philippe Ariès (trans. Robert Baldick), *Centuries of Childhood: A Social History of
Family Life* (New York, 1962).

commissioned and painted the portraits, wrote and read the medical treatises, and designed and maintained the schools. By extrapolating from Ariès one can imagine a whole range of detailed studies with the same underlying purpose. Attitudes toward childhood become, then, a kind of yardstick for measuring historical trends of the most profound consequence. And work of this type exhibits an obvious resemblance to other studies of basic cultural attitudes: attitudes toward death, for example, or love, or nature.

Here is a vitally important area of inquiry—and an area, too, in which much work remains to be done. This essay, however, will deal with *another* form of the study of childhood—related, and yet significantly different in both purpose and method. There is no easy way to designate this approach, for it has scarcely been contemplated, let alone attempted by historians before now. But what I have in mind is an effort to find certain underlying themes in the experience of children in a given culture or period in order to throw some light on the formation of later personality.[3] The approach assumes the ironic truth that "the child is father to the man"; it also assumes that each culture fosters the development of certain dominant character traits or styles. It requires, in short, something like the concept of "modal personality," which has shaped a very broad range of anthropological and psychological studies.[4]

It is well to bring the anthropologists directly into this discussion, for they have long elaborated many of the chief theoretical issues. There is no way to summarize all of the relevant literature; but perhaps the most valuable work, from the standpoint of historians, is associated with the so-called "culture and personality" school, in which names like Abram Kardiner, Ralph Linton, Margaret Mead, Clyde Kluckhohn, and George P. Murdock might reasonably be joined —and with important contributions from the side of psychology by men like Erik Erikson, Henry Murray, and T. W. Adorno. Kardiner's formulation of the issues is especially clear, and is useful here by way of example. He defines modal personality as "that constellation of person-

3 A book which *does* foreshadow many of the concerns of this paper is David M. Potter, *People of Plenty: Economic Abundance and the American Character* (Chicago, 1954), esp. Ch. 9. See also Hunt, *Parents and Children in History*, Chs. 6–9.

4 For an excellent summary of this work, see Alex Inkeles and Daniel J. Levinson, "National Character: The Study of Modal Personality and Sociocultural Systems," in Gardner Lindzey and Elliott Aronson (eds.), *The Handbook of Social Psychology* (Reading, Mass., 1969; 2nd ed.), IV, 418–506. See also Milton Singer, "A Survey of Culture and Personality Theory and Research," in Bert Kaplan (ed.), *Studying Personality Cross-Culturally* (New York, 1961), 9–90.

ality characteristics which would appear to be congenial with the total range of institutions comprised within a given culture."[5] And he divides the institutions into two broad categories. "Primary institutions" are the major force for shaping personality; but they also have an important influence on other aspects of culture—political and economic systems, mythic and religious belief—which he terms "secondary." Chief among the "primary institutions" are customary practices and commitments in the area of child-rearing. To be sure, the Kardiner definitions have been criticized by other anthropologists,[6] and the priorities implied in the terms "primary" and "secondary" seem especially questionable. Kluckhohn and Murray present a more cautious viewpoint, stating simply: "The members of any organized group tend to manifest certain personality traits more frequently than do other groups."[7]

Every practitioner of the "culture and personality" approach has perforce made certain assumptions about human psychology; and in practice much of this work has been deeply infused with one form or another of psychoanalytic theory. It seems likely, in my opinion, that most serious historical inquiry along these lines will be similarly organized. At any rate, it seems clear that we will need *some* theoretical viewpoint from which to approach the subject. This requires emphasis since virtually all prior comment by historians has implied a static, largely undifferentiated model of childhood. We have settled for general notions on the order of "Puritan children were subjected to severe and repressive discipline," or "slave parents regarded their children with considerable indifference."[8]

Moreover, the source materials bearing on the history of childhood form a large, diverse, and fairly inchoate mass. Simply in order to organize them, one must find some principles for distinguishing the important from the trivial—the events which strengthen, or expand, or inhibit, or traumatize the growing personality from those

5 Abram Kardiner, *The Individual and His Society* (New York, 1939), 24.
6 Some of these criticisms are outlined in Inkeles and Levinson, "National Character," 424–425.
7 Clyde Kluckhohn and Henry A. Murray (eds.), *Personality in Nature, Society, and Culture* (New York, 1962; rev. ed.), 57. On this general topic see also Anthony F. C. Wallace, *Culture and Personality* (New York, 1961). It is not necessary in this paper to enter the controversy over the proper meaning, and usage, of the concept of "modal personality." I am willing for present purposes to accept a very minimal definition, such as the one quoted above from Kluckhohn and Murray.
8 These statements—not actual quotations—are intended to represent viewpoints widely prevalent in previous historical literature.

which leave no lasting impression. In this sense I am urging a "developmental" approach to the subject, and it is indeed from developmental psychology that we may borrow some further procedural guidelines.

Broadly speaking, there are two different but interrelated ways of carving up our materials. One may be called "vertical," since it examines the child's development through time, and the other "horizontal," in that it separates out the different areas of the child's experience.

The "vertical" dimension requires a theory of "phases" or "stages" through which the individual proceeds from his first days of life to full maturity. (Indeed, such theory should logically extend to the adult years, and even to death itself, though this is not of direct concern in the present context.) One valuable contribution of this type—and, in my opinion, the *most* valuable—is Erikson's developmental model of the "eight stages of man." [9] "Basic trust vs. mistrust," "autonomy vs. shame and doubt," "initiative vs. guilt," "industry vs. inferiority," "identity vs. role diffusion": here, according to Erikson, are the critical periods in the life of every young and growing person. The stages are not, of course, rigidly programmed across the board, and no two individuals experience them in exactly the same way. Nonetheless, each one presents certain vital "tasks" that cannot really be avoided; indeed, each one involves a measure of "crisis" that is rooted in common psycho-social determinants.

If we take this kind of theory seriously, we are obliged to investigate how a culture manages on its own terms to distinguish between different periods of childhood. We cannot be content with knowing that discipline was generally harsh, or that parents were often indifferent to their young. We must try to determine whether such tendencies were more manifest at one stage of development than another, whether there was a kind of uneven curve of repressiveness or indifference with visible peaks and valleys over time.

But even this is not enough. We must also ask whether repressiveness, or indulgence, or indifference was more effective in some areas of the child's experience than in others. Most cultures do make certain distinctions among the various human instincts, drives, emotions—however they may be named and defined. A good theoretical picture of these issues can be found in the work of the cross-cultural

9 The best summary of this scheme is in Erik H. Erikson, *Identity and the Life Cycle* (New York, 1959), 50–100.

anthropologists Whiting and Child. Their studies are organized around a five-part division of child development, including sex, aggression, dependency, orality, and anality.[10] They have applied this scheme in the analysis of more than fifty contemporary cultures around the world, and a similar effort might well be made by historians.

Once we are committed in this direction, however, some new difficulties arise. There are many varieties of theory available in the developmental field, and it is difficult to reconcile or choose among them in a systematic way. Erikson may strike some of us as being particularly useful, but others may well form a different set of preferences. I believe, however, that the use of almost *any* developmental model—any serious attempt to differentiate among the varied experiences of childhood on either a "vertical" or a "horizontal" basis—will represent progress for the historian.

Let us consider some substantive ideas about one particular historical setting as a way of exemplifying the larger, "developmental" approach. The ideas presented in the next few paragraphs are based entirely on materials left by those seventeenth-century "Puritans" who founded the colonies of New England. There is no intention here to produce a rounded view of Puritan culture—nor is there space to provide the appropriate sort of documentation. But, hopefully, these comments will serve to characterize a certain way of thinking about historical problems, and to reveal both the gains and the drawbacks inherent in such an approach.

Here, then, are some tentative conclusions about particular aspects of Puritan practice in the treatment of infants and very young children. For the sake of clarity they are separated into seven distinct statements:[11]

(1) All infants were breast-fed for the first twelve to sixteen months of life.

(2) The clothing of infants was light and loosely fitted; there is no evidence in early American materials of the custom of swaddling.

(3) Very young infants often slept in the bed of one or both of their parents. Later they might be transferred to a cradle, or, in some cases, to a trundle-bed shared with one or more older siblings.

(4) Their immediate surroundings were animated, warm, and

10   See John W. M. Whiting and Irvin L. Child, *Child Training and Personality: A Cross-Cultural Study* (New Haven, 1953). Erikson's model also lends itself to a "horizontal" breakdown, since each of the eight stages involves a "task" that is of lasting importance throughout an individual life.

11   These matters are presented at greater length in John Demos, *A Little Commonwealth: Family Life in Plymouth Colony* (New York, 1970), esp. 46-49, 131-144.

intimate. Puritan families tended to be quite large,[12] and most infants would have from the start a number of siblings. At the same time, the houses of this period were small, with most daytime activities being confined to the room known as the "hall." One imagines, therefore, an infant lying in a cradle, which is set near the fireplace for warmth, and with a variety of familiar shapes and faces moving constantly around him. This is, to some degree, conjectural, but there is a fit about it all that seems persuasive. In short, we may conclude that for the first year or so, the Puritan child had a relatively comfortable and unrestricted mode of life. But consider what followed.

(5) As previously noted, breast-feeding ended after twelve to sixteen months. We know little enough about the usual manner of weaning in this culture, but there is fragmentary evidence to suggest that it may have been quite abrupt. Apparently in some instances a bitter substance was applied to the breast so as to curb the infant's wish to suckle. And certain mothers may actually have left the household for a few days in order to make a clean break. Particularly suggestive in this connection is the appearance of weaning as a metaphor in a wide range of Puritan literature. Experiences of misfortune and disappointment were often described as "weaning dispensations," and obviously this usage was meant to convey a poignant sense of loss.

(6) When the child was about two, a new baby would arrive. Most Puritan mothers gave birth at remarkably regular intervals of twenty-two to twenty-six months. The reason for this was the powerful contraceptive influence of lactation. We can, thus, recognize that for many infants in this culture the second year of life was bounded by experiences of profound loss—at the beginning by the loss of the breast (with all that this implies for *emotional* as well as physical sustenance), and at the end by the loss of the mother's special care and attention.

(7) Puritan writings which deal in some direct way with child-rearing share one central theme: The child's inherent "willfulness" must be curbed—indeed, it must be "broken" and "beaten down"—as soon as it begins to appear.[13] All other aspects of character develop-

---

12 Completed families in colonial New England averaged roughly eight children apiece. For a detailed analysis of this point, see Demos, *A Little Commonwealth*, 68–69, 192; Philip J. Greven, Jr., *Four Generations: Population, Land, and Family in Colonial Andover, Massachusetts* (Ithaca, 1970), 30–31, 111–112.

13 See, for example, certain statements in Robert Ashton (ed.), *The Works of John Robinson* (Boston, 1851), I, 246–247. See also Cotton Mather, "Some Special Points, Relating to the Education of My Children," reprinted in Perry Miller and Thomas H. Johnson (eds.), *The Puritans* (New York, 1963), II, 724–727.

ment are dependent on this procedure. Here, for Puritans, lay *the central task* of parenthood; and, in a profound sense, they regarded it as involving a direct confrontation with "original sin."

None of the extant literature specifies the precise age at which such will-training should begin, but most likely it was some time during the second year. For this is the age when every child becomes, for the first time, able to express his own wishes in an organized and effective way. He develops a variety of motor skills: he walks and runs, and he rapidly improves the coordination of hand and eye. He begins to learn speech. And, more generally, he becomes acutely aware of the difference between "I" and "you," "mine" and "yours." Even under the mildest sort of disciplinary regime there is bound to be some degree of conflict with authority, parental or otherwise, for a significant part of the child's new assertiveness is expressed as anger and aggression. This, after all, is the phase which Benjamin Spock discusses under the general rubric "the terrible twos."

And what does the psychologist have to say about it? For Erikson, this is the second of the major developmental stages, the one in which the central task is the formation of "autonomy." "This stage," he writes, "becomes decisive for the ratio between love and hate, for that between freedom of self-expression and its suppression. From a sense of *self-control without loss of self-esteem* comes a lasting sense of autonomy and pride." Moreover, while the goal of this stage is "autonomy," its negative side—and its specific vulnerability—is the possible fixation of lasting shame and doubt. It is absolutely vital that the child receive support in "his wish to 'stand on his own feet,' lest he be overcome by that sense of having exposed himself prematurely and foolishly which we call shame, or that secondary mistrust, that 'double-take' which we call doubt." [14]

Let us return now to the Puritans, in order to pull together these varied materials on their child-rearing patterns. We have, first, a period of perhaps twelve months when the infant is for the most part treated indulgently—followed, in the second year of life, by weaning, by the arrival of a younger sibling, and by a radical shift toward a harsh and restrictive style of discipline. It is necessary to emphasize, above all, the last of these events, since, in Erikson's terms, the determination to crush the child's will is nothing less than an effort to deprive him of a chance to develop a lasting and confident sense of autonomy.

14 Erikson, *Identity and the Life Cycle*, 68.

Clinical experience would argue that these patterns must have exerted a profound influence on all of the people who lived through them. Our next task is to survey some of the larger areas of Puritan life in which such influence can be discerned. Let us consider the whole field of interpersonal behavior—the style of relating to one another that was characteristic of this culture. It presents, in fact, a strikingly two-sided aspect. On the one hand, the Puritans placed a tremendous emphasis on the value of harmony, unity, and concord; one could cite as evidence literally countless sermons, essays, official decrees, and pronouncements. At the level of aspirations, nothing was more important for these people.[15] On the other hand, if one examines in detail the actual record of life in these communities—through various court and personal records—one discovers an extraordinary atmosphere of contentiousness and outright conflict. "Harmony" was always the preeminent value; yet, in trying to attain it, the Puritans constantly disappointed themselves. There is no paradox here; there is only the core of a pervasive ambivalence, something that was deeply rooted in the people themselves. To a very considerable degree, the inner life of Puritanism turned on a kind of axis between the opposite poles of conflict and conciliation, anger and love, aggression and submissiveness. And *all* of this, I suggest, is a plausible outcome of the pattern of childhood experience as previously described.

Moreover, we must attempt to assess the specific causes of the many conflicts in which Puritans became enmeshed, and the manner in which such conflicts were resolved. Disputes over boundaries were a constant source of trouble in these communities—boundaries between one man's land and his neighbor's, or often between whole townships that were adjacent to one another. A second, closely-related category of actions involved "trespass" of some sort; and here, too, the court cases are very numerous. More generally, many cases in which the immediate problem was something else—debt, or theft, or breach of contract—seem to have been experienced *emotionally*, by those directly involved, as a form of personal "trespass." We may conclude, in short, that "boundaries" were an immensely potent issue for

15   This aspect of Puritan life has been the subject of two recent studies: Kenneth A. Lockridge, *A New England Town: The First Hundred Years* (New York, 1970); Michael Zuckerman, *Peaceable Kingdoms* (New York, 1970). These authors have brilliantly portrayed the *ideal* of community in early New England—and to this extent I am much in their debt. My own analysis, however, diverges somewhat from theirs in finding a large amount of actual conflict-behavior among the individual people in question.

Puritan culture—and that this, in psychological terms, was tightly bound up with the question of autonomy.

We can also investigate these patterns from the *negative* side of the Eriksonian model, recalling that the reverse of autonomy is the distress created by deep inner trends of shame and doubt. Consider the large number of slander and defamation cases in the records which reveal an extreme sensitivity to the threat of public exposure and humiliation. Some of the most common forms of punishment imposed by legally-constituted authorities in these settlements were sitting in the stocks, branding, or being forced to wear badges of infamy. It seems clear that the pain which these punishments inflicted was above all due to the element of shame. As to Erikson's notion of "doubt," once again the Puritans appear to make a striking fit. Traditionally, of course, they have been pictured as smug, dogmatic, self-righteous, and intolerant—and indeed they often did wear this appearance. But how deeply did it penetrate? If one reads a few of the spiritual diaries and autobiographies left by Puritans with this question in mind, something very much like "doubt"—doubt of their faith, of their "standing" in the eyes of God—emerges as the primary *leit-motif* of such documents. If they sometimes acted smugly and self-satisfied, this was perhaps a kind of false front—a defense against profound inner anxieties from which they could never truly escape.

Here we have made a direct contact with their religious experience, and this might well be a particularly fruitful field in which to develop the same line of analysis. Let us consider for a moment some of the most familiar imagery of Puritan belief: the God who was by turns infinitely loving and overwhelmingly angry, and a God, too, who had the very special power to "see" every human action, no matter how secret, and to make the sinner feel deeply shamed; Heaven pictured as the place of total harmony, Hell as the place of everlasting strife; a moral universe in which each man was to struggle to achieve his personal salvation, though God had already entirely predestined the outcome of that struggle. It is tempting, indeed, to regard Puritan religious belief as a kind of screen on which all of their innermost concerns—autonomy, shame, doubt, anger—were projected with a very special clarity.

In order to become persuasive, these interpretations will require an extended treatment, much more so than is possible here. Therefore I propose, in conclusion, simply to point out some of the strategic and theoretical problems that are likely to arise in any analysis of this sort. We must be careful not to underestimate them.

There is, in the first place, an obvious need for work on the other developmental stages besides the earliest ones—work that finally presents childhood as a long and continuing sequence of growth and change. Character is not fixed at age two or three; later socialization is also of major consequence. With respect to the Puritans, one can surmise that there was much in the experience of later childhood to reinforce the training of the first few years. Any overt display of aggression or willfulness would elicit a stern parental response. Shaming was employed as a disciplinary technique, to an extent that directly enhanced the early sensitivities in this area.[16] The religious education of young persons stressed their utter dependence on God, their need to obliterate all traces of selfhood in order to become worthy of salvation. Traditional folklore underscored these lessons; stories of witchcraft, for example, conveyed with particular vividness the aura of danger that clung to manifestly hostile behavior.[17] There was also the general influence imparted by observing one's elders engaged in countless everyday transactions with each other—in which, of course, the same themes were repeatedly elaborated.

We need not contend, therefore, that all of Puritan culture was determined by traumas occurring during the second year of life, or that there is a simple "linear" connection between autonomy issues in early childhood and later adult behavior. At the same time we can believe that what happened during the second year was critical in the development of these people—that "autonomy" was *the* characteristic Puritan conflict, and that all of this was reflected in a variety of important social and cultural forms.

But are there not other, preferable explanations for the same

---

16 Note the following attributed to John Ward, in Cotton Mather, *Magnalia Christi Americana* (Hartford, 1853), I, 522: "Of young persons he would himself give this advice: 'Whatever you do, be sure to maintain shame in them; for if that be once gone, there is no hope that they'll ever come to good.'" In his essay, "Some Special Points, Relating to the Education of My Children," Mather writes: "I cause them to understand, that it is an *hurtful* and a *shameful* thing to do amiss. I aggravate this, on all occasions; and lett them see how *amiable* they will render themselves by well doing. The *first chastisement*, which I inflict for an ordinary fault is, to lett the child see and hear me in an astonishment, and hardly able to beleeve that the child could do so *base* a thing, but beleeving that they will never do it again" (725–276). The shaming effects of this procedure are impossible to miss.

17 See John Demos, "Underlying Themes in the Witchcraft of Colonial New England," *The American Historical Review*, LXXV (1970), 1311–1326.

range of phenomena? Perhaps we should look instead to certain features of Puritan social structure or political process—fields of inquiry with which historians are generally more familiar and more comfortable. It might be argued, for example, that chronic quarreling over boundaries resulted from the entirely "natural" concerns of peasants and yeomen in an overwhelmingly agricultural society. But this interpretation seems dubious for two reasons. First, there are many agricultural societies in which boundaries are not nearly so troublesome an issue; and, second, the empty lands of the New World should, from a practical standpoint, have lessened any competitive pressures of this type.[18]

Another sort of alternative explanation might be developed from our data on shame. Perhaps the frequency of trials for slander and defamation should be viewed as a necessary concomitant of life in little communities. Where so much human interchange was on a face-to-face basis, a man would have to protect his good reputation in order to obtain rewarding work and social contacts. There is substantial merit in this idea, but it need not be construed as opposed to a more psychological mode of explanation. Indeed, these two factors, the psychological and the practical, lock neatly together. One can even see a measure of gain for the people who endured such a harsh system of discipline: When they emerged as adults, they were conditioned to respond to precisely those cues which would ensure their practical welfare. In this respect, Puritan child-rearing was functionally appropriate to the wider Puritan culture.

But to use the word "Puritan" is simply to beg some further questions. How widely should such interpretations be applied? What groups of people can they reasonably be made to cover? We may agree perhaps that the above analysis treats real problems and issues in the lives of New England Puritans of the seventeenth century. But are we concerned here *only* with New England Puritans? Or can the same patterns be found among New Englanders in general, among settlers in other parts of the colonies, among Puritans in both the Old World and the New, among all English-speaking people—or, indeed, throughout all of "Western civilization" in early modern times? In

---

18   This point can be clarified by exploring the contrary case as well. If the concern with boundaries is to be explained in terms of *psychological* functioning, then it is quite plausible that the whole issue should have been sharpened by the literally "unbounded" character of the American wilderness.

short, the problem is to determine the extension of a particular line of analysis in terms of both historical time and cultural space. Until there is good comparative data on other communities from roughly the same period, we cannot be sure to what extent Puritan child-rearing and Puritan personality development were, in fact, distinctively Puritan.

There are, finally, some special methodological problems in this kind of study: They are not by any means insurmountable problems, but it is best to be explicit about what they involve. There is, first, a style of "proof" or "verification" which may seem somewhat novel when set against traditional canons of historical scholarship. We have, on the one hand, certain information about the prescribed method of disciplining young children, and, on the other, certain information about adult behavior in this society—court cases, methods of punishment, statements of ultimate value, and styles of religious concern. The connection between these two matters is not something that we can follow along a visible chain of evidence. Indeed, we can scarcely link them at all except through a process of analogy and inference, and the basis for this process is what we know from clinical experience in our own time. Moreover, because we are dealing in inference, there is a sense in which each side of the sequence confirms the other. That is: if Puritan adults were especially concerned about "boundaries" and "trespass," and especially vulnerable to shame, then we can say that they *must* have been roughly treated at an early age for their assertive and aggressive strivings. Similarly, if handled this way in childhood, then they *must* have behaved more or less as described later on. This may sound like circular reasoning to the historian—but not to the psychologist, who can adduce countless clinical observations to verify the correlation of the critical variables. It is, after all, less a case of circularity, and more a matter of internal consistency.

The second problem can be presented in the form of a warning. Historians are, officially at least, well aware of the pitfalls created by their own bias; but it is sometimes unclear as to how serious they are about this. In any event, the study of childhood and the family, the exploration of the whole inner world of human personality, is particularly open to various forms of projective distortion—vastly more so, for example, than the study of political, economic, or diplomatic history. Political bias or intellectual preferences are relatively easy to recognize and deal with. But the kinds of psychological baggage that we all carry within us—the outcome, in large part, of our own experience as children, as siblings, and as parents—are both much more powerful and much less conscious.

Yet the gains made possible by adopting a developmental approach remain substantial. What I hope I am doing in my own research is re-interpreting, or at least reordering, some of the most significant elements in early American life; and a similar strategy could certainly be applied in the analysis of other historical periods and other cultures. In the effort to make this strategy work, the study of childhood necessarily assumes a central place. It serves to bring into view certain themes which may not have been clearly recognized before, and, more broadly, it adds analytic depth to the entire research enterprise. We might refer once again to the distinction suggested earlier between the two basic types of approach to our subject. In the first instance we can point to Ariès, and no doubt many others who will be following the course he has marked out—scholars who study the child as a kind of mirror which focuses and reflects back cultural themes of central importance. But in the second instance—what I have been trying to outline here—something else is involved: The child becomes not just a mirror, not only the creature, but also the creator of culture, and, in this sense, a dynamic force in his own right.

Kenneth Keniston

Psychological Development and Historical Change

Most efforts to marry psychology and history have ended in divorce or outright cannibalism. In the hands of psychologists and psychiatrists, psychohistorical works have traditionally concentrated upon the psychopathology of great men. Those few historians influenced by psychoanalysis have sometimes insisted that historical movements were "nothing but" repetitive reenactments of the basic themes of *Totem and Taboo*. For their part, the majority of historians and depth psychologists have been rightly skeptical of the usefulness of an approach that left one unable to understand how great men differed from psychiatric patients and did scant justice to historical events of interest primarily because they were *not* literal repetitions of the past. Until the last decade, most psychohistorical inquiries must be judged a failure from both a psychological and a historical point of view; despite the advocacy of distinguished historians like Langer, the union of history and depth psychology languished.[1]

In the last decade, inspired largely by the work of Erikson, new and potentially more fruitful kinds of psychohistorical inquiry have opened up.[2] Erikson's studies of Gandhi and Luther have shown that some of the insights of psychoanalysis can be applied to great men without reducing them to bundles of neurotic urges. In the works of psychiatrists like Lifton, Coles, and others, we see a new interest in the unifying psychological themes that unite historical movements as different as Southern school desegregation and the atomic bombing of Hiroshima. In the studies of younger historians like Demos or Hunt, we find a new sophistication in applying modern psychodynamic

Kenneth Keniston is Professor of Psychology in the Department of Psychiatry at Yale University, and Director of the Behavioral Sciences Study Center at the Yale Medical School. He is the author of *The Uncommitted* (New York, 1965), *Young Radicals* (New York, 1968), and *Youth and Dissent* (New York, 1971).

Parts of this paper were delivered at the Clark University Conference on The History of Childhood and the Family, March 1970. The research on which it is based was supported by a grant from the Ford Foundation. The author is grateful to Frederick Wyatt for his criticisms of an earlier draft.

1 William L. Langer, "The Next Assignment," *American Historical Review*, LXIII (1968), 285–286.
2 See especially Erik H. Erikson, *Young Man Luther: A Study in Psychoanalysis and History* (New York, 1958), and *Gandhi's Truth: On the Origins of Militant Non-Violence* (New York, 1969).

insights to the study of childhood and the family in other epochs.[3] To be sure, no one, least of all the authors of these works, would claim that a final psychohistorical "synthesis" has been achieved, much less that there exists a solid body of method or theory that can be taught to the novice psychiatrist, historian, or psychologist. Psychohistory is more than anything else a series of questions that cannot be answered by psychology or history alone. But the possibilities of fruitful psychohistorical collaborations seem brighter today then ever before.

The relationship between historical and psychological change is one of the problems that has most frequently attracted those interested in a collaboration between these fields. In the theoretical work of men like Reich, Fromm, and Riesman, as in anthropological studies of culture contact between nonliterate and "advanced" societies, we find a growing body of observation and theory concerning the relationship of historical and psychological change.[4] It is now clear, for example, that when so-called "primitive" peoples come into contact with more technologically advanced societies, there generally results not merely the adoption of new mores and technologies, but the erosion of the traditional culture and the demoralization of a whole people. From such studies have come the concepts of national character, social character, or modal personality—concepts which, whatever their limitations and imprecision, help us understand and explain the observable and regular differences between men in distinct cultures and distinct historical eras.[5]

Most theories of national character or modal personality originated in the effort to understand psychological and cultural change—be it the rise of Fascism or the impact of modernization upon primitive

---

3 See especially Robert Jay Lifton, *Thought Reform and the Psychology of Totalism: A Study of "Brainwashing" in China* (New York, 1961); *Death in Life* (New York, 1967); Robert Coles, *Children of Crisis: A Study of Courage and Fear* (Boston, 1967); Joel Kovel, *White Racism: A Psychohistory* (New York, 1970); Robert Liebert, *Radical and Militant Youth: A Psychoanalytic Inquiry* (New York, 1971); John Demos, *A Little Commonwealth: Family Life in Plymouth Colony* (New York, 1970); David Hunt, *Parents and Children in History: The Psychology of Family Life in Early Modern France* (New York, 1970).

4 Wilheim Reich, *The Mass Psychology of Fascism* (New York, 1946); Erich Fromm, *Escape from Freedom* (New York, 1941); David Riesman, *The Lonely Crowd* (New Haven, 1950); Margaret Mead, *New Lives for Old: Cultural Transformation* (New York, 1956).

5 For a critical review of the concept of national character, see Alex Inkeles and Daniel J. Levinson, "National Character: the Study of Modal Personality and Socio-Cultural Systems" in Gardner Lindzey and Elliot Aronson (eds.), *Handbook of Social Psychology* (Cambridge, Mass., 1968).

societies.[6] But, paradoxically, these theories turned out to be far more useful in explaining historical inertia and cultural stability than in clarifying the mechanisms of change. For theories of national character have depended almost entirely upon the related concepts of socialization and acculturation. These concepts in turn attempt to explain how it is that social norms and cultural symbols are transmitted from generation to generation through the family, educational institutions, and other institutions of cultural transmission. Since a "well-functioning" society is defined as one in which the young are "successfully" socialized and acculturated, the observable facts of social, cultural, and psychological change prove difficult to explain except as a consequence of "failures" in a key set of social institutions.

Stated differently, theories of national character and modal personality have tended to have an implicitly conservative bias, both ideologically and theoretically. As a result, they have proved particularly useful in explaining such phenomena as cultural disintegration, social anomie, and psychological disorientation. These concepts help us understand the high incidence of addiction, apathy, and retreatism among non-literate peoples confronted with cultures that are more technologically advanced. They help illumine the messianic cults that appear to flourish at just that point when an old culture is becoming moribund. But they have proved less useful in understanding those social and historical changes which, all things taken together, seem more constructive than destructive, more synthetic than disintegrative. They help little in understanding the undeniable advances in the human condition brought about by the Industrial Revolution, in explaining how men could make constructive political revolutions, or, for that matter, in clarifying *any* non-degenerative historical change.

But the intertwined concepts of socialization, acculturation, and modal personality do not exhaust the potential contribution of psychology in explaining historical change. Largely ignored so far in the study of historical change have been the emerging concepts of developmental psychology—a small but rapidly growing body of theories about the sequences of stages of human development, the conditions that foster or inhibit development in children, and the consequences of early development for adult roles, symbolizations, and values. I will here argue that, in the long run, developmental concepts are likely to prove more useful than concepts of socialization, acculturation, and

6 Daniel Lerner, *The Passing of Traditional Society: Modernizing the Middle East* (New York, 1964).

national character in explaining historical change, and that the relationship between historical context and psychological development is far more intimate than we have heretofore suspected. Collaboration between developmental psychology and history will clearly require major accommodations from the practitioners of both fields, but the result should be a better understanding of both historical and psychological change.

CURRENT VIEWS OF HUMAN DEVELOPMENT   Every epoch tends to freeze its own unique experience into an ahistorical vision of Life-in-General. Modern developmental psychology witnesses this universal trend. Despite recent advances in our understanding of human development, our psychological concepts have generally suffered from a historical parochialism that takes the patterns, timetables, and sequences of development prevalent among middle-class children in contemporary Western societies as the norm of human development. For example, many developmental psychologists, like most laymen, consider it fairly obvious that human life falls naturally into a set of stages that can properly be labeled infancy, the preschool years, childhood, adolescence, early adulthood, middle age, and old age—for these are the stages which we recognize and institutionalize in Western society, and virtually all research on human development has been conducted in America or Western Europe.

Historians or anthropologists, however, quickly note that these segmentations of the life cycle bear little if any relationship to the definitions of life stages in other eras or cultures. During almost any previous historical era in Western societies, the life cycle has been thought to consist of different stages than those we now acknowledge; in virtually every other contemporary culture, as well, the stages of life are quite differently defined. To attend seriously to these facts requires us to re-examine the assumptions of developmental psychology, and, in so doing, to open the door to a new possibility of collaboration between historians and developmental psychologists.

The reasons for the relative neglect of historical and cultural evidence in the study of development must be understood if this neglect is to be remedied. First among these reasons, of course, is the traditional excuse of psychology: It is a new field. It has in fact proven extraordinarily difficult to understand the complexities of human development even in one subculture of one society: understanding the development of upper-middle class American, French, Swiss, German, and English children is far from complete. How much more difficult, then, it is to study development in non-Western societies, much less in other historical eras.

Yet in addition to the infancy of developmental psychology, there are conceptual and ideological factors that have prevented our attending to historical and anthropological data. First is the generally unspoken assumption that we really *need* not examine development in any other place or time than our own, since the laws, sequences, and stages of human development transcend both culture and history in their universality.[7] Once this assumption is openly stated, it is revealed as parochially acultural and ahistorical. But it is often simply taken for granted in many developmental theories. It is further supported by the widespread psychological assumption that the innate "thrust" of human development is so intense that development cannot be stopped by any "merely" cultural or historical factor. This assumption, in turn, is bolstered by the widespread conceptual confusion between biologically-determined physiological maturation, socially-defined age-grading, and real psychological development—all of which are considered equally inevitable. To open the way for a closer connection between developmental psychology and historical inquiry, we must therefore engage, however briefly, in an analysis of concepts that will challenge this presumption of the inevitability of development.

If we ask what we mean by psychological development, we clearly do not mean simply the accumulation of new facts, the strengthening or weakening of preexisting characteristics, or the repetition of previous attainment. What we can loosely call "quantitative" changes in human behavior are not necessarily developmental. The facts that old people often become more rigid with age, that American girls learn to skip rope more rapidly in the early school years, or that children's vocabulary enlarges with age are not truly developmental changes.

Nor is psychological development equivalent to physical growth or physiological development—that is, to maturation. Maturational changes are indeed virtually universal and inevitable, barring the grossest of insults to the organism. In all cultures, the brain of the child develops rapidly during the first two years of life, although gross malnutrition may slow or impair that development. The historical

---

7 Sigmund Freud's uncompromising views about the biologically-based universality of the developmental sequences are well known. Jean Piaget's acknowledgment that environmental factors play a role in determining the rate of development has always been largely *pro forma*, since he has never defined or studied these environmental differences.

milieu may influence the age of menarche, but it does not prevent the onset of menstruation. In all societies, children pass through puberty, with important changes in their appearance, capacities, and general behavior. Maximal skeletal size is everywhere reached in the early twenties. And, in all eras, the vitality of early adulthood is followed by a progressive decline in physical strength that culminates in old age and death. Yet no one of these changes automatically *entails* developmental change. Maturation may, indeed perhaps usually does, promote or permit psychological development, but it need not. Both folk wisdom and clinical studies indicate that there are physically mature individuals with the psychology of children, and precocious biological children who possess adult developmental characteristics. In a phrase: Maturation and development are empirically correlated, but not *necessarily* related. The virtual inevitability of physiological maturation therefore does not demonstrate the inevitability of psychological development.

A second universal is socially-defined age-grading. A few societies or sub-societies have been or are rigidly age-graded:[8] e.g., classical Spartan society, some modern East African and Melanesian societies, or modern Western school systems. In most other societies, age-grading is somewhat looser: Age cohorts are less sharply demarcated. But, in all societies there are socially-defined differences in what is expected of the young and the old, the infant and the adult, the adult and the elder. In every known society the special status of the dependent and nursing infant is somehow acknowledged. It is also probably universal that societies distinguish the infant-child under the age of six or seven from the older child and/or adult. Every society, too, acknowledges that there is a stage or stages of life which are those of the fullness of life. The blessings and/or curses of old age are recognized. Admittedly, all societies do not divide up the life cycle in precisely the *same* way: On the contrary, they differ enormously in their definition of life stages, of the ages at which new stages begin, and in the substance of their expectations about age-appropriate behavior. But all societies do segment the life cycle in *some* way, and all societies apply formal and informal sanctions to ensure that people will "act their age." Thus, although the content of age-graded expectations varies with culture and history, the general process of age-grading is universal.

But neither maturation nor age-grading is equivalent to psychological development in the precise sense in which I will define this term.

8 On the sociology of age-grading, see S. N. Eisenstadt, *From Generation to Generation* (Glencoe, 1956).

It is clearly possible to possess the social status of an adult but the mentality of a child. It is equally possible to have the body of an adult but the psychological development of a child. Psychological development, then, is related to both maturation and socialization, both of which may at times stimulate or prevent development, but neither of which is identical to development.

What do we mean by psychological development?[9] It can be defined as a process of qualitative change in functioning, in relationship to the world, or to oneself. To qualify as true development, this change must be age-correlated and synthetic—that is, it must involve moving to a progressively "higher" level of functioning, to a new level of organization that in general does not completely negate lower levels but tends to incorporate them. For example, the child who apprehends the grammar and vocabulary of his language, and thus learns to speak, does not lose his capacity to babble and imitate. The adolescent who moves beyond primitive identification with his parents to the more complex syntheses of identity formation described by Erikson still retains the capacity for identification.[10] The child who moves from the world of concrete operations to the hypothetical-deductive world of formal operations still remains capable of concrete operations.[11] Genitality, as defined by Freud, does not entail the disappearance of pregenital sexuality, but rather its inclusion and subordination in a genital orientation. In each case, lower levels of development tend to be subsumed as "special cases" in the next higher level of organization.

Psychological development is also essentially irreversible. This does not mean that regressions, recapitulations, reenactments, and reversions to earlier stages cannot occur in the course of development. On the contrary, most developmental theories find a place for such regressions within their theory. But *essential* irreversibility means that regression to a level is in some sense different from the first experience of that level: e.g., "regressed" behavior tends to be identifiably different; after regression (but not before) it is possible to "leapfrog" levels so as

9 The following account draws heavily upon Bärbel Inhelder, "Some Aspects of Piaget's Approach to Cognition" in *Monograph of the Society for Research in Child Development*, XXVII (1962), 19–33; Laurence Kohlberg, "Stage and Sequence: The Cognitive-Developmental Approach to Socialization," in David A. Goslin (ed.), *Handbook of Socialization Theory and Research* (Chicago, 1969). For a more general discussion of concepts of development, see Dale B. Harris (ed.), *The Concept of Development: An Issue in the Study of Human Behavior* (Minneapolis, 1957).
10 Erik H. Erikson, *Identity: Youth and Crisis* (New York, 1968).
11 Bärbel Inhelder and Jean Piaget (trans. Anne Parsons and Stanley Milgram), *The Growth of Logical Thinking from Childhood to Adolescence* (New York, 1958).

to resume development at the point from which one regressed, and so on. By stressing the sequentiality and essential irreversibility of development, we merely stress that development proceeds in a regular way through stages, each of which constitutes a prerequisite for the next. Stated schematically, Stage B cannot occur before Stage A, while Stage B is in turn a prerequisite for Stage C. Each level thus builds upon the preceding one and is the building block for the one that follows it.

To define further the concept of development or the precise sequences of development would involve controversies and complexities irrelevant to this discussion. What is important is that psychological development as here defined is closely related to social age-grading and physiological maturation, but is not identical to either. In the study of socialization to age-grades we find valuable understanding of the matrix within which development occurs, the catalysts that tend to spur it, and the obstacles that may obstruct it. But an account of social expectations about age-appropriate behavior is not an account of development. Similarly, physiological maturation may be a prerequisite for developmental change or it may be a catalyst for development. But it does not automatically produce psychological development.

THE CONTINGENCY OF HUMAN DEVELOPMENT   These distinctions between socialization to age-grades, maturation, and development enable us to focus more sharply upon the *contingency* of human development. Most developmental theorists have tended to take for granted—or even to allege—that human development is virtually inevitable, barring any but the most traumatic insults to the individual's personality. This assumption springs partly from blurring the distinctions I have just made. For since maturation and socialization are indeed virtually inevitable, if development is not distinguished from them, then development, too, must be inevitable. Thus, despite an accumulating body of research that demonstrates the possibility of irreversible retardations, slowings, arrests, fixations, lags, or foreclosures in development, the logical conclusion has not been drawn, nor have its implications been explored.

In fact, our present understanding suggests that the *extent* of human development is dependent upon the bio-social-historical matrix within which the child grows up; some developmental matrices may demonstrably retard, slow, or stop development; others may speed, accelerate, or stimulate it. We have traditionally seen the human life cycle as an escalator onto which the infant steps at birth and along which he is carried until his death. The view I am proposing here is that human development is instead a very rough road, pitted with obstructions, interspersed with blind alleys, and dotted with seductive stopping places. It can be traversed only with the greatest of support and under the most optimal conditions.

In order to carry the discussion further with any precision, it is now necessary to distinguish between "development-in-general" and development within specific "lines" or sectors of growth. Developmental theories can be roughly grouped on the basis of this distinction: some deal primarily with development in general or broad life stages (Freud, Erikson, Sullivan), while others deal with developmental changes in precisely defined areas of functioning (Piaget, Kohlberg, Perry).[12] It was Anna Freud who first pointed out that what we loosely call "development" in fact consists of a series of changes within distinguishable "developmental lines" or sectors of functioning.[13] Today developmental diagnosticians of childhood define separately the levels attained by each child in a variety of distinct sectors: e.g., fine motor, cognitive, gross motor, interpersonal, affective, defensive-adaptive, verbal-speech, etc.[14] Any global judgment of overall developmental level is based upon a profile derived from sector-specific evaluations. Thus, if we are to speak precisely about the factors that promote an individual's development, we must specify which sectors or lines of development we are talking about.

This apparently technical point is especially relevant to the cross-cultural and historical study of development. For historical or cultural conditions which may stimulate development in one sector of life may well fail to stimulate it or actually retard it in other sectors. For example, many social critics today argue that a narrow kind of cognitive development is over-stimulated in modern Western societies at the

12 For an authoritative summary of the psychoanalytic view of development, see Otto Fenichel, *The Psychoanalytic Theory of Neurosis* (New York, 1945), Chs. IV–VI. Erikson's views are summarized in his "Identity and the Life Cycle," *Psychological Issues*, I (1959), 18–164; Harry Stack Sullivan, *The Interpersonal Theory of Psychiatry* (New York, 1953). The best general introduction to Piaget's immense body of work remains John H. Flavell, *The Developmental Psychology of Jean Piaget* (New York, 1963). For Kohlberg's views, see Kohlberg, "Stage and Sequence," and "The Child as a Moral Philosopher," *Psychology Today*, II (1968), 25–30; William G. Perry, Jr., *Forms of Intellectual and Ethical Development in the College Years* (New York, 1970).

13 *Normality and Pathology in Childhood: Assessments of Development* (New York, 1965).

14 See, e.g., the elaborate forms used to assess early child development by Sally Provence and her colleagues at the Developmental Unit of the Child Study Center at Yale Medical School.

expense of affective and interpersonal development, which are in turn retarded. Freud believed that precocious sexual development tended to retard intellectual development. And it is probably possible to stimulate or over-stimulate some sectors of growth but to understimulate, neglect, or suppress others. The "intellectually precocious, emotionally immature" child in Western societies is a case in point.

Thus, if we are to compare different historical epochs or different cultures from a developmental perspective, we must not merely compare how they define the overall stages of life and study the extent to which individuals actually pass through these global stages, but we must examine specifically how a given cultural and historical context affects each of many specific sub-sectors of human development.

Furthermore, only when we have distinguished between sectors of development does the precise influence of the environmental matrix upon development become truly clear. For example, during the past two decades, the study of children in extreme situations has shown that they may "fail to develop" unless defined environmental conditions are present. The most dramatic examples of developmental failure come from studies of infants institutionalized in antiseptic, hygienic, but impersonal "childrens' homes." The conditions of infant care in such institutions—multiple mothering, unresponsiveness to the child's indications of distress and pleasure, lack of sensory stimulation, and so on—produce specific developmental arrests or retardations in virtually all children subjected to these conditions. Some such children die of extreme reactions to minor physical illnesses; others develop a lethal apathy called marasmus. Those who survive physically are often grossly retarded. And those who live to adulthood tend to be diagnosed as amoral sociopaths.

Until recently, the blame for these developmental failures was laid at the door of heredity: The children who ended up in foundling homes were considered constitutionally defective. But research has made clear that the damage is done not by constitution, but by environment. And research by Provence and Lipton, which carefully distinguishes between development in distinct sectors, has helped pinpoint the areas in which early developmental arrest appear to be irreversible.[15] If the children in question are placed in normal foster homes at approximately the age of two, they soon make up most of the lost ground with regard

15   See René Spitz, "Hospitalism," *The Psychoanalytic Study of the Child*, I (1945), 53–75; John Bowlby, *Maternal Care and Mental Health* (Geneva, 1951); Sally Provence and Rose C. Lipton, *Infants in Institutions* (New York, 1962).

to cognitive development, speech, and gross motor development. But, in other areas, retardation appears enduring: Such children seem never to develop the full capacity for deep personal relationships, for imaginative fantasy, or for the physical grace characteristic of children brought up from birth in natural or foster homes. Each of these fundamental qualities appears to be contingent upon a certain kind of environmental matrix in early life.

The barbarity of "modern" foundling homes is so extreme that if such conditions were societally universal, they would probably produce psychological deformations so extreme that no society could survive for long. In any enduring society, infants can take for granted most of the conditions they need in order to develop. Indeed, as a preliminary hypothesis, we might suggest that until about the age of six or seven, society has relatively little leeway in what it provides children. If the society is to survive, it must provide adequate stimulation—adequate "emotional and cognitive nutriments"—for the infant to become a child. Thereafter, however, we can speculate that the relative contingency of development upon the matrix in which it occurs seems to increase, and we begin to discover a series of truly developmental changes that may or may not occur. For example, Inhelder and Piaget have described at length the development of the capacity for formal operations: i.e., the ability to generate hypotheses and deduce their conclusions regardless of whether or not these conclusions are empirically true.[16] The capacity for formal operations is the capacity for logical-deductive thought. With this capacity, the intellect breaks free from the concrete world into the realm of hypotheses, ideals, and contra-factual conjectures. Upon this cognitive capacity, Piaget insists, philosophies, systems of scientific thought, utopias, and man's awareness of his historicity are based.

With Piaget's well-bred middle-class Swiss youths, the capacity for formal operations emerges at around the age of puberty. And, despite Piaget's *pro forma* acknowledgement that environment plays a role in the development of this capacity, he has associated formal operations firmly with early adolescence. But other studies have questioned this association. In some subcultures and in some societies, including our own, numerous adults seem to lack this capacity.[17] One study of American adolescents from "culturally deprived" backgrounds found that when the capacity for formal operations developed at all, it generally

16 *Growth of Logical Thinking.*
17 Flavell, *Developmental Psychology of Jean Piaget,* 399.

emerged well after puberty.[18] One may further question whether this capacity is likely to emerge at all in non-literate societies. In brief, here is a specific human potential which appears *not* to be actualized in certain environments, but to be crucially dependent upon the catalysts of the surrounding matrix.

Kohlberg's studies of moral development give a still more unequivocal example of developmental levels that are *not* reached by most men and women in American society, or for that matter in any society that has been studied.[19] Kohlberg argues that moral development may proceed from what he calls the preconventional and conventional levels, occurring during childhood and early adolescence, to post-conventional levels. These post-conventional levels are developmental in the precise sense defined above: They are essentially irreversible, sequential, age-related, and synthetic. But Kohlberg's empirical work indicates that the great majority of young Americans, like their parents, do not in fact pass beyond the conventional stage of moral reasoning. The precise psychological and cultural matrix that promotes the development of post-conventional moral reasoning remains largely a matter for speculation.[20] But what seems clear is that Kohlberg has identified measurable stages of moral development which the great majority of Americans do not reach. Research in other cultures suggests that elsewhere these stages are reached even less frequently.[21]

We as yet know very little about the precise sequences of development in each of the areas of human growth that can be distinguished.[22] It will doubtless take decades before we have begun to fill in the chart of human development, much less to understand the impacts of different environmental matrices upon distinct sectors of development. But what

18 Martin P. Deutsch, Remarks at Research Conference, Dept. of Psychology, Yale Medical School, 1968.

19 "Child as a Moral Philosopher."

20 Kenneth Keniston, "Student Activism, Moral Development and Morality," *American Journal of Orthopsychiatry*, XL (1970), 577–592.

21 Kohlberg, "Child as a Moral Philosopher."

22 Stuart T. Hauser, *Black and White Identity Formation* (New York, 1971), demonstrates marked identity foreclosures in black working-class adolescents. Research done in other cultures also suggests different rates and patterns of development that depend on the socio-cultural matrix. See Patricia M. Greenfield and Jerome S. Bruner, "Culture and Cognitive Growth," in Goslin, *Handbook*; Jerome S. Bruner, Rose S. Olver, and Patricia M. Greenfield, *Studies in Cognitive Growth* (New York, 1967), especially Chs. 11–14; Flavell, *Developmental Psychology of Jean Piaget*, 379–402; John Jay and Michael Cole, *The New Mathematics and an Old Culture: A Study of Learning among the Kpelle of Liberia* (New York, 1967).

we do now know consistently supports the hypothesis that human development, from infancy onward, is contingent upon the characteristics of the environmental matrix.

LIFE STAGES AND DEVELOPMENTAL PROFILES   This hypothesis, if correct, has important implications for the study of historical change. For, in general, members of any given society in any given historical epoch tend to share a highly similar developmental matrix. It follows that, despite the variations in human development generated by constitutional and idiosyncratic differences, there should be important constancies in the *modal developmental profile* of adults. Put differently, people in any given society or sub-society tend to resemble each other not only because they have internalized the same roles (socialization) and the same symbols and values (acculturation), but also because they have "leveled off" at approximately the same point in their development in each of the sectors of human growth.

In the past, we have learned to analyze how children internalize shared social roles and how they incorporate common cultural symbols and values. Now we should begin to examine the environments of children, adolescents, and adults in terms of their selective impact on the unfolding of development potentials. We may discover, for example, that certain societies like our own place immense stress upon some kinds of cognitive and intellectual development, while they deemphasize other sectors of development—for example, motoric development and the early development of responsibility. If this is true, then we will require a concept like "modal developmental profile" to characterize the developmental attainments of the average individual in any subculture, society, or historical epoch.

If these hypotheses and concepts prove useful, they may open the possibility of new ways of examining the family, the life cycle, and the phenomenology of human experience in other historical eras. My argument implies that we have been too quick to assume that human development in other societies and other historical eras proceeds in a manner essentially similar to development in our own society. In our rush to reject the arrogance of the nineteenth century vis-à-vis the "savage native," we have been too quick to assume a complete identity of experience between modern man and ancient man, technological man and pre-literate man. In our acceptance of cultural relativism in the realm of values, we may have confused values with facts, generating a twentieth-century pseudo-egalitarianism which is little more than the ethnocentric assumption that all men are "basically" like Western industrialized men. Developmental psychologists have helped us to remember how profoundly different from our own are the mental processes and conceptual maps with which the small child approaches the world. Working together, developmental psychologists, historians, and anthropologists may now help us to recall how profoundly different has been the human experience of growing up in other societies and other times—and how different, as a result, was the inner experience and mind-set of adults in other places and eras.

It may clarify the view I am proposing to consider several problems which might be illumined by this approach. Consider, for one, the observation by anthropologists studying some pre-literate societies and by historians studying earlier eras that the life stage of adolescence has not always been formally recognized or acknowledged. Since puberty obviously occurs in all societies, these same scholars have generally assumed that adolescence as a psychological stage has also occurred, and have devoted their main investigative effort to explaining why so obvious a milestone in human development was not formally noted. But the point of view introduced here suggests a different interpretation. It may well be that adolescence as a stage of psychological development occurs only under specific conditions like those which obtain in modern Western societies. In other societies or historical eras, puberty is therefore not followed by anything like what we consider an adolescent experience.[23]

To state this general hypothesis in its most extreme and provocative form: Some societies may "create" stages of life that do not exist in other societies; some societies may "stop" human development in some sectors far earlier than other societies "choose" to do so. If, therefore, a given stage of life or developmental change is not recognized in a given society, we should seriously entertain the possibility that it simply does not occur in that society. And, if this is the case, then in societies where adolescence does not occur many of the psychological characteristics which we consider the results of an adolescent experience should be extremely rare: For example, a high degree of emancipation

---

[23] Some observers of development after puberty have argued that "adolescence," as commonly defined, is extremely rare in American society as well: see Edgar Z. Friedenberg, *The Vanishing Adolescent* (New York, 1962); Elizabeth Douvan and Joseph Adelson, *The Adolescent Experience* (New York, 1966); Daniel Offer, *Psychological World of the Teenager: A Study of Normal Adolescent Boys* (New York, 1969). These works may be interpreted either to indicate a wide-spread "foreclosure" of development in early adolescence or to indicate that the concept of adolescence has been incorrectly defined.

from family, a well-developed self-identity, a belief system based upon a reexamination of the cultural assumptions learned in childhood, and, perhaps, the cognitive capacity for formal operation.

Let us consider a second example. Elkins has drawn an analogy between what he terms the "Sambo" mentality prevalent until recently among black American slaves and their nominally free descendents and the particular mentality observed amongst the inmates of concentration camps.[24] Elkins' hypothesis focuses upon the impact of extreme and traumatic degradation upon adult personality; he disregards almost completely the possible effects upon children of growing up under the conditions prevalent in slave quarters on North American plantations. As a result, the major intellectual problem in Elkins' formulation is how to explain why the trauma of the middle passage was communicated from generation to generation over so many centuries.

Even with our present limited knowledge of the effects of gross cultural deprivation, illiteracy, discontinuity of mothering, lack of sensory stimulation, and so on, we can readily supplement Elkins' theory by informed speculations about the catastrophic effects upon child development (and, therefore, upon adult personality) of the conditions in which children born into slavery were reared. Such conditions should predictably lead to a dulling of adult cognitive capacities, to resignation, apathy, and indifference, and to a "survival mentality" which stresses manifest acquiescence and covert resistance.

An even more speculative example of the possible connection between developmental and historical concepts may follow from the observations of Ariès, qualified by the later studies of Hunt, concerning the characteristics of child development in sixteenth- and seventeenth-century France.[25] Ariès argues that the concept of childhood as a separate stage of life was unknown during the Middle Ages. Only in the sixteenth and seventeenth centuries, and, initially, only for a small elite, was a separate stage that followed infancy but preceded adulthood socially acknowledged and sanctioned in age-graded schools. If we leap from this datum to the theories of Erikson concerning childhood as a stage of life, we find that the developmental "task" of childhood in Erikson's terms is the achievement of a sense of "industry," which Erikson relates to such human qualities as skill, a sense of workmanship,

24 Stanley M. Elkins, *Slavery: A Problem in American Institutional and Intellectual Life* (Chicago, 1968).
25 Philippe Ariès, *Centuries of Childhood: A Social History of Family Life* (New York, 1962); Hunt, *Parents and Children in History*.

an absence of feelings of inferiority, and a sense of vocational competence. We might argue that in the absence of a stage of childhood, the
psychological quality of industry simply did not develop on a mass
scale, and that its absence thus helps to explain the absence of the
motivations necessary for an entrepreneurial, capitalistic-industrial
society. Perhaps only as childhood was recognized on a mass scale and
as a larger proportion of the population therefore developed a sense of
industry could capitalism and large-scale industrialization proceed. Such
an explanation might help us define the developmental component in
the complex relationship between capitalism, Protestantism, and the
work ethic.

A variety of other topics might be illumined by the application of
developmental concepts. We might ask, for example, how the historical extension of literacy changes the cognitive development and social
behavior of those who can read. Does it enable them to deal more
effectively with complex political questions? Does it make them more
susceptible to mass totalitarian movements? Does literacy help the individual attain that detachment from admired but defeated political
figures which is necessary in a democracy if the opposition is gracefully
to concede defeat? Or does it lay the groundwork for the ideologiza-
tion of political and social controversy? Or we might ask whether,
after the fall of the Roman Empire, the matrix of child development
changed so that children of succeeding generations attained a less advanced cognitive level than that which characterized the aristocracy in
Rome, with the result that original thought ceased for several centuries
throughout most of Western Europe and the Mediterranean.

Finally, turning to our own era, I have elsewhere argued at greater
length[26] that a good part of the untoward restiveness of affluent, educated young people today must be understood as a consequence of a
massive historical change in the developmental matrix. Among other
things, this new matrix promotes the individualization of moral judg-
ments and the relativization of truth. One consequence is that a large
minority of a youthful generation is unable, for better and for worse,
to accept on faith previous moral evaluations or uncritically to accept
traditional ways of viewing the world. These new mind-sets are not
simply matters of the recurrence of perennial generational conflict. On
the contrary, to understand fully the emergence of an oppositional
youthful counter-culture in the most technologically advanced nations

26   Kenneth Keniston, "Youth as a 'New' Stage of Life," *The American Scholar*, XXXIX
(1970), 631–654.

of the world, we must begin to examine how the drastically altered historical conditions of the twentieth century (extended mass education, widespread affluence, exposure to other cultures, threat of holocaust) have in turn changed the modal matrix of human development, "producing" on a mass scale a kind of questioning, restless youth who, if he existed at all in the past, was always part of a tiny and exceptional minority.

In urging that we examine the psychological effects of wide-scale historical changes in the developmental matrix, I am not proposing that we abandon more familiar and traditional modes of psychological and historical inquiry. The concept of national character or modal personality, for example, has emerged from scathing criticism scarred but still useful in the understanding of historical continuity and change. Developmental concepts are in no sense a panacea either to the psychologist or the historian. My only claim is that they may help us understand better the processes by which socio-historical change produces psychological change, and by which psychological change on a mass scale may in turn generate social and political transformations. And, if developmental psychology and historical inquiry can move toward a closer accommodation, we may be less inclined to impose our own culturally ethnocentric and historically parochial world-views and mind-sets upon the experience of those in other cultures and historical eras.

Lois W. Banner

On Writing Women's History

Sexual Politics. By Kate Millet (New York, Doubleday, 1970) 393 pp. $7.95

Essays on Sex Equality. By John Stuart Mill and Harriet Taylor Mill. Edited, with an introductory essay, by Alice S. Rossi (Chicago, University of Chicago Press, 1970) 242 pp. $8.75 ($1.95, paper)

The Lady: Studies of Certain Significant Phases of Her History. By Emily James Putnam (Chicago, University of Chicago Press, 1970) 323 pp. $5.95 ($1.95, paper)

The Southern Lady: From Pedestal to Politics, 1830–1930. By Anne Firor Scott (Chicago, University of Chicago Press, 1970) 247 pp. $5.95

Birth Control in America: The Career of Margaret Sanger. By David M. Kennedy (New Haven, Yale University Press, 1970) 320 pp. $8.75

Daughters of the Promised Land. By Page Smith (Boston, Little, Brown, 1970) 392 pp. $10.00

After a long era of neglect, women are once again becoming a subject of serious historical investigation. The roots of this new interest are twofold. First, a number of advances within historical thought and methodology in general have turned the attention of many social historians toward subjects like adolescence, marriage, the family, and women—subjects once thought peripheral to the central concern of describing the structures and conflicts of social classes. The perspectives of social historians have shifted away from Marxism, with its rigid class divisions and its emphasis on social power, to new sociological theories which view classes as dynamic entities, which focus on the more complex categories of role and status, and which increasingly try to integrate all types of people into their analyses. Second, the feminist movement of the 1960s has thrust the subject of women into public prominence. Once again contemporary militancy has made historians

Lois W. Banner is Assistant Professor of History at Douglass College, Rutgers—The State University.

aware of past oversights, just as the women's rights movement of the early twentieth century prompted a number of noteworthy studies (such as Emily James Putnam's *The Lady: Studies of Significant Phases of Her History*, first published in 1910), and black power more recently has produced black studies. American historians have often studied the immigrant and ethnic groups to which they belong. They have now realized that some central minority groups, from whose ranks few trained and practicing historians had come, have been egregiously overlooked.

Moreover, the critique which some feminists and other radicals have mounted against marriage, the family, and traditional child-rearing methods is beginning to have an impact on scholarly studies. American historians of the 1950s, influenced by the idealism of the war experience and in reaction against the emphasis that Progressive historians like Charles Beard had placed on conflict in the American past, stressed themes of harmony, growth, and accomplishment. Major representatives of the so-called "consensus" school, like Daniel Boorstin and Louis Hartz, celebrated the American past or confined their critical concern primarily to the realm of politics. Present-day historians, however, sensitive to the new sociology and to the widening public debate over the merits of basic social arrangements, increasingly regard studies of marriage, the family, adolescence, generational conflict, and women as enterprises as basic to the understanding of human character and purpose as studies of political power and economic expansion.

The central document of the new feminism is Kate Millet's *Sexual Politics*, just as John Stuart Mill's 1869 essay, *The Subjection of Women*, now edited by Alice S. Rossi in *Essays on Sex Equality* (along with three other essays by Mill and his wife, Harriet Taylor), played an analogous role earlier in this century. The similarities between the two works are striking. Both are compendia of current feminist thought on anthropology, psychology, history, and, in the case of Millet, literature. Both are impassioned pleas for full human equality. Both argue that male domination over the female is the fundamental model for other forms of political and economic domination, although, in a typically Victorian manner, Mill equates freedom with spiritual and mental, not sexual, qualities. The prescriptions for reform put forth by Mill—and especially by Harriet Taylor—are no less radical than Millet's: They call for family planning, new communal marital arrangements and day-care centers for children, and the end to an economic system under which the female half of the population is barred from employment because there are not enough jobs for all.

As historians, however, both authors are disappointing. Neither is interested in the subtleties of historical analysis; both are concerned mainly with proving their theme of universal female suppression. Influenced by the liberal optimism and the vogue of universal history of his day, Mill finds that Western history has passed through two stages: first, in primitive times, the strong came to control the weak, initially in marriage, and then through slavery and political tyranny; and, second, since primitive times, the slow growth of freedom, culminating in Mill's own era of liberal revolutions, had brought an end to political despotism and human slavery. Such a progressive scheme of historical development not only sounds naive to the modern historian, and slights problems of class and economic exploitation, but it also places Mill in the curious position of arguing that over time the position of women has actually improved. He thereby implies that the Victorian woman, despite all of her difficulties, was actually better off than females in previous ages. His sociology and his history are at odds. Sensitive on one level to the repressive attitudes of his own era toward women, he does not consider the possibility that Victorian standards were historically regressive or that his argument for inevitable historical progress made his eloquent catalogue of the ills of Victorian society sound partly contrived.

As a historian, Millet is not so optimistic. What interests her is not the movement of political liberalism, but the existence of that extreme sexual oppression which reached its height during Mill's own age and which reappeared in the twentieth century in reaction to the new sexual and social freedom which feminists and others in the new century had attained. One cannot deny the validity of this interpretation: Indeed, from the point of view of the modern woman, Millet's emphasis on the movement of sexual repression in the twentieth century, rather than on those currents of sexual liberation which so many historians have heretofore stressed, is refreshing. What is unsatisfying about her book as history, however, is her selection and organization of evidence. She has little interest in collective data: the analysis of individual authors of her choice proves all. She dismisses the history of women from the primitive introduction of patriarchy to nineteenth-century reform movements as unimportant because, she implies, nothing essential changed over those centuries. Her discussion of the twentieth-century conservative reaction focuses on Soviet Russia and Nazi Germany (exactly why she includes this aberration on the European body politic is unclear), and on Freud and certain literary figures, even though her discussion of Victorianism and women's movements deals with England and the United States. As a historical polemic, then, Millet's book is superb; but as history, it is flawed. We learn something about individual authors and about general social attitudes, while the total picture is far from complete.

Despite the flaws in both Millet's and Mill's sense of history, no historian of women can fail to take into account the significant thesis which both works present. Implicit in Millet and explicit in Mill is the notion that the position of the woman has been, historically, comparable to the position of the slave. (Indeed, Mill even argues that slaves were better off because after their labors were done they had free time and because the female slave who repelled her master's advances had strong community sentiment in her favor. Women, Mill argues, were accorded neither right.) Ought the history of women be the history of another form of slavery? Will the historians of women find the most important models for their work in the sophisticated studies of American Negro slavery and racial prejudice that are now available? The possibility is not farfetched. One might view the socialization of women, particularly before the twentieth century, like the rearing of the slave—as a combination of rewards and punishments designed to produce a simpleminded subordinate. One might reason that, like the slave, the woman was given domestic labor or childbearing as her duty, was encouraged to become religious as a way of learning fortitude and to read novels for sublimation, and was denied the education that might have provided self-realization. With regard to the twentieth century, the historian might emphasize repression rather than liberation, as Millet does, and view male chauvinist attitudes as being as deeply imbedded in the human psyche as racial prejudice. Is the history of women, as Mill's and Millet's works imply, in reality the history of men—of male attitudes, male schemes, and male manipulations?

An alternative hypothesis is equally feasible. In the first place, power is a dynamic relationship, and it is reasonable to assume that, over time, those who possess power will be influenced in new directions by their subordinates. American slavery was not a static institution: It had a history. And so have women. How do we explain, for example, the appearance of the doctrine of courtly love in the twelfth century which, no one denies, women introduced? Did it represent an incipient feminism growing out of the decline of patriarchal institutions in the high Middle Ages? Did it have any impact on women's role expectations or men's attitudes, or were both sexes able to regard it as simply another manifestation of women's proper role as the guardians of the emotions and all nobler virtues? In the second place, anyone familiar with the literature on slavery knows that there are different ways to approach the problem once the fundamental legal and traditional liabilities of the bondservant are granted. Either the slaves were content with their lot; or the system had forced them to undergo an extreme psychological adjustment which produced acceptance of their condition; or they were continually in rebellion against their fate, whether through running away or through direct or subtle attempts to sabotage the system. The same possibilities exist for the history of women.

Some women's historians would take the third alternative. The most important of these is Mary Beard, who, in her provocative and largely ignored study, *Woman as Force in History* (New York, 1946), argued that from the Middle Ages to the twentieth century there were many informal arguments and conflicting traditions whereby legal and social anti-feminism could be bypassed and that many women had directly defied the myths of female inferiority to hold positions of power or, as able politicians, were able to manipulate power through men.[1] Most histories, she implied, have been flawed because historians were not interested in taking the female factor into account. (Interestingly, Millet overlooks Beard's book—an astounding oversight which leads her to some questionable conclusions about, among other things, the operation of the common law doctrine of *femme couverte* in the United States. Millet bases her conclusions largely, or so it appears, on Mill's discussion of the subject in *The Subjection of Women*.)

Within the slave analogy, Beard's work offers some interesting possibilities. We have no idea, for example, of the extent to which women of past ages tried to escape from unhappy marriages, either through divorce or through some other expedient. We do not know the number of women who chose to remain single rather than enter the married state, which, under the common law, made them legally chattels of their husbands. Nor do we know how many women, after the death of a husband, chose to maintain the role of widowhood which, for the woman of some means, provided much freedom. Under the common law the widow, as *femme sole*, could manage her

1 See also Gerda Lerner, "New Approaches to the Study of Women in American History," *Journal of Social History*, III (1969), 53–62.

own property, was entitled by dower right to one-third of her husband's estate, and had relative social freedom since she was no longer a virgin. Indeed, we do not know to what extent the various life experiences of the woman changed her perspective about herself and her role. House slaves, field slaves, and slaves in the cities made various kinds of psychological adjustments to their condition: Is such variety observable among women on a geographic, class, and ethnic basis?[2] Furthermore, as Beard makes clear, we have no systematic idea as to how many women took on roles other than that of wife and mother. Nor do we know to what degree women with extended roles affected the role definition of their entire society. What impact, for example, did a queen have on the women in her society? Was the institution simply an atavism dating back to primitive mother cults, or did women throughout English society, for example, identify in a special way with Elizabeth, Anne, and Victoria?

It is clear at this point that the most significant advances in understanding the history of women will be made by those historians who, while taking both the Millet-Mill and the Beard hypotheses into account, are able to find some more neutral ground from which to proceed. At the moment, it seems to me that role analysis offers the most fruitful method: Historians ought to chart the definitions of women's roles, the ways in which women have acted out those roles, and the changes in their definitions over time. The task is not an easy one, for what other member of society has had available such a wide variety of parts to play—virgin, spinster, wife, mother, widow, courtesan, queen, and lady, in addition to other roles commonly defined as masculine, such as intellectual, professional, or innovator?

An excellent introduction to the ways in which the historian might proceed is provided by Emily James Putnam, who, in *The Lady: Studies of Certain Significant Phases of Her History*, traced the origins, characteristics, and development of that complex female role which,

2 In the final analysis, however, if the slave analogy proves to be too weak for any consistent application, at least a glance at recent studies of American slavery ought to point women's historians toward the comparative dimension. We know, for example, a good deal about the women's suffrage movement in England and America, but almost nothing about any similar movement on the continent. What does continental feminism, or the lack of it, tell us about Anglo-American feminism? What different roles did continental women play in comparison with their Anglo-American counterparts? Historians of comparative slavery have come to two valuable conclusions: first, that actual social arrangements often differed from those prescribed by the slave laws; and second, that the nature of slavery varied widely from country to country and even from region to region. It is conceivable that the same has been true for women.

on the one hand, tied most women more firmly to their dependent status and, on the other hand, offered some women a way of escape. The lady could be, according to Putnam, a woman of leisure whose conspicuous consumption bespoke her husband's status; or she could be a woman of grace and refinement whose very being was a reflection of humankind's natural drive for beauty; or she could be a forceful woman whose independence was rooted in the echoes of the Amazonian tradition that lingered on from primitive times. Status, aesthetics, and feminism all played a part in her creation. Historically, the three elements of the role were combined in various ways: According to Putnam, the lady abbess of the Middle Ages was above all a feminist, the woman of the Renaissance an aesthete. The French *salonière* of the eighteenth century paid much attention to status and aesthetics and little attention to feminism, while her eighteenth-century English counterpart, the much-maligned bluestocking, may have been ludicrous in her striving after art and beauty, but she made articulate elite Englishwomen ever after self-conscious of their role as women.

The ease with which Putnam's historical periods fall into place, and her use of impressionistic rather than analytic data, makes the modern historian suspicious of her whole scheme. Putnam was herself a spirited feminist, and her personal identification with the lady abbesses and the bluestockings is clear. Yet in a number of ways her book points to the future: not only in her investigation of a significant female role, but also, for example, in her attempts to relate the history of the lady to the houses in which she lived and the styles of dress she wore. Finally, Putnam makes clear her belief that the history of women is much more complicated than the history of men, for male roles are free of the complexities that a subordinate position necessitates. A man—whether bachelor or father, widower or gentleman—is always primarily a man. A woman, on the other hand, is defined by the role she plays.

Putnam ends her book with a brief discussion of the lady of the plantation in the American South; Anne Firor Scott, in *The Southern Lady*, begins her discussion at this point and traces her subject through various phases of her history to 1930. Scott's book is brief, general, and unsatisfying, and it may be that a subject of such complexity cannot be dealt with in so short a space. Her main theme is that because of the impact of the new roles that women assumed during the Civil War and in various socially acceptable reform movements, like temperance, after the war, the southern lady was psychologically able to cast off her acceptance of an inferior role and to take up whatever influential positions interested and were available to her. But is this the entire story? Scott provides us with stimulating and new analyses of the importance of temperance and Methodist missions in raising southern female consciousness; she also charts a new direction in her convincing argument that southern progressivism in the 1920s did not die— because women carried on the reform tradition. But the reader has little sense of the numbers and kinds of ladies involved (other than that they came largely from the cities). One would assume, and Scott herself admits, that the number of female activists in the South was small. What about the majority of ladies who defined their role in a more traditional way? Does belonging to a ladies' club necessarily make one a progressive? What reinforcements did women receive from doctors, from ladies' magazines, and from the male world? What was the impact of the so-called "sexual revolution" of the early twentieth century in the South? Was female activism and a possibly new sexuality related in any way to the southern paranoia about blacks in the 1890s and 1910s? Scott has provided us with an interesting analysis of one aspect of the role of the southern lady; but the full specifications of the part are missing.

Similarly, Scott's discussion of the lady of the plantation misses some analytic possibilities. She stresses, as have Putnam and other authors, the "orientalism" of the female role and the heavy responsibilities the wife bore for managing the plantation. She investigates the question of female sensuality and argues on the basis of a limited number of diaries that many women did enjoy sex. But what about the impact of Victorian attitudes on the South? She takes up the issue of male cohabitation with female slaves and concludes that wives knew about it and did not like it. But did it not have a damaging psychological effect on women's attitudes towards themselves, their husbands, and their slaves? She argues that the existing evidence proves that some marriages were happy and some unhappy, but she fails to investigate the evidence that court records and census figures might provide. For the eighteenth century, Julia Spruill, in *Woman's Life and Work in the Southern Colonies* (Chapel Hill, 1938), found as many advertisements in southern newspapers for runaway wives as for runaway slaves. Did this end in the nineteenth century? Above all, Scott fails to take any comparative perspective into account. Was the lady in evidence only on large plantations, or did her role and expectations differ on small estates? Was her legal status in any way comparable to the slaves' and did she ever see it as such? Did her position in any way change in the 1830s, when the institution of slavery became more rigid? Was the lady in Virginia different in any way from the lady in, say, Mississippi or New Orleans?

Finally, Scott argues, again on the basis of a limited number of diaries, that most southern ladies disliked slavery and wanted it abolished. The reader is not convinced. Southern ladies may have remained close to mammies and domestic servants, but what about their attitude toward female concubines and male slaves? Were they not, as their husbands, afraid of the slaves' potential for violence? Did not the revolts of Toussaint l'Ouverture, Gabriel Prosser, and Nat Turner raise the specter, not only of destruction and death, but of rape? Does not the very uniqueness of Angelina and Sarah Grimké (the daughters of a prominent Charleston, South Carolina, slaveholding family who became major antislavery spokesmen in the north) prove that most women accepted the system and fulminated against it only in their most discontented moments? Scott has provided us with an introduction to the subject of the southern lady; a definitive analysis remains to be written.

Neither Scott nor Putnam are entirely successful at analyzing a significant role played uniquely by females. Similarly, Page Smith's *Daughters of the Promised Land* and David Kennedy's *Birth Control in America: The Career of Margaret Sanger* are off balance. Together they illustrate that the most serious problem in writing women's history is how to strike a sensitive balance between past and present concerns. In the case of Kennedy's book, the difficulty is not a major one. He has written an exemplary study of the development of an organization, although its major leader, Margaret Sanger, is somewhat lost in the midst of legislative battles and organizational intrigues. We learn a great deal about how an important progressive reform was brought to fruition, but we learn much less about the changing nature of women's roles. Where Kennedy's judgment goes astray, in particular, is in his insensitivity to certain feminist concerns. First, he cavalierly dismisses Sanger's primary emphasis on free sexuality as an antidote to human anxiety—an argument which, a modern feminist might retort, is as profound as it is partial. Second, in his criticism of Sanger as a leader, he fails to take into account the dominant anti-feminism in the face of which she forged her career. Granted, Sanger was a difficult personality; but is it then correct to argue, as Kennedy does, that she was wrong in refusing to relinquish her leadership of the birth control movement to a male doctor in order to gain the support of the obviously anti-feminist American Medical Association? Kennedy has written a good book, but his perspective is a male one.

The same criticism in much harsher terms can be directed against Smith's *Daughters of the Promised Land*. Here we have an extremely present-minded book, whose primary virtue is its combination of discussions of marriage and sexuality with a description of the more dramatic women's rights movement which previous histories of the American woman have stressed. Still, the full dimensions of women's roles are left unplumbed: Smith mentions little about the past and present legal status of women, nor does he tell us much about women of various ethnic groups, about women in the lower classes, or about women on the western frontier.

Two themes dominate the book. The first stresses that because of the rise of capitalism and the introduction of European social standards into America, the relative sexual freedom and job mobility allowed to women in the colonial period came to an end. An age of "great repression" ensued. This interpretation is not new (although it does make one pause again before Millet's failure to investigate the prehistory of the Victorian age). What is new is Smith's bold assertion that because of Victorian anti-feminism and sexual repression, most nineteenth-century marriages were failures. In most cases the husband was overworked and anxious, and the wife, although a devoted mother, was constantly ailing, "and soon went to seed." Whether or not such a thesis can ever be proved—and Scott wisely argues that it may be impossible—Smith fails to do so. To counter the few cases of unhappy marriages which Smith cites, like that of Elizabeth Cady and Henry Stanton, it is easy to refer to as many happy marriages, like that of Angelina Grimké and Theodore Weld. Nor does Smith provide us with any clue as to what Victorian partners expected from their marriages: If they consciously avoided sensuality, as Smith argues, why must we then assume that the lack of it cast a permanent blight on marriages? If we do not happen to like Victorian marriages, does that necessarily mean that the Victorians did not? The real question here is to what extent women—and men, too—had internalized within marriage the roles that their society expected. To what extent had "repression" (as interpreted by Smith) become a way of life? It took many decades before even urban dwellers began to cast off traditional moral and religious beliefs about the nature of marriage as a life-long institution, and to read contemporary concerns explicitly into the minds of nineteenth-century predecessors is to confuse the present with the past.

The second major theme of Smith's book is equally unsatisfactory. It is, in addition, insulting to the subjects of his study. Millet argues that women throughout history have been manipulated by men; Smith turns the argument on its head by contending that the energy for female emancipation originally came from men. According to him, most female activists gained their strength from strong fathers (hence the title of his book). The Beecher family, in which father Lyman Beecher dominated the lives of daughters Catharine and Harriet, was a paradigm for the entire century. Yet, in analyzing this theme, Smith makes no reference to the kind of evidence one would expect: What kinds of modern psychological data exist on the relationship between father and daughter and mother and daughter in female ego formation? Would most daughters in the nineteenth century have had by definition strong fathers, since the concept of patriarchy was still in force? To what degree were these daughters reacting, not to the strength of their fathers, but against the weakness of their mothers, in this new age of "repression"? At the very least, one expects some detailed collective biographical data; Smith bases his case—if my count is correct—on six examples.

It is not that Smith dislikes women, for he is careful to point out that modern society is lacking in those very emotional qualities which supposedly have always been a part of woman's nature. But, from a woman's perspective, his attitude is patronizing. Thus he contends that American men (which? how many? of what class?) did not like women, yet made them sentimental objects of devotion. And it was because of this male regard that women have been able to liberalize their situation in America. "The deep and profoundly American feeling that, in the vernacular, 'Nothing is too good for the little woman,' made it possible for women to emerge from their state of dependence" (93). If this is so, why did it take over a century for women to achieve the vote? And why is discrimination against women in male-dominated professions an open scandal? It is more reasonable, if regrettable, to argue that most men have bitterly fought against female emancipation. Moreover, Smith's attitude is made clearer in the two chapters of half-baked psychological and sociological analysis which close the book. Here we learn that women are intensely loyal, incapable of compromise, lovers of intrigue, and able to perform routine tasks better than men. They are good performers but bad politicians (could it be possible that no one would elect them to office?), and good cooks but not great chefs: the old clichés again!

Yet Kennedy's and Smith's difficulty in fully understanding their subjects is not a unique contemporary phenomenon. It is an important part of the limitations of Mill's *Subjection of Women*. One of the most interesting features of the new edition of this essay is that Rossi has astutely included three other essays long attributed to Mill and to Harriet Taylor (his lifelong confidante and eventually his wife) written in 1832 and 1851. The 1832 essays are replete with Victorian ideas, but the 1851 essay, while containing many of the ideas which Mill incorporated in the 1869 version, is more forceful and more radical. The significance here is, as Rossi definitely proves in her introduction, that Taylor, and not Mill, wrote the 1851 endeavor. From her female perspective, Taylor gives no quarter: men and women are equal, no more and no less. In contrast, Mill nearly gives away his case before it is won. He contends that even when they have job freedom, most women should choose marriage as their occupation, and, like Smith, he involves himself in a curious discussion of the differing abilities of men and women in which, while explaining away most differences on the basis of environment, he concludes that women's talents lie in the direction of the practical, not the imaginative. Such was the difficulty that even a liberal male like Mill had in rising above the male chauvinism of his day. It may be that we ask too much of today's historians when we hope they will triumph over the same old problem. But should we not?

Etienne van de Walle

Recent Approaches
to Past Childhoods

Parents and Children in History: The Psychology of Family Life in Early Modern France. By David Hunt (New York, Basic Books, 1970) 226 pp. $6.95

Children in English Society. Volume I: From Tudor Times to the Eighteenth Century. By Ivy Pinchbeck and Margaret Hewitt (Toronto, University of Toronto Press, 1969) 346 pp. $9.50

Presumably the point in asking a demographer to review two books on childhood in history is to ensure a fresh, interdisciplinary point of view. Demographic knowledge, however, can contribute little more than a realization of two basic facts: (1) mortality was much higher in the past, and therefore the risk of being orphaned or (from the parent's point of view) of losing a child in infancy was much greater prior to the nineteenth century than it is now; and (2) fertility also was much higher, and therefore a younger age distribution existed, and children made up a larger part of the population. The ramifications and consequences of these two facts are probably essential to an understanding of the past—although they hardly allow us to differentiate among all of the societies in that largest part (by far) of human history when mortality and fertility were high. And both books pay lip service to the reality of high mortality in their period. According to Hunt, "the fact that infants were so vulnerable . . . is the fundamental precondition which we of a more comfortable milieu must grasp if we are to understand what childhood was like in the seventeenth century" (117). Pinchbeck and Hewitt attribute "the preoccupation with death and sin" (300) that was so much a part of religious and cultural education in the 1700s partly to high infant mortality.

This does not go very far, and I must broaden the vantage point.

Etienne van de Walle is a Research Demographer at Princeton University. He co-authored *The Demography of Tropical Africa* (Princeton, 1968), and is completing a book entitled "The Female Population of France, 1801–1901," which concerns the decline of fertility in France.

As a social scientist, I shall insist on universe definition and representativeness of sources. Are the facts discussed truly characteristic of the period considered? Would they apply to other periods? Are they restricted to a small part of the universe (e.g., seventeenth-century France)?

Furthermore, by virtue of my status as an outsider, I shall be unfair to the volume by Pinchbeck and Hewitt on English children. Although it reflects an impressive amount of scholarship, to the non-historian it looks like a rather dull, nonintegrated enumeration of material. Except for a chapter on childhood and family in pre-Restoration England, comparable to some of Hunt's material on France, and one on child marriage, the book deals mostly not with childhood, but with welfare schemes involving children. The thesis of the book appears to be that Tudor England was paternalistic in its concern with children, while subsequent periods witnessed a failure of the early schemes and an increasingly critical degradation of the condition of poor children.

The book by Hunt, on the contrary, is a fascinating and controversial attempt to explain the child-rearing habits of a previous era. Such customs as swaddling, the resort to wet nurses by the upper classes, the function of marriage as a contract between families rather than between individuals, the role of whipping for "breaking in" the child: All of these seem to be alien to our notions of education. Hunt provides keys toward an understanding of French attitudes about childhood from psychoanalysis. The book is truly interdisciplinary. Hunt attempts to steer a course between the cultural relativism of the historian and the reductionism of psychoanalysis—between Ariès and Erikson. In particular, he uses Erikson's theory of stages in the development of the ego as an aid for the comprehension of seventeenth-century texts. He shows how parents, by their attitude toward education, had shaped their children, but he stops short of the final link that would have been most useful to historians—how did the particular education influence seventeenth-century society? Hunt very cautiously states: "We simplify the task of relating child-rearing to socio-historical issues by studying parental behavior" (20). Yet the author is the first to recognize this failure. (Here, as elsewhere, lucidity is one of the most engaging qualities of the book. I found repeatedly that points that I wanted to make had been shamelessly granted at a later point, and turned to advantage.)

In particular, Hunt is candid about the problems of sources and representativity. "The list of sources has one obvious weakness: it tells us only about a limited segment of seventeenth-century society" (7).

Much of the book is devoted to an analysis of Héroard's journal[1] from the point of view of Erikson's theory of child development. There is no doubt that the approach is fascinating, and it throws much light on this document. Héroard was a doctor attached to the person of the future Louis XIII from birth, and he left a detailed and candid account of every action of the royal child. The result is an extraordinary document about the extraordinary education of an extraordinary child, the dauphin of France. Hunt finds a number of details that fit into the Eriksonian scheme: He shows how the conflicts of the oral stage, of the anal stage, and, finally, of the onset of infantile sexuality were more or less successfully resolved in Louis' education. The diary has been widely quoted by scandal-seeking popularizers of history (e.g., Guy Breton, in his best selling series, *Histoires d'amour de l'histoire de France* [Paris, 1960], III). It is a classic (and probably highly unrepresentative) example of bawdy mores, and is full of incredible entries about the child's initiation to sex. One cannot help feeling that he was abused by the adults who were entrusted with his education, and exposed to shameless sexual play by them. Hunt notes rightly that the child was deeply affected by this education. "I am sure that careful analysis would enable us to follow the process whereby the child who was treated like a little pet by adults of the court grew up into the king known to contemporaries as Louis the Chaste" (174). In view of this suggestion, it seems that Hunt resorts to sophistry when he argues that Louis' upbringing allows us to generalize about children and parents in the seventeenth century. Although he states that he does not believe "that we can assume that the journal describes a representative sample of seventeenth-century sexual morality" (165), he then subtly turns the argument inside out. "If the evidence shows that, even in this free and licentious atmosphere, sex was a source of anxiety and conflict for both adults and children, it would necessarily follow that the same conclusion also applies to the rest of society, where mores were almost certainly more sober and conservative" (166). Again and again, his case rests on *a fortiori* arguments based upon the dauphin's upbringing. He suggests, for example, that infants in the seventeenth century had special problems in getting proper feeding. His evidence once again is largely drawn from Héroard's diary: The dauphin could find no adequate wet nurse for some time, and was famished. "Here, as elsewhere, the experience of the

[1] Jean Héroard (ed. Eud. Soulié and Ed. de Barthélemy), *Journal de Jean Héroard sur l'enfance et la jeunesse de Louis XIII (1601–1628)* (Paris, 1868), 2v., as cited in Hunt, *Parents and Children in History.*

most precious child in the kingdom enables us to imagine the even more somber circumstances of his less fortunate peers" (116). As a social statistician, I find this use of a sample of one shocking.

The book is concerned with the period between 1550 and 1700 in France and claims, at least by inference, some relevance to all social classes and regions of France. By the same token, it claims for seventeenth-century France some characteristics that are not generally common in pre-modern societies. For example, seventeenth-century England or fifteenth-century France would not fit into the same mold. Of course, it is easy to nitpick on such claims. In its laws and customs, its languages, and its religions, France under Henry IV was a mosaic of cultures; also, its social classes presented a vertical stratification which complicated the horizontal one of the regions. Furthermore, Hunt defines his periods rather sloppily. In one early discussion of Ariès' thesis, for example, he seems to agree with the following restatement: "In the Middle Ages, child care was one of the minor responsibilities of the extended family. Eventually a new institution . . . the collège was organized to share with the family the obligation of looking after children" (39). This text opposes the seventeenth century to the Middle Ages, a rather vague terminology—and the extended family, an ill-defined concept at best, rears its ugly head (as it does in the Pinchbeck and Hewitt volume).[2]

The risks inherent in generalization, and, at the same time, their necessity for intellectual syntheses, come to the fore in what is perhaps the most intriguing hypothesis proposed by Hunt for understanding seventeenth-century French society: namely, his view of a society torn by conflicts between the sexes and the generations. "Marriage was an institution rather than a companionship . . . a contract negotiated by two families" (57–58). On the one hand, Hunt appears to believe that the kinship system, which he says molded the character of the seventeenth-century family, was a remnant from the past—"the medieval and early modern period." On the other hand, he suggests that unique

---

2 I suspect specialists of one period are prone to oppose it to a somewhat mythical past. Edwige Peymans, a historian who is studying Latin encyclopedias and education manuals of the Middle Ages in Western Europe, pointed out that they never contain any evidence of the extended family as a frame of reference; they always refer to the relationship between the child and his parent (only one parent at that). And, when Ariès (and Hunt) refer to the role of the collèges (secondary schools) in taking over one of the family's functions, one must keep a sense of proportion and remember that even by the nineteenth century only a very small minority of the population of France was going to school at all.

demographic situations were in the making at the time: what Hajnal has called the European pattern of marriage.[3] Seventeenth-century culture knew no ways of rewarding "the good family man. ... Men in the families felt threatened, their self-respect compromised by the fact of being husbands and fathers" (176). Hunt may indeed have a case that this is characteristic of seventeenth-century France. One is struck by the number of attacks against marriage. They represent a cliché of the literature of the period. And it is possible that the trend is related to an increasing prevalence of celibacy and late marriage in Western Europe. Hunt views the family as an area of bitter conflicts. "The real trouble with marriage was that it subjected men to their wives" (73). One of the causes of conflict were children. The child was competing with the husband for the woman's presence and attention. Louis was hardly ever in contact with his mother because the king could afford to hire surrogates. But ordinary parents felt threatened by their children: first the father by rivals for his wife's possession, and later by potential contesters of his authority; the mother by the famished, bloodthirsty child's demands. (Medical opinion of the time held that mother's milk was actually whitened blood.) The children, because it was so difficult for them to get enough feeding, became "oral sadists" and prospered only at the expense of their mothers, who in return developed, according to Hunt, "a picture of the small child as a predatory animal and frightening creature harming the women whose duty it was to care for him" (121). Hunt sees this perception as a fundamental cause for the hiring of wet nurses. He admits that similar themes appear in other cultures. "At the same time, I believe that images of the child as a greedy little animal has a special power in the seventeenth century" (121–122). They would explain the reluctance of women of the upper classes to feed their own children, and, because they inhibited the supply of milk, the difficulty wet nurses had in coping with the appetite of their nurslings.

Hunt, however, fails to present convincing arguments that prove his "feeling" about the specificity of the seventeenth century in this respect. The custom of hiring wet nurses is something of a mystery. But it is not typical of the time. Arguments in favor of women nursing their own children (followed typically by a long list of advice on the choice of the nurse) were given by the Greek Soranos; they are given by Zola

---

3 John Hajnal, "European Marriage Patterns in Perspective," in D. V. Glass and D. E. C. Eversley (eds.), *Population in History: Essays in Historical Demography* (Chicago, 1965).

eighteen centuries later in *Fécondité*.[4] I suspect that the custom originated, not in the fear of the women, not in the husband's jealousy, but simply because it was widely accepted that a breast-feeding woman should not have sexual intercourse. As for the incapacity of nurses to cope with the appetite of the child, I see more likely explanations than a psychological inhibition. In most cases, the nurse had already weaned her own child. A law in 1762 forbade nurses from offering their services unless their own child was at least nine months old; parish studies indicate that this was the custom in earlier times. The supply of milk was often running out, the more so since some time may have elapsed between weaning and hiring out.

The rivalry of the child with his father is not a characteristic of seventeenth-century France. Hunt's generalizations, such as "whipping was an almost universal custom" (134), or about the emphatic and "unanimous insistence on the obedience of children as indispensable to the survival of society" (149) are not convincing. Educations tended to differ greatly. There are many texts preaching exactly the opposite, including Montaigne's description of his own permissive childhood.[5] (Pinchbeck and Hewitt tell us that the translation of Montaigne was influential in countering the abuse of whipping in England.) There is some exaggeration in stating that the terrorizing of children into submission was "a telling indictment of the Old Regime" (157). Fénelon, for one, was recommending "une éducation douce et patiente."[6]

In brief, I think that Hunt's historicism fails, and that he is not able to draw from scanty documents a characterization of seventeenth-century child-rearing habits. He is most successful when he shows that psychoanalysis provides keys to the understanding of historical events and texts (e.g., Héroard's journal). Hunt spends time clearing some issues of other historians' making, and that no layman in his right mind would ever have questioned. For example, Burgess[7] has suggested that there was no companionship in the marriages of the past; therefore, the author makes rather pathetic attempts at proving the obvious, namely

---

4 Emile Zola, *Les Quatre évangiles—Fécondité* (Paris, 1903). The future Mme. Roland, in the late eighteenth century, wanted to make it a condition in her marriage contract that her future husband would allow her to nurse. This was a post-Rousseauian attitude. In the late nineteenth century, Parisians imported thousands of nurses from the countryside, and sent thousand of babies to be nursed there.

5 Michel de Montaigne, *Essais* (Paris, 1969), I, Ch. 26.

6 [François de Salignac de La Mothe] Fénelon, *De l'éducation des filles* (Paris, n.d.), 18.

7 Ernest Burgess and Harvey Locke, *The Family: From Institution to Companionship* (New York, 1953).

that affection was not absent from the seventeenth-century marriage. Or, Ariès suggested that in the early modern period the kinship system was important in the education of children; Hunt concludes that the French kinship system was not structured. Finally, he is driven back to human constants, the limitations of marriage as an institution and the difficulty of finding perfect companionship within it, the weakness of the wife in the marital relationship, the conflict between generations, and the irreplaceable character of the parent-child relationship.

David J. Rothman

Documents in Search of a Historian: Toward a History of Childhood and Youth in America

Children and Youth in America: A Documentary History. Edited by Robert H. Bremner (Cambridge, Mass., Harvard University Press, 1970–71) I, 836 pp. $10.00

By exploring a new area of investigation, like the history of childhood and youth in America, we are forced to confront fundamental issues. What do we need to know if we are to write such a history? What issues must be resolved before we can determine whether the subject merits the attention of historians? What are the critical questions that must be answered if such categories are to become central to historical analysis?

First, and most obvious, do age groups in fact have histories? Have fundamental changes occurred in the experiences of children and youth from the colonial period to the present? Although at first the inquiry may seem a bit forced (surely something must have happened to them between 1607 and 1971), the matter is far from clear. There may be no way, for example, to trace changes in patterns of parental discipline. In the seventeenth century some fathers were lenient, others harsh; in the twentieth, the same holds true. Or take the question of youth culture. It is perfectly possible that seventeenth-century youths banded together with the same self-consciousness and frequency as did their urban counterparts several hundred years later. Because the *concept* of adolescence was invented only at the end of the nineteenth century is no indication that the *actual* experience of the young had changed. It is also unclear as to whether there have been shifts in the ages at which the young left home, took their first job, underwent religious initiation, adopted adult clothing, or married. As Philip Greven recently noted, it seems that the young left their father's household at

David J. Rothman is Professor of History at Columbia University and an Associate Editor of the JIH. He is the author of *Politics and Power: The United States Senate, 1869–1901* (Cambridge, Mass., 1966), and *The Discovery of the Asylum: Social Order and Disorder in the New Republic* (Boston, 1971).

about the same age in colonial Andover, Massachusetts as in post-Civil-War Union Park, Chicago.[1]

If changes did occur, however, what influences promoted them? What forces shaped the nature of childhood and youth? Were demographic shifts decisive? Did a reduction in the rates of infant mortality revolutionize parental attitudes and practices? Did the movement from farm to village to town to city prompt adults to adopt new styles of child-rearing, or encourage the child to assume a different stance toward the community? Were the most significant variables economic, with industrialization standing as a major divide in the history of childhood? Or did military organizations, educational theories, religious enthusiasm, or some combination, cause major shifts?

Equally important is an understanding of the significance of the stage of pre-adulthood in causing historical change. Do the young provoke change or reflect it? Is this notion a dependent variable which is interesting but ultimately of secondary importance to the historian's story, or an independent variable that is crucial to his analysis? What does a study of childhood attempt to explain? Is it a collection of trivia, or does it uncover elements essential to a history of society?

The books reviewed here touch on some of these points, but they are too few in number to answer many questions, and too flawed intellectually to stand as models. Wishy's *The Child and the Republic*[2] is an exercise in intellectual rather than social history. Using child-rearing literature and childrens' books, Wishy focuses exclusively on the "debate about child nurture," between 1830 and 1900, and not on the child himself. He finds changes in attitudes, but fails to present a convincing explanation for the changes, or an understanding of their implications. Nor does he inform us about the actualities of childhood in these years, which puts us in the position of trying to recreate the battle of Gettysburg by reading only Karl von Clausewitz.

Certainly we cannot fault Demos' *A Little Commonwealth*[3] for not trying to recreate the actualities of childhood. His examination of family life in the Plymouth colony is based upon the designs and architectural remains of the houses and their furnishings, demographic data,

1 An interesting conference at Princeton University in April, 1971, organized by John Gillis and devoted to childhood and youth, was the occasion for these remarks. The conference also helped me to conceptualize many of the issues raised here.

2 Bernard Wishy, *The Child and the Republic: The Dawn of American Child Nurture* (Philadelphia, 1968).

3 John Demos, *A Little Commonwealth: Family Life in Plymouth Colony* (New York, 1970).

styles of dress, and the content of wills; much of the argument depends on psychological theory. But his observations are admittedly speculative, and his results are so thin and inconclusive that they intensify a nagging fear that a history of childhood may well be impracticable.

Demos describes the typical environment surrounding the newborn infant: "for his first year or so a baby had a relatively comfortable and tranquil time" (134). To support this idea, he notes that the houses were usually small, the clothing light, and the infants breast-fed.[4] But these same facts lead just as easily to an opposite conclusion: Since the household was small and the mother burdened with many duties, the infant always seemed underfoot; breast feeding was rushed and impersonal, at the mother's convenience. The noise level in the house was high (with people working, eating, playing, and visiting), so that the baby slept fitfully and was frequently startled; when he added his own cries to the din, he was perfunctorily moved or attended to.

Demos then describes the dramatic consequences of weaning between the infant's first and second year, generally compounded by the probable arrival of a second child, and a new paternal insistence, backed by social and religious doctrines, on breaking the child's will. Demos posits, through Erikson's theories on aggression, a pattern of indulgence-severity in infancy that affected adult behavior. The result of this childhood syndrome was that Plymouth's citizens were prone to take each other to court with incredible regularity. But might it not be that other siblings took an increased interest in the growing infant, so that in fact the household was more pleasant for him as he matured? And the resorting to courts could be explained by any number of other influences including the need to rely upon formal mechanisms to settle disputes because comity was important. Many historians have experienced that middle-of-the-night panic when contemplating how thin a line sometimes separates their work from fiction. But on this score the study of childhood seems especially nerve-racking, threatening to turn us all into novelists.

A third approach to the field may be found in Sennett's *Families Against the City*[5], which utilizes quantitative data on family size and social mobility. Analyzing manuscript census data between 1850 and 1880 for Chicago's Union Park, Sennett contends that a decline in family size led to internal family tensions that ultimately weakened the

4 *Ibid.*, Ch. 9.
5 Richard Sennett, *Families Against the City: Middle Class Homes of Industrial Chicago, 1872–1890* (Cambridge, Mass., 1970).

sons' ability to master the external environment. Yet the quantitative data are often skimpy (in that Sennett generalizes from a handful of cases), several of his procedures are dubious (as when he sets up a "traditional" upper middle-class extended family from one diary), the thoroughness of his research is questionable (surely there were some voluntary associations in Union Park, and the schools must have exerted some influence), and we are finally asked to accept the idea of an injurious small family dynamic without a shred of internal supporting evidence. Even if one grants that children from smaller families were not upwardly mobile, that their fathers actually behaved as Sennett claims they did—in that they were jealous of their children and unable to guide them intelligently in life choices—the entire hypothesis remains speculative. There is less reason to believe that one of Union Park's larger families—typically bigger because a maiden aunt lived with it—would have helped a youngster to adjust. The data are on one side, and the child in the family on the other—with no connection between them.

Despite the many methodological and substantive difficulties apparent in the literature, historians are understandably reluctant to quit the field. It seems too important. Well aware of the work in other social science disciplines in which childhood in particular and socialization in general is so crucial an element, they cannot help but wonder about the effects of childhood and family training on the structure of past societies, and about the changes that have occurred. Given the vast bibliographies compiled in psychological, anthropological, and sociological research, historians would have to be intellectual recluses to avoid pursuing the subject. The unprecedented energy now being devoted to social history also makes this area a prime candidate for investigation. If, to date, failures outnumber advances, that would seem to be the price for asking new questions.

The newest and in many ways most ambitious venture in this area is a documentary history, *Children and Youth in America*, compiled under the direction of Robert Bremner. Volume I, upon which I will focus here, takes the subject from 1600 to 1865. Volume II, whose appearance is imminent, will bring the story to 1932, and Volume III will come to the present. This is no ordinary gathering of documents. The size of Volume I alone makes that obvious—813 double-columned pages of handsomely printed text. Most of the space goes to the documents themselves, but introductions to the various sections and subsections of the book put the material into context.

The project was funded by the Children's Bureau, with the specific charge to update Grace Abbott's *The Child and the State* (Chicago, 1947; 2v.). Helping Bremner were three associate editors, a five-man executive committee, two editorial assistants, thirty-one research assistants, and thirty-six advisers. Given the obviously large expenditure of energy, one approaches the volume with keen anticipation. It might well supply a broad structure and interpretation, bringing some coherence to the study of the child. To be sure, its mandate was more limited, but surely the project intended to do more than add a few recent documents to Abbott's book.

Bremner's preface defines the focus of the volume narrowly: The collection will not treat the history of children and youth in America, but the history of public policy toward them. The differentiation is certainly intellectually valid, and one can trace public policy without entering directly into the actualities of family life or child behavior. But Bremner does not maintain this distinction. The premises underlying the organization of the volume, as well as the substance of many of the documents reprinted, reveal a major concern with the experience of the family and the child in America.

The scope and perspective of the volume emerge clearly in its periodization. Bremner divides the story into three stages. First, between 1600 and 1735, the child was the subject not the citizen of the family. The father was master and the child was to serve both him and the state. Child-rearing practices were rigid, intended to secure the immediate and complete submission of the child to parental will. By 1735, however, in practice but not in theory, New World conditions had undermined this scheme. Following the interpretations of Handlin and Bailyn,[6] Bremner argues that the wilderness and the availability of land quickly began to liberate the child from external controls. Then, in the next period (1735–1820), the child, although still officially subject to family authority, increasingly practiced the doctrines of self-help, independence, and self-interest. He became more and more autonomous, and concomitantly the family's influence weakened. The trends evident in the era of settlement continued to gather momentum under the influence of Enlightenment thought, the Great Awakening,

6 See Oscar Handlin's opening chapter in James M. Smith (ed.), *Seventeenth Century America: Essays in Colonial History* (Chapel Hill, 1959); Bernard Bailyn, *Education in the Forming of American Society: Needs and Opportunities for Study* (Chapel Hill, 1960). For an elaboration of this point, see David J. Rothman, "A Note on the Study of the Colonial Family," *William and Mary Quarterly*, XXIII (1966), 627–634.

the American Revolution, and the spread of the idea of progress. Each of these elements encouraged the intellectual acceptance of the child as worthy and promoted the social conditions under which he could exercise a wide degree of initiative. Even the nascent industrialism of New England worked to the same end, with the mills decreasing still further the power of the family. What the wilderness began the factories continued. Sensing a possible discrepancy in treating industrialism as part of a story of child liberation, Bremner notes that "one can only speculate on the impact of factory labor on the independence of child workers. The meager wages earned went into the family pocket." Still, he insists, "the factory experience occasionally produced experts at an early age" (148).

In the third period, 1820 to 1865, the child was part of a society undergoing extensive political and social change whose sum effects, Bremner concedes, were varied and elusive. "No brief formula adequately explains or summarizes the varieties of family and child life that existed in the United States by the early nineteenth century." What did the slave child, immigrant child, slum child, frontier child, and plantation child have in common? Yet, after issuing this warning, Bremner elaborates the line of argument developed earlier. Labeling this section "The American Child," he contends that for the middle classes the principles of individualism, *laissez-faire*, and democracy permeated not only the economy, the government, and the church, but the family as well, with revolutionary results. "The Western world had not seen the like of the American family before," or the like of the American child. He was, in essence, "a new creature," the culmination of 200 years of New World history. Having once been the subject of the family, the child was now "independent, individualistic." The family which had once treated him as a servant now made his welfare its preeminent goal (343–346).

The critical assumption underlying this framework is that there was an appropriate, convenient, and beneficial match between the evolution of American society and the family. In this interpretation the family reflects without distortion the triumph of freedom and democracy that transformed other institutions. The history of the child is the victory of liberty over dictatorship, of opportunity over rigidity, and of initiative over authority. The child is the quintessential American, and no other story better exemplifies the triumph of republicanism. The decline of the father's influence in the household coincides with the decline of the prerogatives of the crown and the royal governor in politics. They all represented unbridled and autocratic authority at the top of hierarchical structures, and all of them succumbed to republican principles and a fluid social order. The only lamentable fact is that not all social classes were equally affected: Indian, immigrant, and slave children did not share in these changes—just as their parents did not enjoy the same political or social privileges as native-born whites. Nevertheless, for the middle classes—those Americans who were not immigrants, or red, or black—the story of the child is the story of liberation, and one worthy of celebration.

But the problem is that we have gone far beyond this facile and triumphant interpretation in our study of other institutions. Apply the key elements in the family framework to politics or economics, and its simplifications become immediately apparent. An equivalent argument in political history would suggest that the seventeenth-century colonies took the first steps to liberty (the Puritan charter? Bacon's Rebellion?), that developments proceeded predictably and smoothly into the 1700s leading inevitably to the victory of republican principles first in the Revolution, and then by steady stages through the Jacksonian period. The economy ostensibly followed an identical course: State authority in the marketplace began to weaken in the seventeenth century and declined still further in the eighteenth; *laissez-faire* triumphed, again smoothly and predictably, in the nineteenth. Although these contentions are not without some basis in historical reality, and are not completely unreasonable, modern scholarship has made our sense of them far more complex. Few serious researchers would insist that these developments emerged without major conflicts; nor would they be so certain that political and economic developments were ultimately to the best interests of everyone in the society, that there were only gains, no losses. Were Jacksonians the great democrats? Was colonial Massachusetts a middle-class democracy? The matter is more complex and major qualifications are in order. Yet the history of children and youth is in so rudimentary a state that what passes as too simplistic in other areas here remains the basic structure of interpretation. The field, by a measure of equivalency, is still in the hands of a George Bancroft.

But not altogether. For all of the weaknesses and methodological limitations of the recent studies, several do highlight the inadequacies of traditional interpretations. The work of Greven is a case in point.[7] Meticulously tracing the transfer of land in colonial Andover, he

7 Philip J. Greven, Jr., *Four Generations: Population, Land, and Family in Colonial Andover, Massachusetts* (Ithaca. N.Y., 1970),

attempts to use the resultant data to interpret father-son relations. He remains very much on the outside looking in, recreating family dynamics from external behavior. The links between the deeding or willing of land and the exercise of personal authority in the household are weakly forged since substantive evidence is lacking. Nevertheless, Greven does make clear that the interests of fathers and sons frequently diverged, and that a fundamental tension over the transfer of land pervaded these colonial families. Moreover, he argues persuasively that the father's authority did not automatically or rapidly decline in the 1600s. Although it had probably weakened by the mid-1700s, the decisive element was not the munificence of life in the New World but the growing shortage of town land. Crowded settlements rather than open wilderness may have reduced paternal prerogatives.

The image of family life that emerges from the Demos and Sennett studies also points to conflict and maladaptation. Demos argues that family training in Plymouth (e.g., the vacillation between permissiveness and rigid discipline for the infant) did not prepare the child well for community life. As adults, citizens were constantly at odds with one another. And, if his contentions remain speculative, they still undermine the facile assumption that family dynamics conformed to social needs in the colonial period.

Sennett's work is perhaps the most self-conscious attack on the notion that the American family served its children and its society well. He vigorously disputes the idea of the functionalism of the nuclear family. And although he is more polemical than convincing, his work does stand as an important corrective to the bland and equally unsubstantiated optimism inherent in the traditional viewpoint.

The more one reads in this field, the more apparent it becomes that the history of childhood and youth is central to the study of social change. The many documents that Bremner collects are filled with pertinent information, and he and his assistants have made extraordinary efforts to bring to light relevant archival and published sources. They have reprinted fascinating excerpts from the original records of the New York House of Refuge and included little-known but important selections on early factory life from the papers of Samuel Slater. They have also been acutely aware of the fate of minorities. Moreover, the kinds of materials they omit—descriptions or pictures of artifacts, and demographic data—are available elsewhere. Ultimately, all of these documents will find historians. Almost certainly the new works will devote greater attention to the dysfunctional elements, to the conflict of interests, and to the tensions in the story. Precisely at the points of stress and opposition, childhood and youth become germane to an analysis of social change.

Among the problems that most demand a new perspective is the exercise of parental authority. Bremner and others connect a decline in the influence of the parent to the democratization of American society; ostensibly everyone acquiesced in the change for it fitted so well into other developments. Bremner delights in the story of Frederick Marryat, a visitor to the U.S. in the Jacksonian period, who witnessed an incident in which an American child steadfastly refused to obey his parents; his father's reaction was to inform Marryat that the boy was "a sturdy republican," all the while "smiling at the boy's resolute disobedience" (344).

But, in fact, the interaction between the young, the family, and the community provoked much greater strain and dissension than this interpretation allows. In the colonial period, and lasting well into the 1700s, family and community were so intertwined that one cannot talk of children escaping parental authority without considering whether this also meant a rejection of community values. The family's charge was to make children serviceable to their generation and God-fearing Christians, and to fulfill such wider obligations as boarding the poor, educating and caring for apprentices, and managing delinquents. So what does it mean to describe a gradual weakening of parental influence in the colonial years? The child practiced self-help and self-interest, declares Bremner. But the other side of the coin may have been a disregard of the general welfare for narrow private ends. We must recognize that such change would have been controversial, and that the community and the parents would have done battle with the young over it. Coercion, conflict, and a divergence of goals might have been more integral to these events than grand celebration.

Indeed, there is much evidence to suggest that paternal authority had not simply withered away by the end of the Jacksonian period. Perhaps the most obvious manifestation of its survival appears in the lower-class families of both immigrants and natives. The interests of the father and the child clearly diverged, and the father usually won. The youngster's self-interest dictated a fairly lengthy schooling period, while the father preferred an immediate cash return and put him to work as quickly as possible. The father's victory brought a greater accumulation of property to the family, but a life in unskilled or semi-skilled jobs to the youngster.

In the middle classes, too, parental authority may have maintained itself through a shift in tactics. The manipulation of the child, rather than his outright coercion, became more prevalent in Jacksonian America—and this change was not a necessary concomitant of democracy warranting the fulsome applause of historians. We cannot assume that every remark in a child-rearing manual recommending affection represents progress for the child or for the society. The normative literature of the period insisted that strict obedience be the ultimate goal of parental training, but now authors had a wider variety of fresh strategies to recommend before resorting to the rod. Although they counseled greater displays of affection than their eighteenth-century counterparts, they were no less insistent on denying the child autonomy.

Even more compelling is the evidence pointing to a war between the community and the young, which contradicts any simple notion of a neat fit between the child and the state. The spread of common schools, the erection of houses of refuge, the multiplication of orphan asylums, and the nature of college training did not necessarily indicate improvements and reforms. The coercive elements in the pre-Civil-War common schools, both in practice and in concept, are so obvious that it is a testimony to the strength of democratic ideology that historians could ignore them for so long. An element of social control runs through almost everything that Horace Mann wrote. The houses of refuge and orphan asylums were an overt attempt to infantilize the young, to put delinquents, vagrants, and the homeless into a rigid and disciplined environment where they would acquire the obedience that their parents had failed to inculcate. Behind these institutions was the assumption that any manifestation of public disorder in the young was evidence of future depravity. The behavior that a later generation (G. Stanley Hall's) would diagnose as part of a stage of youthful storm and stress, and therefore to be tolerated, was labeled deviant and suppressed by Americans in the Jacksonian period. Universities were also more intent on socializing the young than educating them—and were not particularly successful in either task. To judge from all of these materials, it is hardly accurate to posit a fundamental harmony between the family, the community, and the young.[8]

8   These themes emerge in Stephan Thernstrom, *Poverty and Progress: Social Mobility in a Nineteenth Century City* (Cambridge, Mass., 1964); Michael B. Katz, *The Irony of Early School Reform: Educational Innovation in Mid-Nineteenth Century Massachusetts* (Cambridge, Mass.,1968); Oscar and Mary Handlin, *The American College and the American Culture: Socialization as a Function of Higher Education* (New York, 1970). They are also elaborated in my study, *TheDiscovery of the Asylum: Social Order and Disorder in the New Republic* (Boston,1971).

Other crucial shifts occurred, but their import is lost when historians focus so exclusively on the theme of family democratization. It seems that many institutions affecting the young, from the school to the church to the reformatory, were more carefully and precisely age-graded in the Jacksonian period than before. Traditional interpretations view this phenomenon as evidence of an increasing sensitivity to the various stages of childhood and youth, and another step in the rise of child welfare. But there is a darker side that should not be so completely ignored. Age-grading may have been part of an effort to lock-step the child into rigid and predetermined modes of behavior. The change looked not to his benefit, but to the rationalization of childhood so that behavior would become more predictable and manageable. This altered perspective raises questions about the ideology and reality of social order and disorder, and leads to the general issue of social change. As soon as one drops the assumption that innovation equals reform, that men of good will invariably took the next and logical step to maximize child welfare—that the history of the child in America is one of uninterrupted progress—then this field becomes even more critical for the social historian.

Similarly, one cannot assume that the norms set down in the child-rearing literature or actually inculcated by the family were invariably appropriate for community needs. Is there not enough evidence of friction and maladaptation in American society to make historians skeptical? Was the emphasis on rigid training, order, obedience, rote learning, and bell-ringing punctuality in the schools and asylums of the period, and to some degree in the families as well, necessarily functional for all social classes? It is true that we lack social and psychological theories that unambiguously relate childhood experiences to adult behavior—but our ignorance still makes it at least as appropriate to search for discontinuities as well as neat matches.

It may be difficult for historians to perceive the family as a coercive institution or the community as warring on its young. And perhaps this is not the essential component of the American story. But if we do not explore this theme, if we insist on making progress the exclusive ingredient in our analyses, we are certain to be left with more questions than answers.

James A. Henretta

The Morphology of New England Society in the Colonial Period

A Little Commonwealth: Family Life in Plymouth Colony. By John Demos (New York, Oxford University Press, 1970) 201 pp. $6.75

Four Generations: Population, Land, and Family in Colonial Andover, Massachusetts. By Philip J. Greven, Jr. (Ithaca, Cornell University Press, 1970) 329 pp. $12.50

A New England Town: The First Hundred Years, Dedham, Massachusetts, 1636–1736. By Kenneth A. Lockridge (New York, W. W. Norton, 1970) 208 pp. $6.95

Peaceable Kingdoms: New England Towns in the Eighteenth Century. By Michael Zuckerman (New York, Alfred A. Knopf, 1970) 329 pp. $7.95

For nearly three-quarters of a century the colonial history of New England has been organized around a single dominant theme: the erosion of traditional English institutions, customs, and ideas by the corrosive force of the American wilderness. For the intellectual as much as for the social historian, for Perry Miller no less than for Frederick Jackson Turner, the theme of disintegration, of declension, provided a generalization that was at once elemental in its force, striking in its simplicity, and nationalistic in its impact. The story was simply told: Medieval Englishmen of peasant stock and deep religious beliefs came to the New World intent upon transplanting a traditional communal society to new soil; instead, they were transformed by the American environment. A new type of society was created as the culture of the past was rendered irrelevant by the primitive logic of necessity, and as the constricting social and psychological bonds of the pre-modern world were dissolved by the corrosive forces of nature. This long silent revolution took an explicitly political form in the war for independence, itself the logical culmination of a century and a half of social change.

James A. Henretta is the author of *Salutary Neglect: Colonial Administration Under the Duke of Newcastle, 1724–1754* (Princeton, forthcoming), and has taught history at the University of Sussex and Princeton University. He wishes to thank James M. Banner, Jr. for his comments on an earlier draft of this essay. Bernard Bailyn suggested the concept of a "social morphology" but should not be held responsible for the way this theme is developed here.

Interpretations of this process might differ, but the thrust was the same. The society which appeared in the northern states in the aftermath of revolution was not a positive creation—the end product of the organic growth of a coherent social system. It was the individualistic residue, an atomistic congeries of "new men," which remained in the aftermath of the decay and dissolution of the traditional social fabric of European civilization.

The essay which follows constitutes an extended critique of this "negative" approach to the American past. It builds upon the work of four young historians who have brought the assumptions and techniques of modern social science to bear upon the history of the colonial period. Ultimately, it attempts to make more explicit certain aspects of their findings and to place their results within a common framework. This takes the form of a more positive vision of historical change, a morphology of societal evolution which, like its biological counterpart, seeks an organic explanation for the changing form and structure of colonial society.[1]

Of the four books under review, Lockridge's history of Dedham, Massachusetts conforms most closely to the traditional accounts. If this is not obvious at first sight, it is because Lockridge has translated the old arguments, with their overtones of Darwinian environmentalism, into the language of the modern anthropologist. For fifty years after its foundation in 1636, the author tells us, Dedham was essentially a "Closed Corporate Peasant Community," very similar to those which have formed the substructure of agricultural societies in all parts of the world in many ages. As such, this tightly-knit community of Puritan saints carefully restricted its membership, maintained close control over the distribution and alienation of land, and enforced common standards of behavior:

> The tendency of medieval peasants to look on the villages of an imaginary golden past as their model for the future regeneration of society was repeated in the Puritan idealization of the communes of the primitive Christian church and in the use of these communes as a model for some features of Dedham's organization. . . . Whatever the exact nature of the mixture, Dedham was at once a Puritan and a peasant utopia. [20, 21]

1 For Emile Durkheim, "social morphology" consisted of the study of the environmental basis of social organization and the investigation of population, especially its size, density, and spatial distribution. It is in these senses that the term is used here. The best introduction to the concept of social morphology is Leo F. Schnore, "Social Morphology and Human Ecology," *American Journal of Sociology*, LXIII (1958), 620–635.

This argument is dramatic, but distorted. In this instance, as in others, Lockridge consciously sacrifices historical detail and complexity in his search for the striking generalization and the simplifying concept. In precisely what sense were the first Massachusetts towns "peasant" communities when, as Lockridge himself tells us, they were settled by families drawn "from the broad ranks of the English middle classes"; when the initial inhabitants were complete strangers to each other; and when nearly one-third of the original settlers of Dedham eventually lived in at least three different New England towns? To fashion an *enduring* peasant society from the heterogeneous members of a geographically-mobile middle class would have been an accomplishment. In point of fact, the intense religious ideology which prompted the migration from England was simply not strong enough to recreate the type of community which could only be held together by unconscious assumptions and traditional practices. Within the lifetime of the first generation the open field system had vanished, the nuclear pattern of settlement had been challenged, the control of the original proprietors seriously shaken, and membership in the church reduced to a minority of the inhabitants. From the beginnings of settlement there was an inherent dynamism in these New England communities which made them very different from their medieval counterparts.

For all of its superficial brilliance, Lockridge's interpretation is so schematized, so highly conceptualized, and so removed from the reality it purports to explain, that at times it seems more like arbitrary invention than serious history. Those who came to America were peasants neither in condition nor in consciousness. They were the products of a country already in the process of dramatic social and demographic change. As the work of E. A. Wrigley, Laslett, Stone, and others has demonstrated, the years between 1500 and 1620 were marked by a doubling of the population of England and Wales, extensive enclosures and a remarkably active land market, considerable geographical mobility, and the disruption of traditional economic alignments and social patterns by a sustained rise in prices.[2] In short, the England from which the settlers of Dedham came was at the end of a century-long process of transition which had largely destroyed the earlier peasant society. By

2 See, for example, Peter Laslett, *The World We Have Lost* (New York, 1965); Peter Laslett and John Harrison, "Clayworth and Cogenhoe," in H. E. Bell and R. L. Ollard (eds.), *Historical Essays, 1600–1750, Presented to David Ogg* (London, 1963), 157–184; Lawrence Stone, "Social Mobility in England, 1500–1700," *Past and Present*, XXXIII (1966), 16–55.

1641, as Rich has pointed out, "only 16% of our agricultural population had a hundred years in the same village behind them."[3]

Lockridge's analysis of Dedham is nearly as questionable as his description of its antecedents. Take the matter of chronology. The first half of the book, entitled "A Utopian Commune," carries the story to 1686. Upon inspection, however, it becomes clear that this choice of a date is the result of the author's desire to discuss the history of the town in two periods of equal length; nothing happened in 1686 to cause or even to symbolize the end of the Utopian experiment.

The result has been to distort the real character of those years. On Lockridge's own evidence there were two periods of major change during the first half-century of settlement. The first came in the 1670s with the death of the original minister and of several influential Selectmen, the outbreak of religious controversy, the failure to enforce the laws restricting the entrance of strangers into the town, and the most severe demographic crisis in Dedham's history.[4] The second cluster of important events came in 1691 and 1692 with the acceptance of the Halfway Covenant, after a resistance of thirty years, and the dismissal of all of the Selectmen, apparently because of their acquiescence in the regime of Sir Edmund Andros, the deposed governor of the abortive Dominion of New England. These "natural" turning points are neglected in the pursuit of symmetry and simplicity. As a result, the author's organization of the town's history bears little relation to the actual life experiences of its members. There are brilliant passages and convincing interpretations in every chapter of this book, especially in those sections based upon earlier journal articles, but the total effect is disappointing. The actual Dedham experience is obscured by Lockridge's continual quest for a wider synthesis, and the history of one town is too meager a scaffolding to support a comprehensive interpretation of early American history.

Demos' study of the pattern of social existence in Plymouth colony, between its settlement in 1620 and its incorporation into the province of Massachusetts Bay in 1691, is much better in depicting the

---

3 E. E. Rich, "The Population of Elizabethan England," *Economic History Review*, II (1950), 247–265, as quoted in Greven, *Four Generations*, 265. See also Jack M. Potter, May N. Diaz, and George M. Foster, *Peasant Society: A Reader* (Boston, 1967), esp. 2–14, 35–41, 230–245, 300–323.

4 There were twenty-five recorded deaths in the year 1675–1676, many caused directly or indirectly by an Indian war. See Kenneth A. Lockridge, "The Population of Dedham, Massachusetts, 1636–1736," *Economic History Review*, XIX (1966), 318–344.

concrete reality of the early settlements. Eschewing chronological analysis, Demos offers us a careful topical investigation of the character of family life and of the nature and functioning of the household unit. Within these rather narrow limits he is remarkably successful. In consecutive chapters on the housing, furnishings, and clothing of the colonists, Demos evokes the physical setting of these relatively primitive village communities with considerable skill and understanding. He does not resort to dramatic coloration or curious anecdote to bring these historical materials to life. Instead, he captures the attention of the general reader by explicitly casting the historian in the role of a detective attempting to extract the essence of the past from the barren artifacts which it has bequeathed to posterity.

And there is a larger historical purpose behind Demos' excursion into the mundane description of housing arrangements in Plymouth. It is his contention that the crowded confines of the rough houses of the seventeenth century exacerbated the normal frustrations and problems inherent in family life, and at the same time made it imperative that they be controlled. The aggressive behavior which was suppressed within the household, Demos suggests, was then "displaced" upon other members of the community. As corroborating evidence, Demos points to the relatively large number of inter-family disputes which found their way into the courts, especially when compared to the relative harmony within the nuclear family unit.

Like so much else in *A Little Commonwealth*, this suggestion is frankly presented as an hypothesis without proof in the hope that it will stimulate further research and thought. This is fair enough, but it is important at the outset to establish the *a priori* character of this type of argument and to insist upon the formulation of testable propositions. Yet Zuckerman by combining different psychological and anthropological assumptions with Puritan literary evidence enjoining the suppression of anti-social impulses, arrives at another conclusion. Zuckerman's argument is simply that New England towns were "Peaceable Kingdoms," in large measure because the socialization of children and the political institutions of the society were functionally designed to make them so. In his view, familial aggression was not displaced upon others; it was either sublimated or directed into more socially acceptable channels.

Demos and Zuckerman are in greater agreement with regard to the significance of the clothing worn by children during the colonial period. Building on the foundations laid by Ariès in his *Centuries of*

Childhood,[5] both authors argue persuasively that the identity of dress among children and adults implies a view of human development in which the young are conceived of as adults in minature. Starting from this aesthetic observation, Demos then proceeds to adduce considerable evidence from other sources in support of this proposition. In the final and most original section of his book, entitled "Themes of Individual Development," Demos maintains that significant biological changes occur in all children at precisely that age at which the young in Plymouth colony began to be dressed as adults. Further, he contends, it was exactly at this point as well that considerable numbers of children (perhaps one-third) were sent to serve as apprentices or servants in the homes of others. In this instance, at least, there would seem to be a clear fit between traditional types of historical evidence and the eight-stage model of human development proposed by Erik Erikson and used by Demos as a guide to the life-cycle of the inhabitants of Plymouth colony during the first two generations of settlement.

In other cases the relationship between fact and theory is not conclusively demonstrated. The paucity of written evidence prevents the author from proving that the Puritans systematically repressed their childrens' "natural" impulse for autonomy during the early years of life. More disturbing is Demos' failure to indicate the effect of such child-training on the development of the adult personality; or to consider at length the personality structure of the mature members of the Puritan community. Did the authoritarian nature of family life produce, as Bushman has suggested, "steady and resolute personalities sure of the world in which they lived"?[6] Demos skirts this question at several points in the text, and always refuses to confront it directly.

The limited range of many of the statements in *A Little Commonwealth* and their hypothetical nature are not as serious as the author's unwillingness to exploit the full potential of the Eriksonian model. For Erikson, human development is the result of a continuing interplay among individual propensities, cultural traditions, and environmental forces. A change in any one of these variables inevitably affects the others; this alteration, and the chain of events it sets in motion, also reveals the precise influence of a given factor in the behavior of the human organism. It is therefore crucial for the historian to utilize this model over

5 Philippe Ariès (trans. Robert Baldick), *Centuries of Childhood: A Social History of Family Life* (New York, 1962).

6 Richard Bushman, *From Puritan to Yankee: Character and the Social Order in Connecticut, 1690–1765* (Cambridge, Mass., 1967), 20.

time, to indicate the ways in which small changes in the wider social environment effect subtle mutations in the cultural pattern and in the life experiences of a particular generation. Both because of his methodological commitment to the approach of a developmental psychologist and because of his choice of a narrow chronological period, Demos is not sufficiently appreciative of changes which occur over time—the alterations in the historical context which made family life very different for successive generations, even as it left largely undisturbed the basic structure of the household unit.

For a detailed analysis of historical change, we must turn to the work of Greven. If Demos' study of Plymouth will appeal primarily to the well-educated general reader, and Lockridge's history of Dedham to the eager undergraduate, then Greven's investigation of the relationship between land, population, and family in colonial Andover will win the patronage of the professional historian. In addition to the wealth of data presented in the text, there are twenty-nine tables and five graphs covering a multitude of demographic and social phenomena. While this profusion of detail occasionally makes for heavy reading, it also provides us with a most complete and suggestive analysis of the ecological basis of early American society.

From an isolated settlement of twenty families in 1646, Andover grew rapidly to a town of 600 inhabitants by 1685. This number more than doubled during the next forty years, as the population climbed to 1,305 in 1725; by 1764, there were 2,356 people within the once-ample boundaries of the town. A major factor in this impressive rate of population growth was a low death rate. Plague and famine, the twin scourges of Europe until the mid-eighteenth century, were largely absent from the New England colonies. In the case of famine, this was especially true once the initial settlements had exploited the fruitfulness of the land, and because of the closeness of most towns and villages to navigable water. Except in the port cities along the Atlantic coast, there were relatively few epidemics during the first century of settlement.

The result was little less than spectacular. At the age of twenty the average colonist in America could expect to live well past his sixtieth birthday. This was true not only in Andover, but in Dedham and Plymouth as well; and this long expectancy of life at maturity continued in New England until the end of the colonial period. The situation was rather different in Europe. It was only the generation of children born to British *ducal* families between 1730 and 1779 whose life expectancy at age twenty equalled that of the early settlers of Massachusetts Bay; and only in the first decades of the nineteenth century did the general population of Norway achieve the same expectation of life at maturity.[7]

The data on child mortality are even more striking and, indeed, hold perhaps the main key to the rapid expansion of American population. Both in Andover and in Plymouth, nearly nine of every ten infants born during the first years of settlement survived to age twenty, although this percentage decreased considerably during succeeding generations. Of those born in Andover between 1670 and 1699, only about 80 per cent lived to maturity; this proportion then dropped to 66 per cent of those born during the first three decades of the eighteenth century, and to 50 per cent of those born between 1730 and 1759. At mid-century the rate of childhood mortality in Andover had regressed to the European standard.[8]

Behind this continuous decline was the increased incidence of scarlet fever, dysentery, and diphtheria, epidemic diseases which struck particularly hard at the ranks of the young but which left relatively unscathed the mature portion of the population. In time this increase in child mortality affected the rate of population growth as a smaller percentage of the young survived to bear offspring themselves. The first generation of settlers in Andover produced an average of 8.3 children per completed marriage (where both partners survive until the woman reaches the end of her childbearing years). Of these, 7.2 survived to maturity. These totals fell to 8.1 and 6.6 respectively by the time the second generation began to have children in the years between 1670 and 1690. The offspring of the third generation, born mostly between 1705 and 1735, were still fewer in number. Only 7.2 children were born on an average per completed marriage, and of these only 5.1 survived to adulthood.

As these figures indicate, it was not only the increase in childhood mortality which was responsible for the steady decline in the rate of population growth. Those who did survive to adulthood were having

---

7   T. H. Hollingsworth, "A Demographic Study of British Ducal Families," in D. V. Glass and D. E. C. Eversley (eds.), *Population in History: Essays in Historical Demography* (Chicago, 1965), 361 (Table 9); Michael Drake, *Population and Society in Norway 1735–1865* (Cambridge, 1969), 45–49 and Table 3.5.

8   See, for example, the mortality data in Louis Henry, "The Population of France in the Eighteenth Century," in Glass and Eversley, *Population*, 445–448; Thomas McKeow and R. G. Brown, "Medical Evidence Related to English Population Changes in the Eighteenth Century," in *ibid.*, 298–299.

fewer children as well. There was a continual decline in the number of births per marriage in Andover during the eighteenth century. From an average of 7.6 in 1700, the number dropped to 4.2 by the 1770s. Two factors accounted for this development: an increase in the length of the interval between births and a rise in the marriage age of women. Because of the severely imbalanced sex ratio during the first generation in Andover and in Plymouth, the average age at marriage for women was exceedingly low; at Plymouth twenty years, in Andover a mere nineteen years. In Andover this average rose to 22.3 for the next generation, 24.5 for the third, and then dropped slightly to 23.2 for the fourth generation. The increase of four or five years was particularly dramatic, for it meant that those women who married in the eighteenth century would have at least one and probably two fewer live births during their fertile years than those who had began to raise a family in the preceding century.[9]

The studies of Greven and Demos suggest, therefore, that the high rate of population growth in colonial New England was the result both of low childhood mortality in isolated frontier settlements—a condition duplicated in certain parts of Scandinavia—and a sharp decrease in the age of marriage for women during the first fifty years of a new community. Because the area of settlement was continually expanding during the eighteenth century, it seems likely that these prime demographic conditions were repeated again and again. This assumption would account for the fact that in 1800, when the first national figures are available, the crude birth rate of the white population of the United States was in the range of forty to fifty per 1,000, or an average of five or six births per marriage.[10]

By that date the number of births per marriage in Andover had fallen to 3.0. Given the high incidence of death in childhood, it was

9 At Crulai in France, in the period from 1674 to 1742, "The mean number of children per completed family is approximately 8, 6, and 4, for women who marry at 20, 25, and 30 respectively." (Henry, "Population of France," 450.) It is also likely, as Robert Wells has pointed out to me, that the continual decline in births per marriage was caused in part by the migration of couples married in Andover who departed before the end of the woman's childbearing period. This is suggested by the fact that the number of births per completed marriage falls much less slowly than does the number of births for all marriages. See Greven, *Four Generations*, Tables 6, 15, and 21.

10 J. Potter, "The Growth of Population in America, 1700–1860," in Glass and Eversley, *Population*, 672; Ansley J. Coale and Melvin Zelnik, *New Estimates of Fertility and Population in the United States: A Study of Annual White Births from 1855 to 1960 and of Completeness of Enumeration in the Censuses from 1880 to 1960* (Princeton, 1963), Ch. 4; Gustaf Utterström, "Two Essays on Population in Eighteenth-Century Scandinavia," in

doubtful if the members of the town were even reproducing themselves. Indeed, the total population of the town actually declined between 1776 and 1800. The cause of this depopulation, the conjunction of a high age at marriage for women, high infant and child mortality, and declining marital fertility (as measured by an increase in the average interval between births), appeared also in Colyton, Devon during a period of disease and economic decline.[11] The simultaneous appearance of three demographic characteristics of a stationary or declining population was not accidental and points directly to the central ecological question: the intricate interaction between land, population, technology, and culture.

To state this problem is easier than resolving it, but the valuable investigations of Greven and Lockridge permit us to begin.[12] Three distinct phases, corresponding roughly to the passage of generations, appear to characterize the social life of the towns of colonial New England. The first, which Greven has referred to as a reversion to a "traditional" patriarchal society, was inaugurated by the first settlers and persisted, to some extent, during the lifetimes of their sons and daughters. Its distinctive features were an elitist political system in which effective authority resided in the hands of long-serving Selectmen; patriarchal control over the disposition of family lands, a practice which kept the age of marriage for men at a European level; and low rates of geographical mobility. In Dedham, for example, less than one per cent of the adult males of the town would emigrate in a given year. The inhabitants of these first communities were content to farm their ample lands and to take directions from their ministers and leaders; their sons likewise acquiesced in the hierarchical pattern of authority because of limited economic opportunities elsewhere and their expectation of a considerable landed inheritance.

There was a dynamic element to these settlements as well, and it

---

Glass and Eversley, *Population*, 528, 530. The lower fertility of women in long-settled areas (more spinsters and later age at marriage because of disproportionate male immigration to the frontier) would be more than offset by the increased birth rates in the new areas, and especially by the much lower rates of child mortality there.

11 E. A. Wrigley, "Family Limitation in Pre-industrial England," *Economic History Review*, XIX (1966), 101–105. As Wrigley is at pains to point out, this rather strange mixture of demographic characteristics can only be explained by reference to a wider ecological crisis.

12 Two fine articles by Lockridge are "Land, Population, and the Evolution of New England Society, 1630–1790," *Past and Present*, XXXIX (1968), 62–80, and (with Alan Krieder) "The Evolution of Massachusetts Town Government, 1640 to 1740," *William and Mary Quarterly*, XXIII (1968), 549–574.

was this feature which soon became the predominant one. For sixteen years following the initial settlement at Plymouth in 1620, Governor William Bradford led a successful effort to prevent the dispersion of population. Then, in a massive surge caused both by internal discontent and external immigration, seven new towns were founded between 1636 and 1641. The chronology was much the same *within* the geographically more extensive towns of Massachusetts Bay. During the first twenty years of settlement the proprietors of Dedham distributed only 3,000 acres of the 200 square miles bestowed upon them by the General Court; the next twelve years, however, witnessed the allocation of an additional 15,000 acres. In Andover, three divisions of land between 1646 and 1658 resulted only in the allotment of 2,700 acres; but, in the fourth division of 1662, the settlers divided up more than 5,000 acres. The immediate effect of this expansion was the breakup of the nucleated open field pattern and the increase in the significance of the individual family, now settled on lands of its own at an appreciable distance from the center of the community.

A second dynamic factor was the growth in the size of the family. The birth rate reached 50 per 1,000 in Dedham during the first decade of settlement, a level that was never subsequently surpassed. In Andover and Plymouth, the process was slower. The number of births per marriage rose from the first generation to the second, just at the time that the town was beginning to make a liberal dispensation of its landed wealth. Significantly, this increase in marital fertility occurred at the same time as an increase in the average age of women at marriage. This rise in age was more than offset, however, by a decrease in the average interval between births from twenty-eight to twenty-four months. This development, in turn, would seem to have been the result of the perception of favorable economic conditions and of the great demand for labor.

If the connection between agricultural abundance and marital fertility is conjectural, the relationship between inheritance patterns and geographical mobility in this first phase of town history was clear. In Andover, Greven found that partible inheritance was endorsed in practice as well as in theory. Over 96 per cent of the sons of the first generation of settlers eventually received land from their fathers. As a result, 78 per cent of the men of the second generation remained in the town for their entire lives. And why not? With large tracts of land still untouched by a plow, there was no incentive to move on in search of a landed estate.

This abundance had decreased significantly by the time the third generation came to maturity during the first decades of the eighteenth century, and this change marked the beginning of the second stage in the social morphology of the New England town. Only two-thirds of the male members of the third generation received land from their fathers, and only 60 per cent of those who survived to the age of twenty-one in Andover remained in the town all of their lives. Many of these men purchased their inheritance from their fathers; other sons were given gifts of money in lieu of a section of land. Finally, a large proportion (20–25 per cent) of the male members of this generation took up a trade, an index not only of growing occupational specialization within the community, but also of the need for an alternative means of support. The diminishing agricultural resources of the family had been accompanied by a decrease in the extent of patriarchal authority within the household. Unable to provide for his offspring, the father could not hope to control them.

It was at this point in the history of the community that the average number of births per marriage began to decline. Those married between 1700 and 1710 averaged 7.5 births per completed family. This rate dropped sharply to 5.7 for those beginning married life in the succeeding ten years, and to 4.8, 4.1, and 4.0 in the three decades between 1720 and 1750.

By the time the fourth generation came to maturity between 1730 and 1769, Andover had become overcrowded. The density of the population reached forty-one per square mile in 1764, and fifty per square mile in 1776, relatively high figures given the relatively primitive agrarian technology of the period. There was a consequent decrease in the number of estates which were divided among all sons as Andover moved into the "static" phase of its colonial history. Whereas 95 per cent of all the estates of the first generation had been divided among all of the male heirs, only 75 per cent were so distributed by the next generation. And this proportion declined even further, to 58 per cent, when the third generation came to divide its property in the second half of the eighteenth century. The result was that only 43 per cent of the males of the fourth generation who survived to maturity remained in Andover for the rest of their lives. The majority of men moved off into other localities, often with the assistance of their families, and settled in no fewer than fifty-two different New England communities. The dynamic of natural population increase, present since the early years of the town, had finally outrun the capacity of the land to sustain it, given the essential continuity of economic production, agrarian technology, and social organization.

Andover was not the only town to experience the oppressive effects of the pressure of population upon resources. Grant's study of Kent, Connecticut delineates the same configuration. Settled in 1738 by forty families, many of which were composed of fourth generation descendants of the original immigrants, Kent supported an adult male population of 321 forty years later. But 500 different adult males had lived in the town between 1774 and 1777; over fifty men were moving out of the community each year in search of new land. This process continued until 1796, when a census of the town indicated that 209 adult males were settled on 103 separate homesteads; the subdivided farms of Kent would support only a single heir. New England society had to expand geographically or it would die.[13]

By the time of the American revolution Kent, like Andover, had reached the third—the static—phase of its social development. There was an inner dynamic to this process. Once unleashed by the favorable ecological conditions of the New World, the deep-rooted biological force of sustained population growth had come to constitute an independent variable in the historical process, shaping and molding the cultural patterns of the past. The "traditional" community of the first generations, with its emphasis on patriarchy, hierarchy, and stability, had been inexorably superseded by an "expanding" society with very different social characteristics. And this, in turn, gave way to the "static" town of the late eighteenth century. Epidemics, technological advances, religious conflicts, increased trade—all of these could (and sometimes did) impinge upon or distort the basic morphology of the life cycle of the town. But, in much of New England during the colonial period, these exogenous variables were so weak in their substance and so scattered in their incidence that they can best be considered as deviations from the norm, as "accidents" within a larger framework of organic historical development.

Before making one very important qualification to this social morphology of the New England town, it is necessary to establish the connection between demographic change and political development. As Lockridge brilliantly demonstrates in the case of Dedham, there was a direct causal link between the growth of population and certain types of political change. The doubling of the town's size within a period of

13   Charles Grant, *Democracy in the Connecticut Frontier Town of Kent* (New York, 1961), 99–103.

forty years produced a surplus of potential political leaders. Because of the increased competition for the same number of offices, the average length of service for the Selectmen of the town dropped from 7.6 years to 4.8 years. Nor was this all. The number and length of town meetings increased during the second stage of Dedham's social development. There were more issues to discuss and more voices to be heard. New institutional procedures were adopted as *ad hoc* committees were named to deal with specific problems.

In the end these various developments converged to transform the basic political character of the town. A small group of respected and experienced Selectmen, well advanced in age, no longer decided the affairs of the town in informal meetings; the pressure of population had created new leaders and a more open, more responsive, and more democratic town meeting. Like many other aspects of town life, "middle class democracy" was the manifestation of a discrete and transient stage of political development. In time it would give way to the "organized social system" which Adams discerned in his compelling portrait of New England in 1800 as "the cordial union between the clergy, the magistracy, the bench and the bar" which dominated the life of the community.[14]

This evolution was related to significant changes in the social structure. From 1740 until 1777 the permanent "proletarians" in Kent, Connecticut had never numbered more than 4 per cent of the adult male population; by 1796, this proportion had risen to 11 per cent. In Dedham, the share of the town's wealth owned by the poorest 20 per cent of the taxpayers fell from 10 per cent in 1690 to half that ratio in 1730. During the same period, the landless element in the population increased from 5 to 10 per cent of the adult males. As geographical mobility was hampered by the custom of partible inheritance, the members of this new subgroup of landless workers would eventually facilitate the establishment of small industrial enterprises in New England at the beginning of the nineteenth century. Here, then, was the important legacy of the third phase of town development: a surplus population which could be utilized in a subsequent process of technological and industrial advance.[15]

The interrelationship between demographic change and the poli-

14 Henry Adams, *The United States in 1800* (Ithaca, 1955), 54.
15 A number of English historians have demonstrated the link between partible inheritance and the rise of important centers of domestic industry. See Joan Thirsk, "Industries in the Countryside," in F. J. Fisher (ed.), *Essays in the Economic and Social History of*

tical and social life cycle of a town could be traced in greater detail,[16] but the argument is clear enough. It remains only to place this social morphology within a larger chronological context. The members of the fourth Andover generation who left the town of their birth to settle in fifty-two different New England communities did not have the same religious fervor, social attitudes, and political outlook as did the original settlers of the town. The history of the settlements they would help to create, therefore, would not be completely congruent with that of Andover despite the existence of certain demographic similarities. The maturing of a money economy, itself an index of cumulative economic development, had disrupted the character of the old subsistence-oriented agricultural communities. When Kent was founded in 1738, it took the proprietors only two years to distribute the greater part of the town's land, and ownership of property was not restricted to those who intended to migrate to the new settlement. Only 60 per cent of the men who owned land in Kent during the subsequent twenty-five years ever became members of the community; the rest preferred to speculate with their holdings, hoping to profit from the steadily rising land values in the frontier town. This was a far cry from the close communal consciousness which had prevailed when Dedham had been settled in 1636, when men sought land as much for the sake of community as for the love of money. As Bushman has shown in his study of Connecticut, the New England towns had not been able completely to withstand the processes of historical change.

It is with this point firmly in mind that we must now turn to the fine work of Zuckerman, *Peaceable Kingdoms; New England Towns in the Eighteenth Century*. For it is Zuckerman's contention that the basic *values* and *behavior* of the inhabitants of these towns did not change significantly between 1691 and 1776. On the basis of a close reading of

Tudor and Stuart England (London, 1961); H. J. Habakkuk, "Family Structure and Economic Change in Nineteenth Century Europe," *Journal of Economic History*, XV (1955), 1–12.

16   For example, it was not completely fortuitous that epidemic diseases appeared during the "expansive" phase of the history of Andover. "Given a constant birth rate," Caulfield has noted, "a steady growth in population density obviously produced a more and more rapid renewal of concentrated groups of nonimmune children, a fact which explains the orderly increase in frequency of epidemics." Ernest Caulfield, "Some Common Diseases of Colonial Children," *Publications* of the Colonial Society of Massachusetts, XXXV (1942–46), 13; "A History of the Terrible Epidemic, Vulgarly Called the Throat Distemper, as it occurred in His Majesty's New England Colonies Between 1735 and 1740," *Yale Journal of Biology and Medicine*, XI (1938–39), 334.

the reports of hundreds of town meetings, Zuckerman concludes that "the consciousness of community, in Massachusetts, continued at least three quarters of the way through the eighteenth century as a prime value of public life, an abiding core of provincial culture" (vii).

There is much to be said in support of this interpretation (and of the many other stimulating arguments in this rich book which, because of space limitations and emphasis, cannot be considered here). When the men of the colonial period reflected on the nature of the social order, they did not espouse the ethic of individualism and its attendant values of pluralism, toleration, and majority rule. Rather, they emphasized the harmful effects of political factionalism and of religious and cultural diversity. Simultaneously, the men of the eighteenth century exalted the virtues of harmony, conformity, and consensus. Real freedom (though they would not have formulated it precisely in this way) was possible only within a community of like-minded men. Time after time, the secession of a dissident group inevitably resulted in the creation of a new and more acceptable form of social authority. Men continued to define themselves and their goals in terms of the community rather than in opposition to it.

Zuckerman is therefore on strong grounds when he points to the persistence of the values of uniformity and consensus in eighteenth-century New England. As he is careful to point out, the methods which were used to achieve these social ends shifted gradually over time from physical coercion to moral persuasion. There was little alternative. Lacking a powerful constabulary and a highly developed legal system, the towns had no choice but to rely on the good will and internal discipline of the inhabitants to secure the implementation of legislation and the payment of taxes. The function of the town meeting was not to determine the will of the majority but to ascertain the General Will, the verdict which would be accepted as law by all of the members of the community. Consciously using the "consensus" approach to American history as an analytical tool, Zuckerman points out that it is only in terms of this larger context that the *de facto* acceptance of universal male suffrage in town affairs can be understood; for unless a man participated in the formulation of law, he could not be expected to obey it. "Whatever the stated business written in the warrant," Zuckerman claims at one point, "the real business of a public meeting was always the consolidation of the community" (184).

This statement, like Zuckerman's general argument, must be

qualified in several important respects. The purpose of the town meeting was, in fact, the transaction of substantive business, although the conditions demanded that this be done in a manner that was acceptable to the group as a whole and not to a bare majority. It was only when a particular measure threatened the internal cohesion of the community that the inhabitants were forced to articulate the principles upon which their society was based. Only then did the communal nature of the enterprise take on the explicitly self-conscious character that Zuckerman has detected.

There is a further point to be made in this regard. The system of values, upon which this communal culture was based, was enunciated most clearly and most frequently when its ethical norms were most under attack, precisely at the moment at which they were not accepted as binding by a significant number of the inhabitants. It is not accidental, therefore, that most of the affirmations of consensus and community which Zuckerman cites in the text of his book come from the 1750s or later, for it was then that the changed economic and religious conditions of New England had undermined the traditional foundations of town life. An increasingly diverse and rapidly growing society needed a new ethic; until this new system of values was found, men would continue to invoke the old precepts of uniformity, harmony, and community. By the eve of the revolution, however, these were little more than futile calls to a vanished past or the first adumbrations of the new sense of community which would appear at the beginning of the nineteenth century.

This interpretation is supported by Zuckerman's own evidence, but his sources and his methodology—the stress placed upon values and goals rather than upon behavior and events—have prevented him from developing it fully. In his third appendix, for example, Zuckerman provides us with a chronological analysis of those local disputes which came to the attention of the Massachusetts legislature. The results are revealing. Only thirty-two disputes were referred to the authorities in Boston for discussion and resolution in the four decades between 1691 and 1732, but there were thirty-six such referrals between 1730 and 1742, and at least forty-four in the nine subsequent years. The peak came between 1751 and 1755 when more than seventy local disputes were transmitted to the central government for adjudication.

The change in the nature of the disputes which defied a local solution was equally significant. The data presented in his Appendix III indicate that eighteen of the thirty-two controversies which came to the attention of the legislature before 1732 related to "disputes within the town," and only five to the "rearrangement of the community." It was this latter category which constituted the obsessive concern of the next generation. The dispersion of settlement as a result of the growth of population caused an impressive increase in the number of political struggles in the town meetings, as outlying groups of settlers sought to form new churches and new communities. Of the sixty-four disputes relating to the fragmentation of existing settlements, fifty-one arose in the period after 1742. Likewise, fifty of the fifty-seven battles between local town meetings and absentee proprietors occurred after this date, a revealing testimony to the increase in land speculation and absentee ownership. Because of Zuckerman's concern with values and with rhetoric, he is blind to the changing nature of the social reality which was gradually emerging behind the façade of the traditional clichés.

Yet Zuckerman's tightly-woven argument does point to the essential nature of the evolution of New England society during the colonial period. And it does not correspond to the image of declension and disintegration. Even in the new and unfamiliar circumstances brought about by a decline in religious cohesiveness and by an increase in the extent of market economy, land speculation, and geographical mobility, men continued to define themselves as members of a harmonious community and sought a new and more acceptable definition of commonwealth. The substance of community had changed, but not the value of its existence in the minds of men.

There was a concrete index to this quest for community. The new settlements of eighteenth-century New England were not formed, on the whole, by individuals moving off into the wilderness; rather, they were the result of coalescence of "fragments" of several existing communities. Nearly 60 per cent of the original settlers of Concord, New Hampshire, in the 1720s came from the towns of Andover and Haverhill. At the same time, at least twenty-one members of five Andover families were migrating to Windham county in Connecticut. In Kent during the period from 1738 to 1760, there were eight Beemans, ten Fullers, fourteen Rowlees, and over twenty other families with four or more adult male members. When the pressure of population upon resources came to be felt at Kent, no fewer than ten different families moved across the border to the frontier town of Amenia, New York. Like their fathers and grandfathers before them, these migrants resettled in communities in which the ties of friendship and personal relation mitigated the psychological strains of geographical mobility.

In short, the decline in community was paralleled and to some extent offset by the rise of the family. During the eighteenth century the basic social unit took on more of the tasks of socialization and acculturalization. Between the time of the waning of the influence of the church and the emergence of the public school, the family unit assumed the burden of the education of the young. It was the family, likewise, which became the prime economic institution in the society. With the town lands distributed among the proprietors, it was up to the family to provide for its numerous members. Greven has shown with considerable skill and sensitivity how the traditional structure of the colonial family—nuclear household units with an extended kinship group residing in the community—adapted itself to deal with these new conditions. Instead of settling their sons in separate households on family land, the members of the third generation of fathers in Andover bought land for some of their male heirs in other communities, defrayed the cost of education or apprenticeship for others, and bestowed small but useful sums of money upon those sons who wished to migrate. The structure of the colonial American family thus facilitated geographical mobility and economic expansion. Patriarchy had given way to parental solicitude and aid by the eighteenth century, but the ties of family and kinship remained as stable, organic, and positive factors in the lives of the colonists, smoothing the passage from one generation and one community to the next.[17]

The elements of orderly coherent growth were even more evident in those towns which had reached the "static" phase of their social development. Five members of the third generation of the Abbot family of Andover—three brothers and two sisters—left the town of their birth to resettle together in Brookfield, Massachusetts. But in 1755 there were still thirty-one adult male members of the family in the old town, all descendants of George Abbot I. Intermarried into a dozen different Andover families, these men could count as kin a significant portion of the town's population. This interlocking web of family

17   This interpretation was derived from a review article by David Rothman ("A Note on the Study of the Colonial Family," *William and Mary Quarterly*, XXIII [1966], 627–634), in which he discusses two important works on the American colonial family: Edmund S. Morgan, *The Puritan Family: Religion and Domestic Relations in Seventeenth-Century New England* (New York, 1966; rev. ed.), and Bernard Bailyn, *Education in the Forming of American Society: Needs and Opportunities for Study* (Chapel Hill, 1960).

and kinship gave the community a strong sense of unity and cohesiveness; and it presents us with a picture of social reality which belies the traditional image of disintegration and decay. There was a strong element of organic growth and rebirth in the society of colonial New England, and it is time that we began to write its history in the positive terms that its substance demands.

Tamara K. Hareven

The History of the Family as an
Interdisciplinary Field   As a new field, the history of
the family is broadly interpreted, its boundaries undefined. "Family" is
loosely used in reference to the historical study of childhood and youth,
certain aspects of the history of education, and the history of women
and feminist movements. The field is frequently confused with what
might be considered some of its parts. It has also been identified with
"psychohistory," although not all aspects of the history of the family
have involved psychological interpretations. The future definition and
character of the field will depend on the nature of work done in the
next decade.

Studies of the family have come into vogue only within the past
decade, specifically since the publication of Ariès' *Centuries of Childhood*.[1] Prior to this book's appearance, historians' references to the
family were generally limited to institutional treatments, with occasional allusions to changes in the manners and mores in society.[2] Any
systematic study of the family, excepting biographies, was left to the
sociologists and anthropologists. Childhood and youth, insofar as they
were discussed, were treated in a monolithic, idealized fashion, as if
they remained the same throughout history. Little attention was given
to the possibility that the meaning of various stages of the life cycle
changed over time, and that the treatment, perception, and experience
of the stages of human development differed in various societies and
among different social groups.

Tamara K. Hareven is Associate Professor of History at Clark University. She is the
author of *Eleanor Roosevelt: An American Conscience* (Chicago, 1968); editor of *Anonymous Americans: Explorations in Nineteenth Century Social History* (Englewood Cliffs, N.J.,
1971); associate editor of Robert H. Bremner (ed.), *Children and Youth in America: A
Documentary History* (Cambridge, Mass., 1970–71), 2v.

The author wishes to express her gratitude to Bernard Kaplan, William Koelsch,
Howard Stanton, David Savage, and Anne Buttimer for their constructive criticisms.
Kaplan was a patient tutor in psychological theory.

1 Philippe Ariès (trans. Robert Baldick), *Centuries of Childhood: A Social History of
Family Life* (New York, 1962; originally pub. as *L'Enfant et la vie Familiale sous l'Ancien
Régime* [Paris, 1960]).
2 The classic and still useful history of the American family is Arthur W. Calhoun, *A
Social History of the American Family from Colonial Times to the Present* (Cleveland, 1917–
19), 3v. Roland Berthoff, *An Unsettled People : Social Order and Disorder in American
History* (New York, 1971) is the first American social history text to devote a chapter
to the family. An early exception is Edmund S. Morgan, *The Puritan Family* (New
York, 1966; 1st ed. 1944).

This haphazard treatment of the subject continued despite Morgan's pioneer study of the Puritan family, Bailyn's provocative statements on the family in early America, and Handlin's emphasis on the importance of the family in cities.[3] It was symptomatic of historians' general tendency to focus exclusively on public events rather than on private experience, except where biography was concerned. It also reflected the profession's long-standing indifference to the study of the lives of common people in the past and its concentration on elites.

Even those historians who recognized the importance of the family were awed by practical considerations: the scarcity of documentary materials and the feeling of inadequacy in dealing with the social sciences.[4] Yet, as more recent work has demonstrated, the obstacle was not only in a lack of methodology or materials, but in the failure to ask certain questions.

Recently the historical study of the family has been undertaken by a group of younger scholars committed to an understanding of the total society.[5] They share the common assumption that "the family is . . . an extremely fundamental and durable institution: it often provides a kind of common denominator, or baseline, for a whole culture whose various parts may differ substantially in other respects."[6] They believe that a study of the family provides an understanding of political and social structure, economic developments, and ideology, and assume that the key to an understanding of the interaction between personal development and social change lies in the family.

The renewed interest in the field is a result of changes in outlook and methodology. But it undoubtedly also received its impetus from a sereies of recent crises relating to the conflict between generations, the rebellion of youth, the changing status of women, and growing doubts and anxieties over the future of the family.

---

3   Bernard Bailyn, *Education in the Forming of American Society* (Chapel Hill, 1960); Oscar Handlin, "The Horror," in Oscar Handlin (ed.), *Race and Nationality in American Life* (New York, 1957); and *The Uprooted* (New York, 1951).
4   For a discussion of the limitations of individual family papers, see Edward Saveth, "The Problem of American Family History," *American Quarterly*, XXI (1969), 311–312.
5   For a formulation of the "credo" of the historians of the family, see Philip J. Greven, Jr., *Four Generations: Population, Land, and Family in Colonial Andover, Massachusetts* (Ithaca, 1970), viii. On the relationship of the history of the family to the "new urban history" and the "new social history," see also the introduction in Tamara K. Hareven (ed.), *Anonymous Americans: Explorations in Nineteenth Century Social History* (Englewood Cliffs, N.J., 1971).
6   John Demos, *A Little Commonwealth: Family Life in Plymouth Colony* (New York, 1970), lx.

THE INTERDISCIPLINARY INFLUENCE   As an interdisciplinary field, the history of the family utilizes the tools of demography and the conceptual models of anthropology, psychology, and sociology.

The Anthropological Perspective   The underlying assumptions of cultural anthropology—that the family is universal and that child-rearing is the link between individual character and the dominant values of the culture—are implicit in all studies of the family.[7] More specifically, anthropology has influenced the "cultural history" approach to the family and the national character school. Calhoun's classic *Social History of the American Family* represents an early attempt at "cultural" history. Although it attempted a "sociological" study of the family, it was based on a sequence of impressionistic literary sources.

The cultural approach is expressed in several recent, more sophisticated essays on the nineteenth-century American family.[8] It is no coincidence that all of these focus on the early Republic. Their assumptions are traceable to Alexis de Tocqueville and to the less perceptive barrage of nineteenth-century travelers' accounts. Not unlike the sources upon which they are based, these essays are more concerned with the emergence of a national character than with the family. Nevertheless, this period of concentration was well chosen. As subsequent research has indicated, by the early part of the 1800s, significant changes in family size and function had become evident. Yet, these essays provide no perceptive analysis on the nature of the family and its internal development.[9]

Underlying the cultural history approach is a body of theory derived from the culture and personality school in anthropology—that

7 The culture and personality approach is itself a synthesis between anthropology and psychoanalysis, formulated by Abram Kardiner and Ralph Linton, *The Psychological Frontiers of Society* (New York, 1945); Alex Inkeles and D. J. Levinson, "National Character: The Study of Model Personality and Socio-cultural Systems," in Gardner Lindzey (ed.), *Handbook of Social Psychology* (Cambridge, Mass., 1954), II, 977-1020; Bert Kaplan (ed.), *Studying Personality Cross Culturally* (Evanston, Ill., 1961). For an application of the culture and personality theory to the comparative study of child-rearing, see Margaret Mead and Martha Wolfenstein (eds.), *Childhood in Contemporary Cultures* (Chicago, 1955). For a recent critique of the link between personality, culture, and socialization, see Jehudi A. Cohen, "On Alternative Views of the Individual in Culture and Personality Studies," *American Anthropologist*, LXVIII (1966), 355-361.

8 For example, Richard L. Rapson, "The American Child as Seen by British Travelers, 1845-1935," *American Quarterly*, XVIII (1965), 520-534; Paul Connor, "Patriarch —Old World and New," *ibid.*, XVII (1965), 48.

9 Bernard Wishy, *The Child and the Republic: The Dawn of Modern American Child Nurture* (Philadelphia, 1968).

the socialization process contains the key to the understanding of a whole society. The link between child nurture and national character is conceptualized in Riesman's *The Lonely Crowd*. Riesman provides a developmental sequel to de Tocqueville's original comments on individualism and the American character: "The link between character and society—certainly not the only one, but one of the most significant—is to be found in the way in which society issues some degree of conformity from the individuals who make it up. In each society such a mode of assuring conformity is built into the child, and then either encouraged or frustrated in later adult experience." Riesman concludes that nuclear families tended to produce an inner-directed personality.[10]

The relationship between child-rearing and national character is explored to its fullest by Potter in the context of American affluence. Potter sees the influence of abundance in the feeding, clothing, and housing of the infant, in the frequent availability of the child's parents, in the child's relationship to other adults, and, finally, in the extension of childhood and adolescence into a moratorium from adult responsibilities. But, although he offers significant insights into the impact of social and economic conditions on child-rearing and parent-child relations, he does not explain the end result: the formation of adult personality.[11]

This weakness is generally typical of the cultural approach. Unlike the anthropological "culture and personality" school which it follows, it fails to place the relationship between child-rearing and national character in a social context. While anthropologists study *whole* societies, historians of national character generalize on the representative phenomena of "national behavior." They portray the "typical" family as a representative of the social order, but they lack an analysis of the family as an institution reflecting class differences, population movements, and economic change. By treating the family as the microscopic representation of the social order, they fail to focus on the dynamics shaping family life and organization. The result is a study of cultural attitudes rather than social conditions. The typology of a national character represents only the dominant culture, and leaves out the varieties of family experience among other groups in society.

An entirely different approach to the cultural history of the family is presented by Ariès. His investigation of the concept and condition of childhood in French society reveals that childhood as we know it

10 David Riesman, *The Lonely Crowd* (New Haven, 1967), 5.
11 David Potter, *People of Plenty* (Chicago, 1966), esp. Ch. 12.

emerged only in the early modern period, and that its discovery was closely linked with the emergence of the "modern family." The relativity of childhood experience was established by anthropologists. Ariès' contribution lies in the application of this relativity model of historical change, and in his imaginative use of previously neglected sources.[12] By linking the development of childhood with the varieties of family structure, social class, and economic and demographic changes, Ariès provides a model for the exploration of the stages in the life cycle in relation to the changing conditions of the family in society.

Ariès' approach is developmental only insofar as he recognizes and traces the socio-cultural formation of the stages of human development. He does not study individual development and experience in various stages of the life cycle—childhood, youth, maturity, or old age.[13] This remains the task of the psychohistorian.

Demography   Although initially developed for the study of general population trends and local history, demography has become crucial for the history of the family. The French demographic school, which developed after World War II, provided historians with essential tools for the measurement of population changes, mobility, fertility, birth control, infant mortality, and marriage patterns. More important, the family reconstitution technique has enabled historians to reconstruct the family patterns of vast numbers of anonymous people and to trace them over several generations.[14] Contrary to previous misconceptions, it now appears that preindustrial population turnover had been larger than was generally assumed, that the predominant family structure was nuclear rather than extended, and that birth control came into practice by the eighteenth century.[15]

12   The best evaluation of Ariès' usefulness to the study of the family is by David Hunt, *Parents and Children in History: The Psychology of Family Life in Early Modern France* (New York, 1970), 27–51.
13   The limitations of Ariès model are discussed by Demos, *Little Commonwealth*, 130; Hunt, *Parents and Children*, 46–49.
14   The family reconstitution system was first developed by Louis Henry, who established the Société de demographie historique in 1966. It was then adapted to English records by the Cambridge Group for the History of Population and Social Structure. On the origin of the French group and the development of its methods, see Pierre Goubert, "Historical Demography and the Reinterpretation of Early Modern French History: A Research Review," *Journal of Interdisciplinary History*, I (1970), 37–48.
15   John Demos, "Notes on Family Life in Plymouth Colony," *William and Mary Quarterly*, XXII (1965), 264–286; Philip J. Greven, Jr., "Family Structure in Seventeenth-Century Andover, Massachusetts," *ibid.*, XXIII (1966), 23–56; Kenneth A. Lockridge, "The Population of Dedham, Massachusetts, 1636–1876," *Economic History Review*, XIX

What does all of this mean for the understanding of the family as well as the larger society? Greven and Demos have attempted an answer to this question for Colonial America.

By using the family reconstitution technique, Greven analyzed the demographic patterns of the population of Andover, Massachusetts from 1650 to 1800, and, at the same time, reconstructed the structures of individual families over four generations. The broader implications of Greven's study are his linkage of demographic data with landholding patterns in the family. The family unit thus emerges as the crucial focus of all economic transactions and as the basis of stability in an agrarian society. By relating demographic data with landholdings and inheritance patterns, Greven hoped to reveal the subtle relationships between fathers and sons, the powers of patriarchy in colonial society, and the extent of the son's autonomy within a complicated pattern of kinship networks. The tracing of these relationships over four generations provides our only long-term study of family patterns.

Demos, in contrast, uses demography as the backbone for a psychosocial reconstruction of family experience in Plymouth colony. To achieve this, he relates the demographic data—marriage age, birth rates, longevity, and occupation with the "themes of individual development" in the various stages of the life cycle.

The Psychological Impact: A Developmental Approach   The influence of psychology on the history of the family is currently limited to Erikson's developmental model, which is a composite of psychoanalytic theory, anthropological concepts of culture and personality, and a historical perspective. This model enables historians to transfer psychohistory from individual biography to the larger social sphere.[16]

The application of the Eriksonian model is exemplified in Demos' study of Plymouth and Hunt's exploration of the French family during the old regime. Both authors chose the Eriksonian model because of the "need to discover the dynamic interconnections between experience at an earlier stage and a later stage, to appreciate that a child is always *developing* according to influences that proceed from within as well as

---

(1966), 82–109. For summaries of the new demographic evidence of preindustrial Western societies, see Goubert, "Historical Demography."

16 For a formulation of the Eriksonian model, see Erik H. Erikson, *Childhood and Society* (New York, 1963); *Identity and the Life Cycle* (New York, 1959). The best discussion of the Eriksonian theory in relationship to the family is Hunt, *Parents and Children*, 11–26.

from the wider environment."[17] This would hold equally true for all stages of human growth beyond childhood. Historical data permitting, the historian would be able to understand the experience itself, not only the social and cultural attitudes toward a developmental stage. This goal, as expressed by Demos and Hunt in slight variations, could be defined as an existential approach to the history of the family. Sennett and Greven, although not insensitive to psychological issues, take a more sociological structural-functional perspective.[18]

The Eriksonian model is based on the assumption of ego development throughout life, and provides a psychological setting for the interaction between the individual and society. Individual development and the crises of each stage are determined by the social and cultural environment. For although psycho-sexual development is universal, the ego qualities peculiar to each stage as well as the nature of the transition are culturally (historically) determined. It is this flexibility that renders the Eriksonian framework so useful to historians. Like members of the culture and personality school, Erikson sees a relationship between childhood experiences and the larger society. His theory of social modalities is based on the assumption that stages of infancy are linked with specific institutions in society. Group action is therefore articulated in terms of modes of behavior formed during the first stages of life. When applied to colonial Plymouth, for example, this approach offers insights not only into the child-rearing practices of the Puritans, but also relates the social meaning of the Eriksonian childhood stage of autonomy to the Puritans' fixation on anger and aggression.

There are problems, however, with the Eriksonian model. One major obstacle is in the availability and interpretation of adequate documentation of the interrelationship between individual development and social values. Erikson isolates developmental patterns; but his model is descriptive rather than explanatory. The model itself is derived from contemporary psychoanalytic experience and from observation of the Sioux Indians. Erikson's own historical application of his model has centered on individual biography in the past. Demos and Hunt, in contrast, have refined the model, thus enriching not only our historical perception, but also the possibility of its future uses. Demos used the model in order to understand the experience of "common" people in the past. He placed them within a social and demographic context, and attempted to relate family structure to individual

17 Demos, *A Little Commonwealth*, 130.
18 Hunt, *Parents and Children*, 18–21.

development. With a different emphasis, Hunt has broadened the interpretation of the Eriksonian model to allow for an explanation of interaction between parents and children at each developmental stage.

In addition to the application of psychological models to the family in the past, several historians and psychologists have studied the history of psychosocial concepts, such as childhood, adolescence, and youth, in historical perspective.[19] All of these studies merge the Eriksonian framework with anthropological theories on rites of passage, cultural discontinuities, and the role of peer groups as forces competing with family cohesion.[20] They seem to suggest ways in which an understanding of the historical conditions of various stages in the life cycle is significant for the study of larger social processes. The meaning of childhood, adolescence, and youth, as well as the definition of aging in a society, are not only related to family experience. They also carry serious implications for educational theory and practice, for the understanding of work patterns, sex roles, and the relationship between generations. Yet these interconnections have barely been touched. New studies of public policies toward children suggest that the social recognition of developmental stages is intimately connected with public child welfare and child protection policies. Yet, until very recently, historical studies of child welfare, juvenile delinquency, and governmental attitudes toward the family were carried out in a developmental vacuum.[21]

19 John and Virginia Demos, "Adolescence in Historical Perspective," *Journal of Marriage and the Family*, XXXI (1969), 632, 638. Greven and Kett have attempted to connect the passage from childhood into adulthood in early nineteenth-century America to the religious experience of the Great Awakening. Philip J. Greven, Jr., "Identity, Youth and the Great Awakening"; Joseph F. Kett, "The Definitions of Youth in America, 1800–1880"; Tamara K. Hareven, has related the "discovery" of childhood in nineteenth-century America to the crisis of a rapidly urbanizing society in "The Discovery of Childhood in American History," all delivered at the Clark University conference on "Childhood and Youth in History." The most complete and important conceptualization of this approach is Kenneth Keniston, "Youth as a Stage of Life," *The American Scholar* XXXIX (1970), 631–654.

20 See Ruth Benedict, "Continuities and Discontinuities in Cultural Conditioning," *Psychiatry*, I (1938), 161–167; Kingley Davis, "The Sociology of Parent-Youth Conflict," *American Sociological Review*, V (1940), 525–535; Kenneth Keniston," Social change and youth in America," *Daedalus* XCI (1962), 145–171.

21 The first attempt to relate changes in the concept of childhood with public policies is Robert Bremner (ed.), *Children and Youth in America: A Documentary History* (Cambridge, Mass., 1970–71), 2v. A fascinating analysis of the relationship between private schools and the discovery of childhood is in James McLachlan, *American Boarding Schools: A Historical Study* (New York, 1970). On the development of the sociology of the family, see Norman W. Bell and Ezra F. Vogel (eds.), *A Modern Introduction to the Family* (New York, 1962); Harold T. Christensen, "Development of the Family Field of Study," in

Despite its great promise, the study of developmental stages in the past is still at the embryonic level. These studies are still handicapped by the same limitations as the cultural history of the family: a reliance on child-rearing literature or autobiography, and a concentration on the middle class. If we assume that the social meaning of developmental stages is relative to various classes, ethnic, and racial groups within the larger society, we must study the experiences of other groups as well. Such studies would be more complete if augmented by demographic analyses of the age structure of the population, age of commencement of work, age of marriage, and the work patterns of the larger society. Finally, because of the preoccupation with childhood and youth in American culture, most historical studies of the life cycle tend to concentrate on the early rather than the later stages of life.

The Sociological Dimension   Although psychology has contributed significantly to the recent revival in the historical study of the family, this subject is essentially a descendant of sociology. But sociologists have beset historians with several problems.[22]

First, they relied on general census computations to determine trends in family patterns over time instead of studying such changes in relation to specific groups, classes, and patterns of settlement. Second, they used historical data to illustrate sociological theory, thus divorcing most of their evidence from its historical context. Most importantly, however, their biases as to the nature of the ideal family dictated their historical interpretations.[23] They typed all family forms that deviated from the middle class American family as symptoms of social disorganization. Finally, because of their emphasis on a narrow interpretation of "structure" and "function," they neglected a developmental perspective.[24]

Harold T. Christensen (ed.), *Handbook of Marriage and the Family* (Chicago, 1964), 3–32. For the sociologists as historians, see John Sirjamaki, *The American Family in the Twentieth Century* (Cambridge, Mass., 1953).

22   William F. Ogburn, "Changing Family Functions," in the President's Commission on Recent Social Trends, *Recent Social Trends* (New York, 1933), 661–708; E. Franklin Frazier, *The Negro Family in Chicago* (Chicago, 1932), and *The Negro Family in the United States* (Chicago, 1939).

23   See, for example, Ernest W. Burgess and H. J. Locke, *The Family* (New York, 1960; 1st ed. 1945); E. R. Groves, *The American Family* (Philadelphia, 1934), 8v.

24   Sociologists are not oblivious to a developmental approach, but they apply a structural framework, rather than a psychological one. See Reuben Hill and Roy H. Rodgers, "The Developmental Approach," in Christensen (ed.), *Handbook of Marriage and the Family*.

The application of sociological models to recent historical studies of the family converges on three crucial questions: What constitutes a family? What is the relationship between family structure and parental authority? What are the family's mechanisms for adaptations to social change?

In attempting to answer these questions, historians have relied heavily upon Parson's structural-functional model of the family.[25] The Parsonian theory provides a central framework for both Greven's study of Andover and Sennett's analysis of the reaction of middle class families to urban life in Chicago.[26] Although Greven links the question of parental authority to landholding in a colonial town, Sennett examines parental authority in relation to the adaptability of the family to the city in general and to the "world of work" specifically. Both explain stability and instability, familial solidarity and filial mobility on the basis of family structure. Thus, they place the burden of proof on the difference between "nuclear" and "extended" families. When historians first took these concepts from the sociologists and anthropologists, they also accepted the standard characterization of the extended family as the dominant form typical of the preindustrial period, and the nuclear family as the product of industrialization.[27] But Demos, Greven, and the Cambridge Group have shown that the nuclear family was the dominant form even in the preindustrial period. In this respect, the historical data are now seriously modifying sociological assumptions.[28]

If family structure did not change drastically over time, what, then, are the profound historical changes within the family over the last 300

25 Talcott Parsons, et al., *Family, Socialization and the Interaction Process* (Glencoe, Ill., 1955); Parsons, "The Kinship System of the Contemporary United States," *American Anthropologist*, XLV (1943), 22–38.

26 Richard Sennett, *Families Against the City* (Cambridge, Mass., 1964). The Parsonian approach has received its historical formulation in Neil Smelser, *Social Change in the Industrial Revolution* (Chicago, 1959).

27 Sidney Greenfield, "Industrialization and the Family in Sociological Theory," *American Journal of Sociology*, LXVII (1961), 312–322; Frank F. Furstenberg, Jr., "Industrialization and the American Family: A Look Backward," *American Sociological Review*, XXXI (1966), 326–337. For a modified form of the extended family system, see Eugene Litwack, "Geographic Mobility and Extended Family Cohesion," *ibid.*, XXV (1960), 385–394.

28 For a recent summary, see E. A. Wrigley, "The Pre-Industrial Family in European Populations," paper delivered at the Organization of American Historians meeting, April 1971; Greven, *Four Generations*, 16. Initially, Greven argued that the families in Andover were "modified–extended." He has since resorted to the definition "extended," but what he is talking about in reality are families living in nuclear households with extended kinship ties outside the home.

years? The answer of Demos and Greven follows the lines of traditional sociologists: The major change occurred in the *functions* of the family. Social change stripped the family of its traditional functions: ". . . broadly speaking, the history of the family has been a history of contraction and withdrawal; its central theme is the gradual surrender to other institutions of functions that once lay very much within the realm of family responsibility."[29] Thus, the history of modernization in the family is a story of the loss of its functions as a school, a church, a correctional institution, a hospital, and a workshop. In Parsonian terms, what occurred here was a process of differentiation: "When one social organization becomes archaic under changing historical circumstances, it differentiates . . . into two or more roles or organizations which function more effectively in the new historical circumstances."[30] Are those functions left to the modern family identical with their corresponding functions in the past? Or, did the loss of various functions, combined with a shrinking membership, have an impact on the quality of family relationships? According to Ariès, this contraction marked the emergence of the modern family: nuclear, intensive, inward turning, and child-centered at the expense of sociability. Ariès concludes that the loss of other functions strengthened the family. Parsons argues that this is precisely the family type most suitable to prepare individuals for their functions in a modern differentiated society.[31]

What family type is most adaptive to the urban, industrial society is a crucial question in Sennett's book. He studied the family patterns of "middle class" residents of a Chicago neighborhood in the 1870s and 1880s. His empirical evidence contradicts Parson's theory that the nuclear family was a means of adaptation to the urban environment. Sennett claims that the nuclear family was used as a refuge from the city, rather than as an adaptive mechanism. Consequently, this family form infringed upon the authority of the father, trapped its members in mother-dominated households, and undermined the sons' chances for social mobility. In times of crisis, "intense nuclear families" were singularly unequipped to deal with urban violence and the general fear of social breakdown.

A similar view is taken by McLaughlin, whose analysis of Italian immigrants in Buffalo in the early 1900s suggests that the extended

29 Demos, *Little Commonwealth*, 183.
30 Smelser, *Social Change*, 2.
31 For a detailed analysis of these two models, see Sennett, *Families Against the City*.

family was not automatically transferred to the New World, but rather was improvised to meet the needs and crises of migration.[32] Surprisingly the common feature in the findings of McLaughlin and Sennett is the minimal percentage of extended families. If the extended household represents the more adaptive form, does the predominancy of nuclear households express the overall failures of middle class or immigrant families to adapt to the city?

The problem here derives from an over-reliance on family structure. Sociologists and historians have often interchangeably employed the terms "family" and "household." The situation is complicated by the fact that most of the historical data available for the 1800s come from the census, which uses the *household* rather than the family unit. This is especially significant in view of several sociologists' recent revisions of their definitions of urban kinship networks. They now increasingly question the validity of examining the nuclear family in isolation from extensive kinship networks outside the household.[33] If this expanded model could be applied to the past, it would considerably revise the historians' notions about anomie and family disorganization.

The question of family adaptability is closely linked with Park and Burgess' theory of social disorganization, the theoretical pitfall which historians have inherited from the Chicago School of Sociology. Frazier, their student, attributed to the city an influence more destructive than slavery. From his study of the Negro family in Chicago he concluded that "In the case of large numbers of Southern migrants who came to the city, the customary and sympathetic bonds that held families together in the rural communities of the South were dissolved. . . ."[34]

Today several historians are trying to exorcise the theory of social disorganization. The onslaught began with Jacobs' defense of the ethnic urban neighborhood as a cohesive community.[35] Research in progress

32 Virginia McLaughlin, "Working Class Immigrant Families: First Generation Italians in Buffalo, New York," paper delivered at the OAH meeting, April 1971. See also her dissertation, "Like the Fingers of the Hand: The Family and Community Life of First-Generation Italian Americans in Buffalo, New York."

33 See Marvin B. Sussman and Lee Burchinal, "Kin Family Network: Unheralded Structure in Current Conceptualizations of Family Functioning," *Marriage and Family Living*, XXIV (1962), 231–240. Alfred M. Mirande, "The Isolated Nuclear Family Hypothesis: A Reanalysis," in John N. Edwards (ed.), *The Family and Change* (New York, 1969), 153–163.

34 Robert E. Park and Ernest W. Burgess (eds.), *The City* (Chicago, 1925); Frazier, *Negro Family in Chicago*, 22. See Lee Rainwater and William L. Yancey, *The Moynihan Report and the Politics of Controversy* (Cambridge, Mass., 1967).

35 Jane Jacobs, *The Death and Life of Great American Cities* (New York, 1961).

on the Negro family structure promises to revise the breakdown stereo-type initiated by Frazier and reinforced by Moynihan.[36] Although attacking a theory, however, one can easily get trapped in its frame-work and expend too much energy in dispelling it. The negative dependency on the social disorganization theory is evident in the revi-sionists' use of the criteria for breakdown employed by the Chicago school: they are trying to demonstrate the existence of stable house-holds and low rates of illegitimacy and delinquency. In the process, however, one might neglect alternative frameworks, such as the study of varieties of family structure within a spatial framework in the city. There is also a danger of forgetting, as Frazier demonstrated, that Negroes in their contact with the urban environment exhibited re-markable adaptability by developing alternative kinship ties.

THE FAMILY AND SOCIAL CHANGE: THE PROBLEM OF INTERAC-TION   Interaction between the family and social change constitutes the fundamental unanswered question underlying most of the issues discussed above. This all-encompassing area still remains the "great unknown" in the history of the family. Existing studies are too limited in time and place to provide an analysis of change in the family. Customarily, historians have resorted to two broad explanatory clichés—urbanization and industrialization—and almost all aspects of change within the family are generally related to one or the other of these phenomena. However, since the terms "urbanization" and "indus-trialization" have not yet been defined precisely, nor have their dy-namics in historical context been explored fully, it would appear futile to attempt an explanation of one unknown by another.

Historians and sociologists have studied the family too frequently as a dependent variable, while giving little attention to its role as an agent of change.[37] With the exception of Smelser, no attempt has been made at a systematic historical study of the family's impact on social change. What occurs within the family that drives its members to accept or re-ject innovation? What is the relationship between family patterns and initiative for migration? What impact does the family have on social mobility?[38] For over a decade, Lampard has urged historians to study

36 Daniel Patrick Moynihan, "The Negro Family: The Case for National Action [1965]," in Rainwater and Yancey, *The Moynihan Report*, 39ff.
37 See William J. Goode, *The Family* (Englewood Cliffs, N.J., 1964), Ch. 1.
38 Thernstrom and Sennett have made important contributions to the understanding of the relationship between family and social mobility.

the *process* of urbanization within an ecological (e.g., demographic, economic, and geographic) framework, but his cry has remained largely unechoed.[39]

An interpretation of the relationship between internal changes in the family and social movements has been attempted in studies on the impact of family experience on ideological change. Keniston has developed a model of multi-generational changes in the family from the Victorian period to the present to explain individual alienation in a fragmented society.[40] On a larger scale, Weinstein and Platt have interpreted the ideological reaction against authority in social movements as an expression of the son's desire for autonomy from the control of the patriarchal father, whose authority in the family had been on the decline since the Industrial Revolution.[41]

The focus on patriarchal decline as an overall explanation of changes in the family is problematic. One can explain the impact of social and economic forces in the post-industrial society by the decline of the father's authority. But can one use the changing father-son constellation in the family as an overall explanation for ideological change? Weinstein and Platt have attempted to relate changes in the family and ideological changes in society. They have established parallels between ideological change in society and the changing authority of the father in the family, but have not succeeded in tracing the interrelationship between these two phenomena and in substantiating it historically.

PROSPECTS   The history of the family is now only in its beginning stages. Before one can form general theories about its historical development and role, a larger number of building blocks are needed. Future studies will therefore have to continue along two complementary levels: first, detailed studies of family experience within distinct communities or limited time periods, such as the studies that have emerged so far for the colonial period; and, second, investigations of macro developments in the family over time. Since change in the family itself is slow, long-term studies will be essential. In both cases, however, one must call for an integrated analysis of all aspects of the

39 Eric E. Lampard, "American Historians and the Study of Urbanization," *American Historical Review*, LXVII (1961), 49–61.

40 Kenneth Keniston, *The Uncommitted: Alienated Youth in American Society* (New York, 1960), and *Young Radicals: Notes on Committed Youth* (New York, 1968). Christopher Lasch, *The New Radicalism in America, 1889–1963* (New York, 1965).

41 Fred Weinstein and Gerald M. Platt, *The Wish to be Free: Society, Psyche, and Value Change* (Berkeley, 1969).

family and its interaction with society. This will involve an integration of subjects such as the history of women, divorce, and birth control, which are now treated as marginal subsidiaries to the history of the family. The study of sex roles and the changing meaning of sexuality must also be incorporated into the study of the family. Similarly, the few available studies on divorce and birth control deal essentially with public policies or social reform, without a systematic relationship to demographic, social, and internal conditions in the family.[42] It is extremely difficult for the historian to bridge the gap between the public institutions and articulated attitudes, on the one hand, and private practice, on the other hand. But the effort to integrate them should be made, especially in the area of education, where the relationship between family socialization and public institutions is intimate.

Future work in the history of the family will have to be comparative. The major limitation imposed on studies discussed so far is their isolation. It is impossible to measure "adjustment," "adaptability," "stability," and change for certain family groups without comparative criteria. Thus, the experience of foreign immigrants must be compared to that of Negro migrants in the cities and to that of rural migrants before any generalizations are made about "immigrant" and "urban" experience. The theoretical debate about the comparison between immigrant families in the Old World and patterns in their places of origin and in the United States will assume a different character when immigrant families in the United States are compared with those of their country of origin.

Interdisciplinary influence has been limited so far to the disciplines discussed above. Not only have possible alternative theories within each discipline been overlooked, but also economic and spatial interaction models have not been utilized. With the exception of studies for the colonial period, recent studies of the family ignore standards of living, the family's relationship to external economic conditions, and the internal management of the household.[43]

Nor has the importance of social space been taken into consideration. Most studies in American social history, even those pertaining to

42   See, for example, William O'Neil, *Divorce in the Progressive Era* (New Haven, 1967). Research in progress on family dissolution in early nineteenth-century America by Christopher Turner analyzes the patterns of family breakdown.

43   Most historians have neglected the work of the nineteenth-century French sociologist Frédéric Le Pley. See, for example, *L'organization de la Famille* (Paris, 1871). Although his family typology is outdated, the connections which he establishes between family, work, and space could be extremely useful to historians.

the urban experience, suffer from a detachment of the spatial environment. Yet the spatial situation in the city, the neighborhood, and the village are crucial for the understading of the family's interaction with other institutions and social groups.[44]

Even within the interdisciplinary modes employed so far, there are serious omissions. Theories of social psychology have barely found their way into the study of the family. Thus, conflict and tension within the family have escaped systematic analysis. Nor has the pull of external forces on members of the family been given sufficient consideration. For example, Festinger's theory of cognitive dissonance could provide an explanation for tensions between the home and the world of work and between parents and children, and help us understand the conflict between family members' perceptions of their respective roles in periods of drastic social change.[45]

Some of the current limitations in the field derive from a narrow perception of the family as a biological unit. Recent sociological and psychological theory is moving away from this limited conception. It attempts to study the family as it does other groups in society. But, for some reason, small group psychology has not been utilized by historians.[46]

The most challenging question facing the historian of the family, or any historian following an interdisciplinary approach, is the adaptation of theory borrowed from another discipline. Should theories borrowed from the social sciences merely sensitize the historian to questions which are not normally asked of the source materials within his field? Should they be used primarily to interpret and explain? Should they simply provide a framework for the integration of apparently disparate elements? Should they provide hypothetical answers about dimensions which one could never obtain from the existing historical sources? Obviously the answer is all of these. But the problem of integration still remains.

44 Frazier's study of the Negro family in Chicago is so far the only historical analysis of the family in the context of urban space. The study suffers, of course, from Burgess' mechanistic model of concentric zones. Sennett promises to study family in the urban context, but his book does not deal with the city. An exciting definition of "social space" developed by French sociologists has not been considered by American historians: Paul-Henri Chombart de Lauwe, *Famille et Habitation* (Paris, 1956–59), 2v. For an analysis and definition of social space in the urban setting, see Anne Buttimer, "Social Space in Interdisciplinary Perspective," *Geographical Review*, LIX (1969), 417–426.

45 Leon Festinger, *Theory of Cognitive Dissonance* (Evanston, Ill., 1957).

46 Robert F. Bales, "Small-Group Theory and Research," in Robert K. Merton, *et al.*, *Sociology Today: Problems and Prospects* (New York, 1959), II, 293–309.

Bibliographic Note

C. John Sommerville

Toward a History of Childhood and Youth

If there is one thing that both sides of the "generation gap" could agree upon, it would probably be the importance of childhood experience to the development of the individual and of society. And, although professional historians have long neglected the history of the child, and of the cultural construct "childhood," the publication record of the past several years is evidence of a surge of interest in this field.[1]

This note will cite the literature in English which relates to the history of childhood, listing existing bibliographies and other works that have escaped them or call for special notice. It will not be possible, however, to take account of the stream of works on the plight of today's youth—the stuff of which historical studies will be made in years to come.

Older attempts at writing the history of childhood and youth are often of great interest because of what they indicate about the attitudes characteristic of the time of their writing. Of course, few of the older histories attack the problems to which social historians are now addressing themselves. One is tempted to say that it was only with such recent works as Edmund S. Morgan's *The Puritan Family: Religion and Domestic Relations in Seventeenth*

C. John Sommerville is Assistant Professor of History at the University of Florida. He is presently working on several studies of popular religion and secularization in late seventeenth-century England.

The author wishes to thank H. C. Erik Midelfort, Mary L. Schofield, David B. Tyack, and Carl Degler, among others, for their suggestions concerning this bibliographic note.

1 Ivy Pinchbeck and Margaret Hewitt, *Children in English Society. Volume I: From Tudor Times to the Eighteenth Century* (Toronto, 1969), bibliog.; Levin Schücking (trans. Brian Battershaw), *The Puritan Family: A Social Study from the Literary Sources* (New York, 1969; 1929, 1st ed.); John Demos, *A Little Commonwealth: Family Life in Plymouth Colony* (New York, 1970); David Hunt, *Parents and Children in History: The Psychology of Family Life in Early Modern France* (New York, 1970); Walter I. Trattner, *Crusade for the Children: A History of the National Child Labor Committee and Child Labor Reform in America* (Chicago, 1970); Richard Rapson (ed.), *The Cult of Youth in Middle-Class America* (Lexington, Mass., 1971); Joseph M. Hawes, *Children in Urban Society: Juvenile Delinquency in Nineteenth-Century America* (New York, 1971); "Generations in Conflict," *Journal of Contemporary History* V (1970); Editors, "The History of the Family," *Journal of Interdisciplinary History*, II (1971); Robert H. Bremner, et al., *Children and Youth in America: A Documentary History* (Cambridge, Mass., 1970–71), 3v.; *British Parliamentary Papers: Children's Employment* (Shannon, 1969), 15v.; *British Parliamentary Papers: Juvenile Offenders* (Shannon, 1970), 6v. See later notes for articles and other new books.

Century New England (New York, 1966; rev. ed.), Philippe Ariès' (trans. Robert Baldick) *Centuries of Childhood: A Social History of Family Life* (New York, 1962), and Bernard Wishy's *The Child and the Republic: The Dawn of Modern American Child Nurture* (Philadelphia, 1968) that the history of childhood came of age, with a new breadth of interest and imagination, and maturity of judgment.[2]

It was Ariès, for instance, who showed how several fields once dominated by antiquarianism could be made to serve a more general cultural history. Antonia Fraser's new *History of Toys* (London, 1966: bibliog.) and Phillis Cunnington and Anne Buck's *Children's Costume in England, from the Fourteenth to the End of the Nineteenth Century* (New York, 1965) illuminate two such areas.[3] Iona and Peter Opie's encyclopedic *Children's Games in Street and Playground* . . . (Oxford, 1969) may enable historians to tackle questions that anthropologists have raised concerning the social significance of the popularity of certain games.[4]

The study of children's literature is served by a spectacular bibliography in Anne Pellowski's *The World of Children's Literature* (New York, 1968), with its 4,500 annotated citations of books, bibliographies, articles, theses, and periodicals. Virtually all historical treatments of the subject may be found here, organized nationally, and the historian will be introduced to the possibilities for comparative research, the evidence for children's actual preferences, and studies of the taste-making power of book reviewers and librarians.[5] F. J. H. Darton's *Children's Books in England: Five Centuries of*

2   Wishy offers the best bibliography on the American child. It is hoped that Pinchbeck and Hewitt's second volume will add to their bibliography on the English child, especially on child labor and public policy. Works not cited elsewhere include: Elizabeth Godfrey [Jessie Bedford], *English Children in the Olden Time* (London, 1907); Isabel Simeral, *Reform Movements in Behalf of Children in England of the Early Nineteenth Century, and the Agents of those Reforms*, (Clifton, N.J., 1971; 1916, 1st. ed.), bibliog.; Marion Lochhead, *Their First Ten Years: Victorian Childhood* (London, 1956); Joseph J. Findlay, *Children of England: A Contribution to Social History and to Education* (London, 1923); Frederick Gordon Roe, *The Victorian Child* (London, 1959); *idem., The Georgian Child* (London, 1961); U. R. Q. Henriques, "Bastardy and the New Poor Law," *Past and Present*, XXXVII (1967), 103–129; C. Crane Brinton, *French Revolutionary Legislation on Illegitimacy, 1789–1804* (Cambridge, Mass., 1936); Lucy Crump, *Nursery Life 300 Years Ago: The Story of a Dauphin of France, 1601–10, Taken from the Journal of Dr. Jean Héroard, Physician-in-Charge, and from Other Sources* (London, 1929).

3   Their bibliography does not include Iris Brooke, *English Children's Costume Since 1775* (London, 1930).

4   John M. Roberts and Brian Sutton-Smith, "Child Training and Game Involvement," *Ethnology*, I (1962), 166–185. See also Henry Bett, *The Games of Children: Their Origin and History* (London, 1929); Leslie Daiken, *Children's Games Throughout the Year* (London, 1949); Foster R. Dulles, *A History of Recreation: America Learns to Play* (New York, 1965; rev. ed.), bibliog.

5   Pellowski does not cite Sara I. Fenwick (ed.), *A Critical Approach to Children's Literature* (Chicago, 1967); Alec Ellis, *A History of Children's Reading and Literature* (Oxford,

Social Life (Cambridge, 1956; rev. ed.) has long provided a model for the social history of children's literature, a subject which would profit from the more systematic collection of materials that has been proposed.[6]

Problems in interpreting the history of children's literature—how far it influences children, and how far its changing fashions reflect adult attitudes— are less acute in dealing with the picture of the child in adult literature. Peter Coveney's excellent treatment of nineteenth-century English literature relates the image of childhood to a broader history of culture.[7] Here, too, some of the bibliographical spadework has already been done in John Mackay Shaw's massive *Childhood in Poetry: A Catalogue* ... (Detroit, 1967; 5v.). Norman Kiell's *The Adolescent Through Fiction: A Psychological Approach* (New York, 1959), and W. T. Witham's *The Adolescent in the American Novel, 1920–1960* (New York, 1964). There are also several examinations of autobiography which suggest questions about how different generations have "remembered" their own childhoods.[8]

1968); Victor Neuburg, *The Penny Histories: A Study of Chapbooks for Young Readers over Two Centuries* (Oxford, 1968); Carolyn Field (ed.), *Subject Collections in Children's Literature* (New York, 1969); Anne Ellis, *The Family Story in the 1960's* (Hamden, Conn., 1970); William Baring-Gould and Ceil Baring-Gould, *The Annotated Mother Goose* (New York, 1962); D'Alte A. Welch (comp.), *A Bibliography of American Children's Books Printed Prior to 1821* (Worcester, Mass., 1963); 5v. She also does not cite the English translation of Bettina Hürlimann (trans. Brian W. Alderson) *Three Centuries of Children's Books in Europe* (Cleveland, 1967), or the revised edition of Cornelia L. Meigs (ed.), *A Critical History of Children's Literature: A Survey of Children's Books in English* (New York, 1969).

6 James Fraser, "Children's Literature as a Scholarly Resource: The Need for a National Plan," *Library Journal*, XCIV (1969), 4490–91.

7 *The Image of Childhood: The Individual and Society: A Study of the Theme in English Literature* (Harmondsworth, 1967; rev. ed.), bibliog. See also Francis L. Janney, *Childhood in English Non-Dramatic Literature from 1557 to 1789* (Grifswald, 1925); Bert Roller, *Children in American Poetry, 1610–1900* (Nashville, 1930); Clifford Parker, *The Defense of the Child by French Novelists* (Menasha, Wisc., 1925); Justin O'Brien, *The Novel of Adolescence in France* (New York, 1937); Sylvia Anthony, *The Child's Discovery of Death: A Study in Child Psychology* (London, 1940); L. C. Martin, "Henry Vaughn and the Theme of Infancy," in J. Dover Wilson (ed.), *Seventeenth Century Studies Presented to Sir Herbert Grierson* (Oxford, 1938), 243–255; Albert Stone, *The Innocent Eye: Childhood in Mark Twain's Imagination* (New Haven, 1961); Barbara Garlitz, "The Immortality Ode: Its Cultural Progeny," *Studies in English Literature*, VI (1966), 639–649; Frank R. Donovan, *Dickens and Youth* (New York, 1968).

8 Walter de la Mare, *Early One Morning in the Spring: Chapters on Children and on Childhood* ... (London, 1935); Alan Warner, (ed.), *Days of Youth: Selections from Autobiography* (London, 1960); Norman Kiell, *The Universal Experience of Adolescence* (New York, 1964). For bibliographies, see Louis Kaplan (comp.), *Bibliography of American Autobiographies* (Madison, 1961), subject index: Childhood Reminiscences; William Matthews (ed.), *British Autobiographies: An Annotated Bibliography of British Autobiography Published or Written Before 1951* (New York, 1968); Edna Oakeshott (ed.), *Childhood in Autobiography* (London, 1960).

George Boas, in *The Cult of Childhood* (London, 1966), has indicated the significance of the child as a symbol of irrationalism and primitivism in the history of philosophy. But the importance of the changing image of the child to various understandings of human nature would justify further investigation. Among the studies of the child in art, one that touches on questions of philosophical importance is Josef Kunstmann's *The Transformation of Eros* (Edinburgh, 1964).[9]

That youth has a political as well as a literary history is clear from several studies of European student movements in this century.[10] The burgeoning field of political socialization has already seen some pioneering historical studies.[11] But the recent international bibliography on the formation of youth societies indicates that even the Scouting movement has yet to find a historian who will show it against its wider background of urbanization and imperialism.[12] George C. Brauer has attempted to study youth when it has been in positions of power rather than in opposition, and suffering the temptations that power brings.[13] But there is room for more study of preparation for leadership and rule, as educational historians have concentrated more on academic disciplines and preparation for citizenship than on the transmission of an aristocratic ethos.

Interest in the history of public policy toward children and child labor seems to be reviving after a postdepression lapse. The documentary history which Bremner and his associates are publishing will partially supersede Grace Abbott's *The Child and the State* (Chicago, 1938; 2v.), and the notes to

9 See also Anita Klein, *Child Life in Greek Art* (New York, 1932); F. M. Godfrey, *Child Portraiture from Bellini to Cezanne* (New York, 1956).

10 Walter Laqueur, *Young Germany: A History of the German Youth Movement* (London, 1962); Lewis S. Feuer, *The Conflict of Generations: The Character and Significance of Student Movements* (New York, 1969); E. Josephson, "Political Youth Organization in Europe, 1900–1950," unpub. Ph.D. thesis, (Columbia University, 1959); Herbert Moller, "Youth as a Force in the Modern World," *Comparative Studies in Society and History*, X (1968), 237–260.

11 Gordon Schochet, "Patriarchalism, Politics, and Mass Attitudes in Stuart England," *Historical Journal*, XII (1969), 413–441; John C. Crandall, "Patriotism and Humanitarian Reform in Children's Literature, 1825–1860," *American Quarterly*, XXI (1969), 3–22.

12 David Gottlieb, John Reeves, and Warren TenHouten, *The Emergence of Youth Societies: A Cross-Cultural Approach* (New York, 1966). The literature on Communist youth organizations has grown considerably since this book appeared. See also Ronald Tuttle Veal, *Classified Bibliography of Boy Life and Organized Work with Boys* (New York, 1919); Ann Duncan Brown (comp.), *Youth Movements in the United States and Foreign Countries* (Washington, D.C., 1936). On Scouting, see Brian Morris, "Ernest Thompson Seton and the Origins of the Woodcraft Movement," *Journal of Contemporary History*, V (1970), 183–194; and the debunking of Lord Baden-Powell in Brian Gardner, *Mafeking: A Victorian Legend* (London, 1966).

13 *The Education of a Gentleman: Theories of Gentlemanly Education in England, 1660–1775* (New York, 1959); *The Young Emperors: Rome, A.D. 193–244* (New York, 1967). See also James McLachlan, *American Boarding Schools: A Historical Study* (New York, 1970).

Walter Trattner's new history of child labor reform supplement the bibliographies in these works. Murray and Adeline Levine have shown the way toward a broadening of the usual institutional focus in this field in their *Social History of the Helping Services: Clinic, Court, School, and Community* (New York, 1970).

The historian whose interests and concepts do not derive from the social sciences has probably already been to the new *International Encyclopedia of the Social Sciences* (New York, 1968) for help. But John Clausen and associates, in *Socialization and Society* (Boston, 1968), offer more useful introductions to the relevant literature in sociology and anthropology, as well as fuller bibliographies which include some historical works. James Bossard and Eleanor Boll's *Sociology of Child Development* (New York, 1960; 3rd ed.) is still useful in citing the older histories of childhood, as well as studies which are no longer scientifically current on such topics as the child and war, depression, law, and discrimination.[14] Much of the discussion of generational conflict begins with S. N. Eisenstadt's *From Generation to Generation: Age Groups and Social Structure* (New York, 1956) and Edgar Friedenberg's *The Vanishing Adolescent* (Boston, 1959), and there is an instructive attempt at a generational periodization of cultural history in Anthony Esler's *The Aspiring Mind of the Elizabethan Younger Generation* (Durham, N.C., 1966).[15] Edward Saveth has surveyed the writing of American "family history,"[16] and Alan Macfarlane has shown how anthropological concepts can be employed with historical materials in *The Family Life of Ralph Josselin, A Seventeenth-Century Clergyman: An Essay in Historical Anthropology* (Cambridge, 1970). Finally, there are several field guides in the social sciences which might suggest what is or is not possible on the basis of historical evidence.[17]

14 See also Louise A. Menefee and M. M. Chambers, *American Youth: An Annotated Bibliography* (Washington, D.C., 1938); Merritt M. Chambers and Elaine Exton, *Youth, Key to America's Future: An Annotated Bibliography* (Washington, D.C., 1949); Thomas Minehan, *Boy and Girl Tramps of America* (New York, 1934); Juliette Despert, *Preliminary Report on Children's Reaction to the War, Including a Critical Survey of the Literature* (New York 1942), bibliog.; *Children and War* (Washington, D.C., 1943); Anna Freud and Dorothy Burlingham, *War and Children* (New York, 1943); Sibylle Escalona (ed.), *Children and the Threat of Nuclear War* (New York, 1962); Martha Wolfenstein and Gilbert Kliman (eds.), *Children and the Death of a President* (Garden City, 1965).

15 Esler cites the European literature on this concept. Erik Erikson edited a symposium on the subject in *Daedalus*, XCI (1961–62), which has been published as *The Challenge of Youth* (New York, 1965).

16 "The Problem of American Family History," *American Quarterly*, XXI (1969), 311–329, bibliog. notes. See also H. R. Trevor-Roper, *Historical Essays* (New York, 1957), 30–34; Lawrence Stone, *The Crisis of the Aristocracy, 1558–1641* (Oxford, 1965), 589–687; William Stephens, *The Family in Cross Cultural Perspective* (New York, 1963), bibliog.

17 John W. M. Whiting, *Field Guide for the Study of Socialization* (New York, 1966); Paul H. Mussen (ed.), *Handbook of Research Methods in Child Development* (New York, 1960); Jerald G. Bachman, et al., *Youth in Transition. Vol. I: Blueprint for a Longitudinal Study of Adolescent Boys* (Ann Arbor, 1967).

Those not already expert in child psychology or child development need not trust their intuitions in these areas since the appearance of surveys (with bibliographies) for the nonspecialist in Martin and Lois Hoffman's *Review of Child Development Research* (New York, 1964–66; 2v.) and Paul Mussen's new edition of *Carmichael's Manual of Child Psychology* (New York, 1970; 2v.). Erik Erikson's works, especially *Childhood and Society* (New York, 1963; rev. ed.) and *Young Man Luther: A Stuay in Psychoanalysis and History* (New York, 1958), will be familiar to anyone with an interest in the study of childhood, and the books by Demos and Hunt[18] show how historians are making a discriminating use of his theories and those of others.

Several fields relating to the professional care of children already have at least embryonic histories, specifically pediatrics, the child study movement, and work with emotionally disturbed children.[19] The story of the recent vicissitudes of child-rearing advice can be collected from a variety of books and articles.[20] And reports of the child-rearing experiments in Israel and the

18 See n. 1, and articles by John Demos (with Virginia Demos), "Adolescence in Historical Perspective," *Journal of Marriage and the Family*, XXXI (1969), 632–638; "Underlying Themes in the Witchcraft of Seventeenth-Century New England," *American Historical Review*, LXXV (1970), 1311–1326. Phyllis Greenacre, in *Swift and Carroll: A Psychological Study of Two Lives* (New York, 1955), studied two men of importance to the history of children's literature. See also Christoph Heinicke and Beatrice B. Whiting (comps.), *Bibliographies on Personality and Social Development of the Child* (New York, 1953).

19 John Ruhräh (comp.), *Pediatrics of the Past: An Anthropology* (New York, 1925); idem., *Pediatric Biographies* (Chicago, 1932); George Still, *The History of Paediatrics: The Progress of the Study of Diseases of Children up to the End of the XVIIIth Century* (London, 1931); I. G. Wickes, "A History of Infant Feeding," *Archives of Diseases in Childhood*, XXVIII (1953), in five parts; Arthur F. Abt, *Abt-Garrison History of Pediatrics* (Philadelphia, 1965); Claire E. Fox, "Pregnancy, Childbirth and Early Infancy in Anglo-American Culture: 1675 to 1830," unpub. Ph.D. thesis, (University of Pennsylvania, 1966); John Anderson, "Child Development: An Historical Perspective," *Child Development*, XXVII (1956), 181–196; Juliette Despert, *The Emotionally Disturbed Child, Then and Now* (New York, 1965); William Kessen (ed.), *The Child* (New York, 1965), bibliog. notes. Milton J. E. Senn is collecting an oral history of the child development movement, to be stored in the National Library of Medicine, Bethesda, Maryland.

20 James Tobey, *The Children's Bureau: Its History, Activities, and Organization* (Baltimore, 1925); Daniel R. Miller and G. E. Swanson, *The Changing American Parent: A Study in the Detroit Area* (New York, 1958); Urie Bronfenbrenner, "The Changing American Child: A Speculative Analysis," *Journal of Social Issues*, XVII (1961), 6–18; Geoffrey H. Steere, "Freudianism and Child-Rearing in the Twenties," *American Quarterly*, XX (1968), 759–767; Margaret Mead and Martha Wolfenstein (eds.), *Childhood in Contemporary Cultures* (Chicago, 1955); other works cited in Bossard, Clausen, and Daniel Calhoun, "The City as Teacher: Historical Problems," *History of Education Quarterly*, IX (1969), 312–325. Journals of special interest: *Annals of the American Academy of Political and Social Science*, *American Journal of Orthopsychiatry*, *Journal of Marriage and the Family*, *Child Study*, *Child Development*, *Journal of Child Psychiatry*, *Journal of Pediatrics*, *Eugenics Quarterly*, *Adolescence*.

Soviet Union are of interest in showing the perplexities which accompany even planned historical change.[21]

The recent development of historical demography is clearly important to the dispute over the status of children at various times, because of the bearing of population structure on the question. E. A. Wrigley's *Population and History* (New York, 1969; bibliog.) provides a guide away from persistent misconceptions in these matters, as well as suggesting the importance of a home-wrecking adult mortality, the reasons why mobility was once predominantly downward, and the function of children as accident, old age, and life insurance.[22]

Keeping up with the literature on the history of education is becoming more difficult as it outgrows its traditional institutional preoccupation. There is room here to cite only an article by David B. Tyack which indicates the extent of the reconceptualization which is in progress and refers to work that will be of wide interest on such topics as the connection of education with urbanization and economic development.[23] Modesty might forbid educational historians to inquire as to the status of teachers in other periods, although the position of those whose work is with children might well be the best indication of the status of their charges. The courtesy and conduct books once so important in education have been catalogued, and the technique of a quantitative content analysis should prove especially suitable for such a convention-bound literature.[24]

Of greater importance than the development of new sources of evidence, however, will be the clarification of the goals of a history of childhood, and

21   Bruno Bettelheim, *The Children of the Dream* (New York, 1969); The earlier literature is cited in A. I. Rabin, *Kibbutz Studies: A Digest of Books and Articles on the Kibbutz* (East Lansing, 1971). Urie Bronfenbrenner, *Two Worlds of Childhood: U.S. and U.S.S.R.* (New York, 1970).

22   See also Frank Musgrove, *Youth and The Social Order* (Bloomington, 1965); Joan Thirsk, "Younger Sons in the Seventeenth Century," *History*, LIV (1969), 358–377; Peter Laslett, *The World We Have Lost* (New York, 1965).

23   "New Perspectives on the History of American Education," in Herbert J. Bass (ed.), *The State of American History* (Chicago, 1970), 22–42. See also Calhoun, "The City as Teacher"; C. Arnold Anderson and Mary Jean Bowman (eds.), *Education and Economic Development* (Chicago, 1965); Carlo Cipolla, *Literacy and Development in the West* (Harmondsworth, 1969); E. G. West, "Resource Allocation and Growth in Early Nineteenth-Century British Education," *Economic History Review*, XXIII (1970), 68–95. Bernard Bailyn's excellent *Education in the Forming of American Society* (New York, 1960) contains a useful bibliography, as do many numbers of the *British Journal of Educational Studies*.

24   Gertrude Noyes, *Bibliography of Courtesy and Conduct Books in Seventeenth-Century England* (New Haven, 1937); Virgil Heltzel, *A Check List of Courtesy Books in the Newberry Library* (Chicago, 1942); John E. Mason, *Gentlefolk in the Making: Studies in the History of English Courtesy Literature and Related Topics from 1531 to 1774* (Philadelphia, 1935), bibliog. See David C. McClelland, *The Achieving Society* (Princeton, 1961), for a use of this technique with important results for the history of socialization.

of the concepts which give it shape. The last century's efforts are unsatisfying because they are so largely one-dimensional, ruled sometimes by no more than tacit preferences for play over work, or amusement over seriousness. Historians continue to be interested in how children were "treated," but are beginning to discriminate between the questions of the economic position of children or youth, the ideological importance of "the child" in the reigning view of human nature, "the child" as the society's hope for the future, and the actual efforts expended on children's welfare. For too long generalization as to the status of children were taken from a society's professions of concern, its permissiveness, or the extent to which children were allowed a world of their own. But, as we are now reminded, permissiveness can be neglect, and interest itself can be a mask for envy. It is becoming clear that these various dimensions—of interest, importance, protectiveness, leniency, and acceptance—are quite separate matters.[25]

The most striking and instructive example of the older prejudices in the context of English or American historiography concern Puritanism. The Puritan was portrayed as the snake in a child's paradise, or else was treated with a dreary facetiousness that obscured the importance of that episode for an understanding of the ideological content of the history of childhood. Morgan has shown, however, that the doctrine of infant depravity was accompanied not only by a new severity, but also by an increased concern for the child and a new interest in child psychology.[26] Puritan concern can be seen in a revolution in the names given to children, and in the first English attempts to produce a literature for them.[27] This child-centeredness need not be put down to middle-class cosseting when the future-orientation of the Puritans offers such a ready explanation. As in other historically-conscious movements, the child was the heir of the new era, although unlike more modern revolutionaries, Puritans could not view the child as the embodiment of an unspoiled human nature.

In general, one would expect the literature on childhood to be especially rich at those points in history when societies felt a need for the protection,

---

25   As against one of the hoariest shibboleths—that the child was being treated as a little adult—see Richard Rapson, "The American Child as Seen by British Travellers, 1845–1935," *American Quarterly*, XVIII (1965), 520–534; Jan H. Van den Berg, *The Changing Nature of Man: Introduction to a Historical Psychology* (New York, 1961).

26   *The Puritan Family*, esp. 87–108. By contrast, Ariès and Coveney show how the effort to preserve a childish "innocence" led to repression and emotional crippling.

27   Charles W. E. Bardsley, *Curiosities of Puritan Nomenclature* (New York, 1880); William Sloane, *Children's Books in England and America in the Seventeenth Century* (New York, 1955). On religious dissent, see also Lewis Schenck, *The Presbyterian Doctrine of Children in the Covenant: An Historical Study of the Significance of Infant Baptism in the Presbyterian Church in America* (New Haven, 1940); William A. C. Stewart, *Quakers and Education as seen in Their Schools in England* (London, 1953); Richard Vann, "Nurture and Conversion in the Early Quaker Family," *Journal of Marriage and the Family*, XXXI (1969), 639–643; and the works of Howard Clive Barnard on Jansenism and education.

restoration, or creation of a truer humanity, or when the creativeness of adult society was in question. Of course, adult attitudes are at issue here, but the same is true in treating children's literature, child-rearing manuals, or the child in art. To be sure, there may have been times when adult attitudes were less important elements in the child's environment than factors such as industrialization, migration, urbanization, or population growth. But it would not be desirable, even were it possible, to dissociate the study of childhood from a complementary history of adulthood. No study of a form of "naughty" behavior, for instance, could neglect its meaning for the adult society which permitted or encouraged it. Similarly, the greatest fears concerning a rising generation should tell us much about their elders, just as studies of the "play element" in a culture ought to relate the experiences of youth to those of age in the society.[28] An awareness of the complementary character of this history will not only enlarge the circle of evidence available, but should also help in history's perennial task—helping adults to understand themselves.

28   See Johan Huizinga, *Homo Ludens: A Study of the Play Element in Culture* (Boston, 1950); Natalie Z. Davis, "The Reasons of Misrule: Youth Groups and Charivaris in Sixteenth-Century France," *Past and Present*, L (1971), 41–75.

Index

Abbott, Grace, 183
Adams, Henry, 204
Adolescence: early ideas on, 95–99
  Hall's concept of, 95, 102–103, 105, 108
  in nineteenth century America, 95–110
  prolonged, 105, 108–109
  psychological development in, 151–152, 154
  religious conversion in, 101–103, 109–110
  youth distinguished from, 97, 105–107
Adorno, T. W., 128
Anthropology, cultural, 213–215
Ariès, Philippe, 127–128, 139, 155, 172, 174, 177, 195–196, 211, 214–215, 221
Ascham, Roger, 96

Bailyn, Bernard, 183, 212
Banner, Lois W., 159
Beard, Charles, 160
Beard, Mary, 163–164
Beecher, Catharine E., 100, 169
Beecher, Lyman, 100, 169
Belgium, illegitimacy in, 72–78
Bloch, Marc, 16
Boorstin, Daniel, 160
Bremner, Robert H., 179, 182–184, 186–187
Brown, Charles Brockden, 108
Brownson, Orestes, 107
Buffalo, N.Y.: Italian families in, 111–126
  Polish families in, 121–122
Burgess, Ernest W., 176, 222
Bushman, Richard, 196, 205
Bushnell, Horace, 107, 110
Butler, Elizabeth Beardsley, 122

Calhoun, Arthur W., 213
Calvinism, 101, 110; see also Protestantism
Child, Irvin L., 131
Childhood: American, documentary history of, 179–189
  in cultural history, 214–215

developmental studies of, 127–139
early American ideas on, 97–101
Erikson's model of developmental stages, 130, 133, 135, 216–218
foundling homes and institutions, 150–151
in France, seventeenth century, 172–177
history of, 127–139, 171–189, 227–235
in New England colonies, 195–200
psychological development in, 144–156
Puritanism and, 97–99, 131–138, 181
Coleman, Emily R., 1
Coles, Robert, 141
Comenius, John Amos, 96
Contraception in France, eighteenth century, 23–25, 68n
Cooper, James Fenimore, 107
Cultural anthropology, 213–215
Culture, personality and, 128–131, 213–214

Danforth, Samuel, 99
Davis, Natalie Z., 26
Demography: of American Quaker families, 85–94
  of France, early modern period, 19–27
  historical, 16–27, 215–216
Demos, John, 97, 100, 127, 141, 180–181, 186, 191, 194–197, 199, 216–218, 220, 221
Demos, Virginia, 100
Divorce, remarriage and, 92–93
Dunglison, Robley, 96–97
Durkheim, Emile, 192n

Education: American, history of, 104–107, 109, 188
  colleges, early nineteenth century, 104–105
Elkins, Stanley M., 155
Elyot, Thomas, 96
England: illegitimacy in, 55, 60–63
  life expectancy, eighteenth century, 197–198
  population changes, sixteenth and seventeenth centuries, 193–194

Erikson, Erik, 128, 130, 131, 133, 135, 141, 147, 149, 155–156, 172, 173, 181, 196, 216–218

Family: American, children's position in, 179–189
    American Quakers, demographic study, 85–94
    history of, as interdisciplinary field, 211–226
    Italians in Buffalo, 111–126
    in New England, 195–202, 208–210
Fathers in America, 183, 184, 186, 187, 202
    in France, seventeenth century, 175–176
Febvre, Lucien, 16
Fénelon, François de Salignac de La Mothe, 176
Fertility rate, 21, 171, 198–201
Festinger, Leon, 226
Fowler, Orson S., 108
France: birth rate, decline, 23
    children in sixteenth and seventeenth centuries, 155, 172–177
    demographic study, early modern period, 19–27
    illegitimacy in, 71–84
    marriage: in Middle Ages, 1–15; in seventeenth century, 174–175
    population growth, 22–23
Frazier, E. Franklin, 222, 223
Freud, Anna, 149
Freud, Sigmund, 145n, 147, 149, 150, 162
Frisch, Rose, 43, 44
Fromm, Erich, 142

Gagnon, John, 53
Garden, Maurice, 26
Gascon, Richard, 26
Germany, illegitimacy in, 60–61, 65–66, 79–82
Girls: adolescence, 103, 107–108
    age at menarche, 28–30
Glick, Paul C., 85–86, 88, 89
Goode, William J., 111
Goubert, Pierre, 16
Grant, Charles, 203
Great Awakening, 101
    Second, 101–103
Greven, Philip, 179–180, 185–186, 191, 197–201, 209, 216, 217, 220, 221

Grimké, Angelina, 167, 168
Grimké, Sarah, 167
Guérard, Benjamin, 1, 9

Hajnal, John, 175
Hall, G., Stanley, 95, 102–103, 105, 106, 108, 109, 188
Hammel, Eugene, 37
Handlin, Oscar, 115, 183, 212
Hareven, Tamara K., 211
Hartz, Louis, 160
Hélin, Etienne, 72
Henretta, James A., 191
Henry, Louis, 18, 20, 21, 61
Héroard, Jean, 173
Hewitt, Graily, 44
Hewitt, Margaret, 171, 172, 174, 176
Hunt, David, 141, 155, 171–177, 216–217

Illegitimacy, 48–84
    age of mothers at birth of children, 32n
    response to illegitimate pregnancy, 64–67
    types of, 54–55
Infant mortality rate, 171
    in France, 21
    in New England, 198–200
Infants: breast feeding, 175–176
    weaning, 132
Inhelder, Bärbel, 151
Italians in Buffalo, 111–126

Jacobs, Jane, 222

Kardiner, Abram, 128–129
Keniston, Kenneth, 141, 224
Kennedy, David M., 159, 167, 169
Kett, Joseph F., 95
Kluckhohn, Clyde, 128, 129
Kohlberg, Laurence, 149, 152

Labrousse, Ernest, 17
Lampard, Eric E., 223–224
Langer, William L., 141
Laslett, Peter, 28, 193
Lifton, Robert Jay, 141
Linton, Ralph, 128
Lipton, Rose C., 150
Lockridge, Kenneth A., 191–194, 200, 203

Longnon, Auguste, 1–2, 9
Louis XIII, childhood of, 173–175

McLaughlin, Virginia Yans, 110, 221–222
Mann, Horace, 188
Marriage: age at, 21–22, 30n, 31–39, 87,
    199–201
  of American Quakers, 85–94
  divorce and remarriage, 92–93
  duration of, 89–91
  in France; medieval, 1–15; seven-
    teenth century, 174–175
  in Victorian period, 168
  widowhood, length of, 91–92
Marryat, Frederick, 187
Marx, Karl, 59
Masturbation, 48, 97
  insanity and, 96, 99
Mather, Cotton, 97, 98n, 136n
Mead, Margaret, 128
Melville, Herman, 108
Men: employment and unemployment,
    113–117
  as fathers: in America, 183, 184, 186,
    187, 202; in France, seventeenth
    century, 175–176
  Italian, as heads of families, 114–119,
    124–125
  in medieval population, ratio, 4–8
  in women's rights movement, 169
Menarche, age at, 28–47
Menopause, age at, 30, 31n
Meuvret, Jean, 17–18
Middle Ages: marriage in, 1–15
  population, ratio of men to women,
    4–8
Mill, Harriet Taylor, 159, 160, 170
Mill, John Stuart, 159–164, 169–170
Millett, Kate, 159–164, 168–169
Möller, Helmut, 51
Montaigne, Michel Eyquem de, 176
Morgan, Edmund S., 212
Moynihan, Daniel P., 114, 125, 223
Murdock, George P., 128
Murray, Henry, 128, 129

New England in colonial period, 191–
    210; see also Puritans
Nisbet, Robert, 60
Noyes, John Humphrey, 107

Odencrantz, Louise, 123

Park, Robert E., 222
Parke, Robert, Jr., 86, 88
Parsons, Talcott, 220, 221
Perry, William G., Jr., 149
Personality: culture and, 128–131, 213–
    214
  modal, and national character, 142–143
Peymans, Edwige, 174n
Piaget, Jean, 145n, 149, 151
Pinchbeck, Ivy, 171, 172, 174, 176
Platt, Gerald M., 59, 224
Polanyi, Karl, 60
Polish-Americans, 121–122
Post, J. B., 30
Potter, David, 214
Protestantism: conversion of young peo-
    ple, 101–103, 109–110
  Great Awakening, Second, 101–103
Provence, Sally, 150
Psychohistorical studies, 141–142
Psychology, developmental, 216–219
  historical change and, 141–157
Puritans: childhood, ideas on, 97–99
  children, treatment of, 131–138, 181
  sociological studies of, 191–210
  youth, ideas on, 97–98
Putnam, Emily James, 159, 160, 164–
    167

Quaker families, demography of, 85–94

Raciborski, M. A., 44, 45
Reich, Wilhelm, 142
Reinhard, Marcel, 17
Revelle, Roger, 43
Rich, E. E., 194
Riesman, David, 142, 214
Rigden, Walter, 44, 45
Roberton, John, 43, 44, 45, 69
Rossi, Alice S., 159, 160, 170
Rothman, David J., 179
Rousseau, Jean Jacques, 96
Rowson, Susanna, 107

Sanger, Margaret, 167
Sauvy, Alfred, 18
Scott, Anne Firor, 159, 165–168
Sennett, Richard, 181–182, 186, 217,
    220–222
Serfdom, marriage and, 1–15
Sexuality: premarital, 48–70
  reasons for intercourse, 52–53
Sexual revolution, 48–84

Shorter, Edward, 48
Simms, William Gilmore, 108
Simon, William, 53
Slavery: children born in, 155
    women's attitudes toward, 166–167
    women's position compared with, 162–164
Smelser, Neil, 223
Smith, Page, 159, 167–170
Social disorganization, theory of, 222–223
Social morphology, 191n, 192
Sociology in study of family, 219–223
Solé, Jacques, 56–57
Somerville, C. John, 227
Soranos, 175
Spock, Benjamin, 133
Spruill, Julia, 166
Stanton, Elizabeth Cady, 168
Stone, Lawrence, 193
Stowe, Harriet Beecher, 169
Sullivan, Harry Stack, 149

Tanner, J. M., 29, 30, 39, 43, 44, 45
TenHouten, Warren, 125
Tissot, Samuel A., 96
Tobenkin, Elias, 122
Tocqueville, Alexis de, 59, 213, 214

van de Walle, Etienne, 171

Weinstein, Fred, 59, 224
Wells, Robert V., 85
Whitehead, James, 44, 45
Whiting, John W. M., 131
Wishy, Bernard, 180
Wolf, Eric R., 60

Women: age at birth of first child: 35–42
    age at marriage, 21–22, 30n, 31–39,
        87, 199–201
    age at menopause, 30, 31n
    age at sexual maturity, 28–47
    breast feeding of children, 175–176
    childbearing period, length of, 88–89
    employment, 111–126
    in family life cycle, 86–94
    feminist movement, 159–160, 168–169
    fertility rate, 21, 171, 198–201
    as heads of families, 111, 115–116,
        124
    history of, 159–170
    Italian, in Buffalo, 111–126
    in medieval population, ratio, 4–8
    roles of, 164–166
    subjection of, 160–163, 168–170
Women's liberation, 159–162
Wrigley, E. A., 61, 72, 193

Youth: adolescence distinguished from,
        97, 105–107
    American, documentary history of, 179–189
    career choices, 109–110
    education, early American, 104–107,
        109
    in nineteenth century America, 95–110
    Puritan ideas on, 97–98
    religious conversion in, 101–103, 109–110

Zola, Emile, 175–176
Zuckerman, Michael, 191, 195–196, 205–208